T0196934

THE ESSENTIAL: GLOBAL HISTORICAL REFLECTIONS

An Intellectual Exception! Introducing
"A Newly Innovative Genre "Histojectory"
A Prospective "Best Seller"

WILLIAM F. WILLIAMS

authorHOUSE®

AuthorHouse™
1663 Liberty Drive
Bloomington, IN 47403
www.authorhouse.com
Phone: 1 (800) 839-8640

Published by AuthorHouse 02/01/2016

ISBN: 978-1-5049-7495-0 (sc)
ISBN: 978-1-5049-7496-7 (e)

Print information available on the last page.

Any people depicted in stock imagery provided by Thinkstock are models,
and such images are being used for illustrative purposes only.
Certain stock imagery © Thinkstock.

This book is printed on acid-free paper.

CONTENTS

PREFACE

The *"Historical Reflections"* presents past and present collective social, economic, and political events that landscaped and structured global societies. The focus of this *history reflects* religious ideals, global conflicts, societal advancements, and innovative economic and social credence that fostered social change. Institutionalized principles, doctrines, and political dominance stagnated (temporarily) evolution, and creative intellectual design from advancing social, economic, and political vision. Notwithstanding, the execution of imposing contradictions towards creative inventiveness was enforced from antiquated legislative principles, doctrines, cultures, and the ruling class structures, to abort social, economic, and political social change; Thusly, religious, governmental, and influential social power structures enforced social dominance. Consequently, scientific, intellectual, social, political, and economic modernization was temporarily stagnated; which inflamed and provoked creative and innovative ingenious individuals to pursue their immediate goals towards social and industrial progression. Therefore, *"The Essential Global Historical Reflections"* revives historical memory of social conquests that fostered and cultivated ingenious individual and social achievements that nourished and enhanced social, industrial, economic, and political global progress. Contrastingly, global societies are cognizant of eras-in-time, when creative and industrial innovation was hindered by social obstacles that challenged social progress, which resulted in restricted individual and social development.

The Essential Global Historical Reflections portrays collective, factual, historiography, and histojectic events indicative of vital global societal innovation that shaped and restructured our global existence, to achieve social, political, economic, and religious reform and development.

Noteworthy, the recently innovative concept "histojectory" reflects a broad history writing ethical *genre* or class standard for principled guidelines divulging either/or inclusive "objective and subjective" historical data accountability; which informs readers of the liability and standards between events that are objective and /or subjective history writing *sourced* accountability. Additionally, *"histojectictory"* presents validity and factual guidelines and standards for historiography, which will result in extensive exploration, investigation, and interpretation of published historical events presented to the global communities, as valid or invalid accountable sourcing of eventful historical data. The merging of factual and non-factual historical sourcing or foundations, exemplified through *"histojectic"* guidelines and standards, will present a creditable innovative genus (categorical classification) to the "World" of historiography, and to accountable research.

The Essential Global Historical Reflections, distinguishes and perceives similarities between *"Christianity and Taoism's" sacraments* or rites, ceremonial procedural practices, convictions and belief similarities, and practices, of their faithful individual religious tenets. ... Lastly, *The Essential Global Historical Reflections* contributes an internal and external assessment of social consciousness and sub-consciousness regarding eventful historical time-frames, from antiquity to the present... With intent to stimulate historical interests within the framework of important and essential events that shaped, structured, and created mental social ingenuity, creativity, skills and social advancements from antiquity to the 21st century. Furthermore, social demands such as advanced social, economic, political, and *moral reconstruction* is continually contemplated in *"The Essential Global Historical Reflections"* objective doctrine. Also, progressive social ideals from antiquity to the present, which gainfully critiques *social, economic, ethics, and religious reformation* towards global continuity that unites global progress. Therefore, its historical events fosters epic, social, economic, political, and religious changes in establishing a historical mindset within academia, to challenge innovative foresight towards eventful creative history research, exploration, and interpretation of past, present, and future historiography.

INTRODUCTION

Histojectory, Histojectic, Histojectical, Histojectically
(An Innovative Word Definition
Guideline for *Historiography*)

The introduction of the newly creative genre *"Histojectory"* structures guidelines and disciplines to distinguish merged *objective and subjective* data presented in published historiography. Its innovative purpose and objective is to set standards within the framework of sourced accountable data (objective) that's factual, from unaccountable (subjective) data; published in historiography, social sciences, science, military, and by all published authors. The *"Histojectic" genus (classification) is created to qualify whether publish data sourcing is a "factual and fictional" contribution. However, unaccountable data presented, which is subjective or imaginary data sourcing,* that accompany or merge with objective data sourcing in published work, is distinguished in publications, after each paragraph, footnote, and bibliography with the symbol *"hty or "tjy"*. Thusly, identifying the merger of data in published publications as collective data sourcing, that contains both accountable and non-accountable sourcing (objective and subjective data). Futuristically, identifying an authentic classification category, and bringing to bear trustworthy published work within its authentic and reputable classification. This *histojectory* discipline applies to all published books, manuals, and manuscripts, presented for social viewing, which includes public and private schools, educational facilities, students and academia alike. Coincidentally, authentic objective publications must be scrutinized extensively for accurate eventful time-accountability, character input (moral fiber), and chronological sequence validation. *"Histojectory"* is established as a precise classified "Social Science" genre, with great inference to the field of historiography, methodology of historians, and the development of history as a discipline, and also to bodies of works written from the critical examination of archived sources, with the selection of *particulars (critical events time-tables)* into a narrative that will stand the test of critical reflective precedence.

CHAPTER I

An Examination of Arnaldo Momigliano's "Works of Art"

The Classical Foundation of Modern Historiography
(A Histojectic Interpretation of Arnaldo Momigliano's ("Works of Art") (Critique By: William F. Williams)

Momigliano urged historiographer's to demonstrate clear lines of permanence between classical or traditional historiography and modern history. This aim is reflected upon in six chapters of *"The Classical Foundation of Modern Historiography".* Momigliano appeared to trace important elements bestowed by the ancients throughout this aforementioned reading. The following important apprehension was his firm belief that echoed historiographer's profession to exemplify *"Leopold Von Ranke's"* methods of research and authentic evidence sources. Ranke represented the era which instituted the modern examination of history, which he structured to be a scientific method of historical investigation. He imparted his expertise and methodology through the introduction of the seminar as an informal but intensive teaching device. He's said to have dismissed the inaccurate romantic historiography of the enlightenment, and implement history as a science. He was distinguished majestically as the "Father of Modern Historiography". Comparatively, reflecting on historiographer's such as the historical deconstructionist *"Haden White",* during that era, whose history had become little more than a branch of rhetoric, which would have no place in Momigliano's scheme of historiography methodology work.

Four areas of Momigliano's research is quiet interesting and they are as follows: What was Momigliano's attitude towards popular generalizations of his historiography research? What was his novel insights in his books? Why was his books enjoyable to read? And what were his inherent issues in the books which attempted to corral his ambitious scope from classical to modern historiography.

Importantly, and notably during the early 20th century Italy's development in historiography had not evolved until 1902, when "Croce" published the "Philosophy of Spirit"; and even then the notion of a professional history created discomfort within the Italian University system. Not that this great Italian civilization failed to make major historiography contributions to historical thought in its revised idealism associated with *"Benedetto Croce"* (1866-1952). Notably during this era *"Croce"* was one of Italy's important statesman, philosopher, and historians. Additionally, he was considered the leading Italian intellectual of the first half of the twentieth century, and one of Europe's best known figures. During this era in Italian history,* distinguished historian's existed *"through the acid of fascism corroding the vision and achievements of those historians who embraced historiography" in the likes of "Volpe"*, who stood superlative within the philosophy, and intellectual Italian arena. However, *"Gaetano Salvemini"* the historian and journalist (1873-1957) introduced economic and social inquiry into Italian historiography. Unfortunately, he spent his later years combating the fascist dictatorship of Mussolini. Unfortunately, *Salvemini* found his intellectual career destroyed, due to his opposition to Italian fascism. Factually, the point at issue is that Italian *historiography* methodology and structural approach, differed from their neighbor's further North (Germany), during the fascist era and prior. Example, *"Ranke's"* method and scientific historiography was required to write Italy's history of the *"Pope"*; and *"Burkhart's"* (German historiographer), expertise was required to explore, research, and celebrate Italian *"art"*. Perhaps, Italian self-identity in the academic field of historiography phenomenon, during that era, was stagnated by fascism. Consequently, causing her *State* formation too festered to permit an easy transition to a professionalized historiography writing capacity of her historical past.

Arnaldo Momigliano (1908-1987), emerged onto the historiography intellectual scene, his ethnic heritage was Italian Jewish. Unfortunately, he was interned during WWII, due to his nationality, from approximately June to November 1940, as an enemy alien. He was subsequently released from fascist Italian internment through public protest by academians; such as "Gilbert Murray", and other Intellectual organizations, who were credited with forming and structuring ways to accumulate resources, and valid references, for the purpose to aid fellow scholars, confronted with social crisis such as fascist internment, as was imposed on *"Momigliano"*. "The Society for The Purpose of Science and Art", and "The Academy Assistance Counsel", continually provided assistance for scholars and their families in distress, which included victims of World War II's fascist system. Arnaldo Momigliano was a pupil of the brilliant academia Francesco de Sanctis (1817-1883). The Italian liberal politician and political critic, who was trained in law, but turned to the study of Italian culture. Several years later, after his three year prison sentence for his involvement in the 1848 revolution against conservative Austrian rule, which caused his banishment from Italy, he returned. Thereafter, returning in 1868 he completed his most creditable *"Storia della letteratura Italiana",* or *"History of Italian Literature".* However, Momigliano recognized at an early stage of his academic training that he was intellectually influenced by *"Karl Julius Beloch"* (1854-1929), a classical and economic historian. Momigliano was also greatly influenced in his late youth by "Fraccaro, an Italian academe whose Intellectual approach to thinking changed Momigliano's approach in forming his thoughts during his youth. Momigliano was introduced to German culture while in Rome as a staff member of the "Enciclopedia Italiana". During this era, he established an intellectual association with *"Benedetto Croce"* (1860-1952), who provided in Momigliano's later years a letter of recommendation, to obtain a lecturer position at Oxford University; which Momigliano could not accept due to his WWII fascist internment, because of his Jewish heritage. After his intern from fascist internment, he was invited to head the new "Instituto Storico", in Naples, Italy, which was headed by "Croce's Humanities Department. *Momigliano* 'began to revive his academic enthusiasm towards his intellectual pursuits, and commitments towards his goals, which were lost during his fascist internment experiences, which coupled psychologically with the murder executions of nine interned mates; thereafter, he regarded history as merely a professional discipline, as opposed to a philosophy or culture. Many "English and / or European historical writers during this era showed by example, the *Mommsenian* traditions of intellectual historiography, such as influential historians "Hugh Last" and "Isobel Henderson.

Additionally, it's imperative to acknowledge Momigliano's most influential literary achievements, which were often presented in *lecture series* at the *"Warburg".* 3 His achievements included: *"The Ancient History and the*

Antiquarian, which was delivered at the *"Warburg"* in 1949; "*Heresies*", a lecture series was delivered in 1951, which topic was an "Unsolved Problem of Historical Forgery; also "*The Scriptores Historia Augustae"* was also a lecture series on Historical forgeries. However, from 1958-1959 he organized these lectures, which were published as "*The Conflict between Paganism and Christianity"* in (1963), as the first volume in the *"New Oxford Warburg"* series.

In continuing his achievements, in (1963) *Momigliano* delivered the essay on *"Time in Ancient Historiography"*, in a series on *"Time Eternity"* 4, and in (1964) he delivered *Roman 'bestioni and Roman 'eroi* in *"Vico's Scienza Nuova"*, that was part of a series on *"Myth and History"* 5. Noteworthy, a year prior (1962), at the age of fifty-four, Momigliano delivered *"The Sather Classical Lecturer's"*, at Berkeley, Calif., introducing *"The classical Foundation of Modern Historiography"*, that established the perimeters of his inquiries. Furthermore, he attempted as a provisional challenge to evaluate the worth of ancient historiography in light of the twentieth century revolution concerning history writing, which is reflected in all six chapters of the aforementioned book.

Momigliano seems to trace important elements bequeathed by the ancients in demonstrating the application of classical historiography, in order to answer the modern quest for a scientific pursuit in the likes of Ranke, and Gibbon's, in the direction of historical continuity; as applied towards the end of each chapter of his books… This underlined his urge to show the clear lines of certainty between classical historiography versus modern historiography. It's obvious that his second concern was to fortify the firm belief that a historians obligation was to display *"Ranke's" "Wie es eigentlich gewesen" (how things actually were);* However, a deconstructionist in the likes of *"Hayden White's* interpretation of history had become little more than a branch of rhetoric, which would certainly have no place in Momigliano's method of working-out historiography principles, theories, or methods of historical research, writing, analysis, evaluation, and interpretation of sourced materials.

Noteworthy, the molding of Momigliano's persona, inhibits his ingenious abilities to view life without social constraints, limitations, and restrictions, due to fascism that he experienced as a Jew during WWII. Therefore, social and psychological impediment restructured impulsive social instabilities within the hereditary and geographical bounds of his ancestral birthright and person, to exist in life's experiences as a free-thinking human-being. Furthermore, as a Jewish social scientist, intellectual, and scholar in war torn Europe, the pressures to articulate humanity, through his ethnic experience stagnated his visionary imagery of his concept of the life he was thrust into; due to his ethnic and historical identity. Thusly, he was a restricted person within his environment to manifest or display one set of humanitarian social principles, which shaped and produced a dualistic survival understanding or comprehension of his shackled state of being. Notwithstanding, mental brilliance was born out of a crucial *survival mode,* that dictated the quest to regard *"the mind",* as his most precious resource and ally, towards humanity and survival; due to the ethnic human social divide created by" *Fascism and Nazism".* Example, Momigliano didn't hesitate to "scornfully" denounce ex-Nazi historiographer "Helmut Berve's <u>"History of Greece"</u> in 1959. Ex-Nazi historians and social scientist's fundamentally altered Momigliano's interest in historiography after WWII, due to the imposed Fascist experience Jewish ethnicity encountered before and during WWII. Nonetheless, he outfitted his compulsion and composure to bear witness to the abuse of scholarship during the fascist era. Retrospective of his past, and the return to *The Classical Foundation of Modern Historiography,* he wrote as a passion for survival, and was published with excellent review, and merit from his peerage. Historian *"Riccardo di Donato's"* foreword of Momigliano's book states as follows; *"This is a crucial event for the understanding of his intellectual development, his social struggles, and cultural limitations, which previously hindered the preparation and publication of this masterpiece; which can now be interpreted as the completion within a specific time frame, from social internment and detainment, to a free self, which has enabled this newly innovative modern approach to historiography...*

Three grand themes had matured in Momigliano's mind during this middle period in England, from 1951-1960. However, three of these aforementioned themes had great impact on English classical scholarship: *"The History of Late Antiquity", "The History of Historiography",* and *"The Origin of Rome".* Therefore, *Momigliano* innovated and designed *scholastical* innovations towards combining historical antiquity with historical modernity (except for Ranke's scholarly unity of judging the past, and of instructing the present for the benefit of future ages). Furthermore, Momigliano's interest in this aged era versus combining modern era histories, originated in his studies of the traditions of *"Christian Seneca"*, and reflective *"Italian"* scholarship which he embraced during his youth.

Momigliano held the distinguished *"grown-breaking"* reputation as being the master of the *opening sentence*, by his peers. However, English scholars following "Robert Browning, Walter Pater, and Bernard Berenson", surmised that there can be few more arresting *opening sentence* beginnings than that of *Momigliano's "British Academy"* Italian lecture of 1955, *"Cassiodorus and Italian Culture of His Time"* as stated:

"When I want to understand Italian history
I catch a train and go to Ravenna.
There, between the tomb of Theodoric
and that of Dante, in the reassuring
Neighborhood of the best manuscript of
Aristophanes and in the less reassuring
One of the best portrait of Empress Theodora,
I begin to feel what Italian history
Has really been".

The first specific historiography contribution of Momigliano's was to insist, in a crucial period on the importance of a non-English activity, the *"History of Ideas"*, as opposed to prosopography (the study of careers of individuals linked by family, economics, social and political relationships, and administrative history). The second important area of scholarship owed to *Momigliano*, is *"The History of Historiography"*. His great series of essays on *"Ancient History"* in England, begins with the readings of *"Herodotus, Thucydides, Polybius and Tacitus"*, in their entirety. These great series of essays has therefore been his most valued contributions to classical studies in the "English" speaking World.

Subsequently, Momigliano's top contribution was within the realm of understanding "English Cultural" bonds to historiography, in the eighteenth and nineteenth centuries; through his introduction of two distinguished *English Masters* of *"Ancient History"* largely unrecognized until *Momigliano's 1950* essay lecture. One of the two distinguished *English Masters* was *"Edward Gibbon's", mostly recognized* as a great stylist, who read aside *"Macaulay"* by every student of *"Modern History"*, as opposed to *"Ancient History"*; Yet, the only aspect of his *"Historical Methods"*, which attracted great scholarship attention was his notorious *"Anti-Clericalism"*. However, in two related papers, *Ancient History and the Antiquarianism"* (1950), preceded *"Gibbon's Contribution to Historical Method"* (1954), which was paramount in Momigliano's success in establishing *"Gibbon's" "as our greatest and most relevant "Master of Historical Methods"* (except for Ranke's title "The Father of Modern Source Based History). Many articles written by "Gibbons" remain the basic fundamental texts understanding his historical methods approaching history writing, which are published in the *"Journals of Roman Studies"* (1983).

Four primary questions in Momigliano's *"The Classical Foundation of Modern Historiography"* begins with an analyzed observation of historical generalizations in chapter one: The analysis of continuity of historical thought by prominent historians illustrates Momigliano's annoyance with weak generalizations of historical data, sources, and objective conformity. He backed each observation with an assortment of evidence that was stunning in historical method capacity and gravity. He cites generalizations concerning the anti-historical consciousness of *"The Greeks"* by T. F. Driver, which was one of Momigliano's prized scholarly subjects he criticized. Such presentation by Driver's was a fallacy to Momigliano, as bad as equating "Plato without a "Greek Mind". In *Driver's historical interpretation of "The Greek's", Momigliano explains* that Polybius *"cyclical notion was confined "only" to the progression of Constitutions, and definitely not to Political and Military History".* Example two, section seven, chapter four emphasizing Momigliano unlocking an inquiry on the origins of Fabius Pictor's historical sourcing data, by discounting *banquet songs* as source material. However, he set-out in a methodical manner discrediting *"Bowra's revitalized "Romantic Notions",* in this chapter. The primary argument was that in early Roman Historical times, popular legends were canonized before annalists documented them. Additionally, Momigliano confirmed that the commonplace version of "Coriolanus's" story was infinitely dissimilar from Fabius account. This predetermined that in Fabius's instance, myths were still developing and only became constant or sanctified in the first century BC. Therefore, confirming the obvious fallacy that Fabius was not informed of any "banquet songs", as an apparatus for historical sourcing; and that it occurred subsequent to Fabius historical arrival

Momigliano established concrete foundations in the mechanics of Classical History, by overturning defective historical simplification to innovating highly developed historical narrative structure in Historiography. Example, he revised the historical dichotomy between Thucydides and Herodotus, by structuring historical antiquarian research and origins of proper historical documentation. In orthodox history it was common place to characterize Thucydides as the truthful historian of events taken place, and Herodotus historical writing as false. In the advent of the "New World" Herodotus stories of events was seen as deceptive and untruthful conclusions. Importantly, scholars during the Renaissance era began to value Herodotus historical conclusions enough to breathe life back into his historical writing conclusions. This justification was revitalized because Herodotus historical concepts, as he allegedly witnessed in history was different, due to his methods of historical implementation. Thucydides was committed to a Political life, as opposed to Herodotus "good humored cosmopolitan lifestyle existence. More importantly, Momigliano viewed Herodotus method of history writing methodically simulated within modern ethnography. Subsequently, Momigliano displayed that antiquarianism or historical antiquity left important heritage to Modern Historiography. Historical antiquarianism linage is traced from modernity to the Hellenistic scholarship or (Greek Culture); that developed five characteristics crucial to proper history writing (historiography) utilities, which are as follows: literary texts, tradition, monuments, biographies, and chronology.

Noteworthy, "Gibbons" formidable *footnotes,* and *"Mommsen's"* fame were the result of these five aforementioned antiquated Hellenistic characteristics structured and defined as conservative empiricism (research) necessary for quality historiography. These five historiography utilities were held as virtues (assets) approvingly their necessary conjoined (five) principles fostered branded *uncertainty, unless* accompanied by *proper documentation, which supposedly erases historical skepticism of events.* Thusly, historical interpretation must be based on solid empirical documentation of historical happenings and events. Historical interpretation should not be based on airy "Romantic" notions of subjective intuition or feelings; which describes Momigliano's historical and personal fears he experienced, that fostered negative social demonic race purity under totalitarian regimes that created Fascism and Nazism.

In the light of Momigliano's ethnic heritage and professional time lost under Fascist political bureaucracy in Italy; he begins to comprehend his strong faith in historical antiquarian data sourcing. Additionally, he grew to distrust "grand schemes of historical interpretations of historiography that was without antiquarian historiography methodology. During the war years he witnessed the tragic departure from coherent reasoning by German scholars, and loathed those Nazi classics that enhanced racial science. After the war he conceded that two issues must be addressed, and they were to establish scholarly, and socially that such fascist atrocities must not be forgotten; and that future historical studies must be firmly grounded in the methodologies imparted or communicated through antiquarian data sourcing. Antiquarian historians (Cicero's era) conscientiously linked documents and quotations into their historiography. With an over-riding concern towards precedent and tradition, possibly due to their fears of being challenged by governance, academic personnel, military and social media, concerning factual data sources. Thusly, motivating and establishing historical events as credibility, professional, and as a necessary structured vocation... Noteworthy, proper historiography documentation is the foremost confirmation of the foundation of *modern* historiography. Momigliano discovered in *"Eusebuis's Ecclesiastical History"* a model of proper documentation, which establishes this expository as *Eusebuis's* greatest contribution to *modern* history; which was continued by *Counter-Reformation* historians. Importantly; initially these *Counter-Reformation* historians were not immediately interested in proper documentation per se, because the *Roman Catholic Church's* quest at that time was establishing the reformation reaffirming the veneration (reverence, honor and respect,) of saints, and the authority of the *Pope (Protestants* objected); however, many of these leaders were *Jesuits.* However, eventually through their ecclesiastic trepidations in time, the *Counter-Reformation* Historians wittingly advanced the facility for proper historical documentation.

Momigliano's beloved ancient's contributed greatly to his methodology of modern historiography, placing him in his element through the discovery of linking antiquarian sourced data to modern historiography; which overturned presupposition for a modern approach to modern historiography.

What makes Momigliano's "*Classical Foundation of Modern Historiography*" enjoyable to read is his "sly wit" in his ability to incorporate narrative experiments, such as in chapters three and six, which reads like a mystery novel. His erudition is sophisticated enough to implement obscure facts in the manner of anecdotes. Both the story of "*de Peirese's dissection of Angora Cat's* and, *Benedetto Bacchini's Fumbling in the Dusty Ducal Library,* served to illustrate a larger visual reflection of their respective chapters, namely *Galilean Methods of Observation* regarding the conflict between primacy of documentary evidence versus doctrinal evidence 11.

Momigliano has questionable faults as other historiographers, by not exposing history writing to the general public, students, peers, and others, in his brilliant conceivable entirety; Therefore, if one wasn't present at his numerous "lectures", his history writing credence was difficult to capture as a quality "work of art"; However, by reading his writings only, the dualism of both "*lectures and readings*" coincides with capturing the brilliant's of his modern historiography innovations. However, argument of his faults in historiography reveals that he certainly does not try to conceal faults, because it would be contrary to his methodological and forthright empirical approach to historiography. However, *Ernest Breisach* perceived faults in his dualism between Thucydides and Herodotus.

He witnessed dualistic characteristics in the relevance of Herodotus traits towards antiquarian historical data sourcing versus *Thucydides*. *Briesach* found it difficult to accept such a restraining theme, because he cites structuralism as not evident throughout *Herodotus* account of the *Persian Wars*. He believed that such dualism could not be used as a distinction *"between right and wrong"* historiography. However, to this author it seems extremely curious in *Breisach's* analysis that he perceives *Momigliano's* dualism between *Herodotus* and *Thucydides* in this way. Momigliano's dualistic methodology was deliberate "structured dualism", as a central theme; consequently, he selected to revive both ancient historiographer's in the quest to nullify one as a liar (due to his selective antiquarian data sourcing), which confirms a more probably accurate assessment (based on historical selection or approval by him to distinguish factual from subjective data, due to his Modern historiography link with Ancient History), in his historical accountability of other's historiography data source methodologies. However, nowhere in Momigliano's expository regarding Herodotus and Thucydides was it implied that Herodotus was right in his historiography of the Wars and, Thucydides was wrong, in his historical presentations. Momigliano alleged to have favored Herodotus historical writing methodology as it relates to his antiquarian foundation conjoined with modern historiography. Therefore, it's documented that *Momigliano breaths life back into Herodotus* historiography, for his expressionist approach to history writing that connects *Momigliano's modern historiography* with *ancient history,* in his interpretation of *"The Classical Foundation of Modern Historiography"*. *Breisach, continues to find fault in Momigliano's* interpretations of characters in his book, and the focus of his criticism concerns what he refers to as the dichotomy or polarity of the theme on *"Tacitism".* In reference to Momigliano's reflections on *"Tacitus", the* Roman Historian famous for his insight into characters, and the construing of motives… the picture he draws of Imperial Rome is revolting. Additionally, he's distinguished for his writings of *"Life of Agricola", "Germania", "Histories", and "Annals",* for their conciseness, vigor and the pregnancy of meaning. Tacitus states as follows "a single word sometimes gives effect to a whole sentence, if the meaning of the word is missed, the sense of the writer is missed". Consequently, I refer and direct the aforementioned sentence to Breisach's misinterpretation of *Momigliano's* interpretation and reflections on *"Tacitism".* Further criticism of *Momigliano's* book by *Breisach* took into account his view of the "excessive expanded flexible use of the terms *Nation and Modern.* Unfortunately, Breisach's life experiences didn't capture *Nazi or Italian Fascism* socially or politically, which explains his mislead criticism regarding Momigliano's *"excessive flexibility he expanded on the two terms in his book Nation and Modern".* Therefore, Momigliano's personal tragic encounters with Fascist experiences colored his perceptions of both *important terminologies* in his composition of both words *"Nation and Modern",* because his vivid understanding of belonging and not belonging to a *Nation* captured his opus or production that generated and bred *Modern* or *Classical* historiography from his insights, motives, conciseness, vigor and the pregnancy of meaning through *Tacitism.* Example, the *"phrase national consciousness"… through Momigliano's conceptual experiences*

15

of life's natural consciousness, which presents an expandable idiom of social and ethnic "choices by the *creator (God)* in Momigliano's values, to be granted and anointed with humanity without favor, in acquiring "life, liberty, and the pursuit of happiness". Thusly, Momigliano clearly exemplify *Modern Historiography* as a *social science* within historical *narrative* and *Classical Modernity* standards of innovation. Breisach's reveals negative reflections on Momigliano's concepts of Persian historians, as written and conceptualized in chapters one-four, claiming that "the lack of annalistic tradition hardly explains nationalistic *Persian* historians". However, as Momigliano explains in chapters one –four in *"The Classical Foundation of Modern Historiography"*, *"The Annals of the Pontiff"* that *Fabius* references, and not *Cicero's* versions, was highly in spirit and character with the *Persian's* chronicles or accounts of Persian nationalistic history and annalistic tradition. The compatible analysis of both *Persian and Roman* annals concludes that both are factual, which disbands Breisach's negative opinion of *Momigliano's* historical analysis of both civilizations, as revealed by *Fabius*. Additionally, *Breisach's* last negative response to *Momigliano's* book referred again to *"Tacitus"*, he states as follows: "Momigliano's argument indicates a break in modernity, that implies a different status for this era; Thusly, quite troublesome for his promise in this title". It is true that the dispute regarding *Tacitus* has passed into another juncture; however, that hardly qualifies *Breisach's* postulation or inference that a breach in *Momigliano's* conceptual analysis of his meaning of modernity, as titled in his book is contradictory to the title, which includes the words, *"Classical Foundation of Modern Historiography".* Exemplary example, *Marxism* over the decades has witnessed many stages in both practical and elucidated gist, practice, and authority; however, that doesn't deny it a place in modernity. Subsequently, *Momigliano* directs attention to the relevance of *"Tacitus"* to modernity, to epitomize the *"social psychology of tyranny"*, which pledges *posterity* and *modernity* through the *origin* of *antiquated* historiography linked to his concept of *"modernity"*. The above cited arguments are pedagogic, quibbling, odious, and informative. Such differences in arguments aforementioned, in point-of-facts, which measures the academic and colloquial weight of interpretation regarding *Momigliano's* critics of his books, as opposed to deficiencies in his sophisticated scholarship, and culture. Example, another lesser critic of *Momigliano's* work was *"Grafton"*, referring to minimal limitations "in the lack of interest in the rediscovery of ancient methods in the exact sciences and, the absence of *Momigliano's* qualifications and reiteration of scholarship in the field of "social history", which he addressed in his book *"The Man who saved History. The New Republic.,* 1991.

Conclusion: most alleged limitations criticized in Momigliano's "Classical Foundation of Modern Historiography" and lectures, are mere misinterpretations of the combination of his life-experiences, coupled with mitigating extenuations engraved in his inharmonious fascist experiences. However, his heighten mental brilliance found reason, emotion, and foundational scholar to foster necessary antiquarian history to evolve modern Historiography… Quote from "Cornelius Tacitus" "a single word gives effect to a whole sentence, if the writing of a word is missed, the sense of the writer is not reached". In Momigliano's conceptual analysis to evolve modern historiography, the sense of his single "life experience, and exposure to fascism" was missed by his critics in misunderstanding his approach or philosophy of modern historiography. Principally,

Momigliano balanced his mastery of concrete facts, with a clear style of contemporary writing, scholarly proficiency, and modern innovation by way of antiquarian history. Noteworthy, reading Momigliano's works and lectures is an intellectually enlightening encounter...

References:

Michael Bentley, Modern Historiography: An Introduction, as found in Gioachimo Volpe (1876-1971), Professor of Modern History, Milan 1905-1924; Rome 1924- 40, Official Historian of the Regime: Storia del Movimento fascist (1939). He had begun as an medievalist (Eretici e Moti Ereticali Sociate dal XI at XIV Secolo (1907), but then wrote on Modern Italian political diplomatic history, as in his study of Guerra Dopoguerra, Fascismo (1928) after the collapse fascism he wrote a two-volume account of L' Italia moderna (1943-1952), For prospective on post-war Italian historiography see Bentley 1997, chapter 22.

Carlo Donizetti, Arnaldo Momigliano e Croce, Belfagor, 43 (1988), 617-641), reprinted in Ricordo di Arnaldo Momigliano (Bologna, 1989),

Contributo alla storia degli studi classical (Rome, 1955) 67-106 also in studies in Historiography (London, 1966)

Momigliano, *the Classical Foundation of Historiography* (Berkeley, 1990).

Secondo Contribution, in *Studies in Historiography*

Contributo and ; also in Studies in Historiography

P. R. Ghosh, "Gibbon's Dark Ages": Some Remarks on "The Genesis of the Decline and fall" Journal of Roman Studies 73 (1983),

The chief source of this memoir are personal knowledge and discussion or correspondence with the following: Peter Brunt, the late Dan Davin, and Carlotta Donizetti ET. al., The Society for the Protection of *Science and Learning (Bodleian Library, Oxford), (Oxford: University Press), and (for the Sather Lectures), The Momigliano papers now at the Scoular Normal in Pisa.*

Ernst Breisach, *"Reflections on Arnaldo Momigliano's*: *The Classical Foundation of Modern Historiography*. Clio. (1993),

Peter Green, *"Tracking down Wisdom: Momigliano's Religion of Scholarship".* (1991)

CHAPTER II

An Analysis and Personal Interpretation By: William Williams

<u>"Bias in Historiography"</u>

This concise essay analyzes and assess historiography with ardent selective judgment and balance; with inference regarding "Bias in historiographies description of sources, interpretations, explanations, and misleading unsupportable historical events published. The intent of histojectory is to regulate standards of history writing that discards or notify the reading audience of unofficial and informal historiography that's published, with total or partial subjective data sourcing; which will be regulated by "histojectic standards to induce *objective writing*, and to *notify the data entry of subjective source data* guidelines; which validates structured authentic objective and subjective published history writing. This newly innovative genre, category, and classification will prescribe, stipulate, and regulate ethical authenticity to eradicate "bias in historiography" by classifying subjective chronology data sourcing as histojectic, histojectory, histojective, histojectivity, and histojectical, primarily to inform readers that this published history source and data, is authentic or, unauthentic, fictional, or imaginative historical information. Thusly, enabling prescribed regulated standards for objective history writing, through the author's and publisher's conscience exactitude, focus, and authentic objective sourced data presentation of events, chronology, character's, and subject matter. Therefore, fostering quality and pervasive precedence for future historical references. In structuring *"bias historiography"* through regulated *"histojectory"* in the social sciences, which requires *examples* of subjective and objective data entry; or subjective sourced data merged or conjoined with objective source data, which must be explained as follows: Example, *"Arnaldo Momigliano's, "The Classic Foundation of Modern Historiography"* is gifted work which engineered his concept of this aforementioned masterpiece from conceptual manifestation, that justify his modern theory of historiography, which is directed and established from historical antiquities, that qualifies the genus "histojectory"; which classifies his historiography concept as objective credence, because of his authentic initial thought and conceptual materialization. Thereafter, he qualified the concept of "chronology-in-time through authentic chronicled events, that innovated, revolutionized, and modernized historiography; However, his focus and concentration between the relationship of "ideas and history", which is under the professional guidelines and genre of "histojectic" validation. Consequently, his ideology within this instance of conceptual cognition fostered his concept and plan for "classic modern historiography", which sealed and forged his oneness of "ideas and history", that structured and legitimized an original state-of-the-art historiography methodology; which now transforms from "conceptual manifestation" (subjective), to (objective) guidelines, standards, and regulations that modified and reformed "historiography". He becomes the equivalents to the "Father of historiography Sourcing", in the likes of *Ranke.* However, Momigliano's modification and modernized methods of historical research, and his mental reflection of placing both "ideas and histories" as the essential components of *Modern Historiography, displayed* reality as a rivalry between accountable vs. unaccountable historical sourcing, research, and interpretation of modern historiography. "Thereafter, he was crowned "The Father of Historiography Methodology".

Coincidentally, the formative question is as follows: "did Momigliano's conceptual foundation of fusing "ideas and histories" authenticate the reason historiography was modernized"? Secondly, "was his motivation concerning his inspiration that "ideas and histories" had upon each other become a question for historians, as a suggestion, or impression, to stimulate historiographer's thinking process towards the modernity of history writings sourced data accountability? Subsequently, historian's debates concerning "bias" in descriptions of past civilizations, and interpretation of events, would not take place, if the attainability of historical sources were objective in their writing, coupled with fair-mindedness as opposed to genetic or hereditary past, present, and future elucidations of civilizations, and historical deviations of people, cultures, and events. Noteworthy, *genetic or inherited historical sourcing breeds unfair and "bias" descriptions, interpretations, and explanations of misleading historiography".* The antonym for inherited or genomic is *acquired learning, which is the leading qualifier that creates debatable dialog amongst historians towards "bias" personal and cultural interpretation of (subjective) historiography.* To learn and acquire skills towards "unbiased" historical description, research, interpretation, and explanation of historical data, requires personal focus towards genuine commitments, standards, and most importantly, conscience acknowledgement towards publishing accurate, objective, and accountable details of the past, present and future historiography. However, the debates between history writer's, confirms "bias" intentions of the past, present, and future, regarding subjective unaccountable informational data input, that stems from professional negligence, and distorted guidelines that fosters "biased" historiographer's. Many reasons occur that lead to "bias" historical events published; namely, selfish motives to acquire literary status, finances, misleading research (secondary data sourcing and subordinate) acquired through cultural and/or personal data, akin to the historians purpose in accelerating time proposed for his publication, and failure to acknowledge literary integrity and professionalism. Furthermore, the question arise from the issue of "cause and effect", which denotes historians "mental acts", beliefs, ideas, and opinions that perpetuates "habitual unaccountable neglected peer-group discipline, and regulatory sub-standard ethical guidelines. These "bias" neglects of integrity and standards has always been the object of accord and solidarity amongst historiographer's, within their cultural interests; therefore, "why rock the boat". Notwithstanding, *"bias" research, investigation, interpretation*, and *explanation* of history, that constitutes a deliberate *"misleading personal bias", in many select instances which has its Big-Brothers endorsements and ratifications".* Noteworthy, historiography standards and levels of quality is enforcement against "bias", which has been enforced upon many writers, yet negligently enforced upon the influential, prestigious, and wealthy historiographer's with membership in prestigious and prominent historical clubs, organizations, and associations.

The newly innovative genre "histojectory" establishes an exacting account, authentic, and standard efficient guideline towards identifying and notifying, the reading audience of subjective data enjoined with objective source data associated with all published material (books, manuals) etc.... Therefore, historian's, historiographer's, and other's, must regulate published historiography without *bias,* and through this select *disciplinary utility priority* "histojectory", the newly innovative word genre that will authenticate and validate historiography; which classifies categorical identities, such as objective and subjective historiography published data. Additionally, it classifies categorical identities by symbolically notifying the general public, students, academe, and scholars that *subjective* research data is amalgamated with *objective* research data sourcing. However, in order for this newly innovative word genus "histojectory" to qualify as the supervisory authority that retard and eliminates "bias" in published historiography, historians *must solemnly* pledge tangible commission and ethical declaration; by signing a written authorized endorsement that's administered by the Historian Associations; which bear the allegiance to the guidelines authorized by the newly innovative genre "histojectory", prior to any published historiography submissions, on a national and international status quo.

How does "histojectory" eliminate "bias" in historiography? It's essential that commitments to standards of rational inquiry, personal bias, cultural bias, bias in evidence, appraisal, adequacy of historical interpretation, and comprehensive descriptions of history written, must be restructured authentic and accountable; within the aforementioned aspects of historiography principles, guidelines, and authority. Historians must acquire and procure a modernized standard and vision of past, present, and future published historiography to insure quality precedence for future valued references, that results in superior statistics and factual quantifiable information. The models to rebuild fair, balanced and, comprehensible historiography output and structure allows history to be rewritten, appraised, and researched by students, academia, social scientist, and others. History written qualifies to be recycled through research, examination, investigation, interpretation, and exploration, for furthering verifiable objective procurement. Thusly, opening avenues for quality professional historians to elevate the profession of historiography within the scope of anthropology, zoology, geography, and geology. This form of historiography will reform the presence of "bias" and colloquial informality, that's published recklessly without abandonment. Thusly, qualifying exactness, discipline, and academic progress towards eradicating subjective imagery, produced by former, and present historiographer's. Importantly, accountable historiography relates to a standard of excellence that correlates to our future progression within the paradigm of efficient and proficient academic discipline. However, unfair accounts of the past (subjective data sourcing) is the result of historiography's *"prejudice or unfairness in documenting historical events".*

Noteworthy, rational standards of inquiry will not be totally sufficient or adequate to avoid "bias of evidence", if the evidence or data published as an historical event, civilization, or people in itself is "biasly" represented. Therefore, the modernized apparatus "histojectory" reforms rules, guidelines, standards, and authenticity, as a vital and valuable utility, that will eliminate "bias historiography" and "bias in evidence", that cannot be permitted or allowed to exist within the assertive mechanism of historiography. It's noted that historians often allowed "bias in evidence", and by further qualified it, by explaining the reconstruction of "past evidence" as allowable. Subsequently, historians constructed "bias" with unauthorized and unauthentic and pointless historical events, that occurred in the past as a routine agreement, or act of consent amongst historiographers.

Histojectory will require the brevity "hty" or "hjy" symbol to be applied after each paragraph, bibliography reference, or indexed reference; which will notify and identify officially any subjective implemented historical data, or standards contrary to "histojectory data or guidelines". Therefore, allowing history students, historians, academia, academe, scholars of historiography, author's, publisher's, and others, "to open the doors", to research, investigation, exploration, translation and interpretation of "all" historiography sourced data, with the noticeable symbol "hty" or "hjy" disclosed in the aforementioned locations as prescribed above.

CHAPTER III

An Interpretive Analysis of the History of Sciences Developed Framework, and Structure that Shaped Global Societies: From Antiquity to Modernity

How was the history of science mentally developed, structured, and advanced through compositions of social, cultural, and politically imminent social conditions? Thereafter, the history of science obtained 21st century industrialized technology in the Western hemisphere (which includes China's technological advancements as a prelude to the introduction of technology for Western industrialization). In acquiring this initial question, it's necessary to pursue rational historical objectives, ideas, goals, and sources pertaining to *The Amalgamation of the history of the sciences.* Beckoning, from antiquity to modernity, selective creative being's internalized and structured technology adaptation, and intellectual focus and vision, within stages of advancing socially, industrially, economically, technologically, and politically; through responsible, reliable, and necessary acclimatized civil maturity. Example, during the initial formative stages of the *Enlightenment Era* in the Western World; *creative idealist or crusaders* rationalized that *material* objects do not exist independent of the mind, and therefore set-out to identify and structure the study of their phenomenal surroundings within the physical and natural *World* they lived in. Example, physical surroundings concerns comparative study of human evolution, variation, and classification through rational measurement and observation. Case in point, natural intellectual reason conforms within the ordinary course of nature; as opposed to the supernatural causes that it rejects; because natural intellect exercises the development *by human reason alone, rather than by revelation or religion. However, by exercising or* using intellectual observation, through normal or usual characteristic identity of events, which follows and links their course of exploration; which distinguish the relevance of observation, investigation, exploration, interpretation, adaptation, and application in understand these *material objects that* surrounds the environment. Therefore, creative idealists initially utilized systematic research, observation, and scientific skills, with extraordinary mental acuity. Noteworthy, mental observation and discovery in this era of "Enlightenment" or "Ages of reason" era, was not governed or administered with authoritative mandate; therefore, discovery and technological innovations efficiently and beneficially exceeded authoritative and regulative governmental design, policy, and proposal; through cognitive independent reflective rational.

Importantly, prior to Western (and Asian) civilizations development of physical and natural sciences; valid precedence established by *primitive* cave dwellers, (Neanderthal's and the likes...) embraced practical utility of environmental situations, through *cause and effect* from natural environmental surroundings, namely, by stumbling accidentally into social or group sustainable physical and natural scientific absorption; such as the discovery of fire, through physical and natural scientific fusion from environmental exposure. Thusly, initiating the framework for advanced civilizations subsequent following from their physical and natural discoveries which furthered their exploits, exploring, interpreting, and natural innovations from environmentally progressive discoveries. "Thusly, initiating *the construction for advanced mentalities to further comprise their quality of life". Universal/ Worldly matter possesses and retains within its natural and physical embodiment and quintessence: existing independent, with timeless virtues and assets within its fundamental nature, that initialized scientific development, framework, and constructive management"...* However, mankind's further ambitions and desirous obligations to acquire scientific knowledge and skills, endeavors the conquest of advancing and expanding *"natural and physical laws". Therefore, r*equiring valid proof of phenomenon that so far is unknown, until discovery; which is invariably under the natural or physical condition of the interactions with *universal matter. Scientific analysis conjoined with exploitive mental* credibility evolves a relationship proven as absolute from both mathematical and logical expressions; Consequently, furthering scientific explorations; *as the reserved regularity of the natural and physical World.* Thusly, over-powering colloquial and pseudo-intellectual gravity, which is enforced and calculated from *"deceptive superficial apparentness"*, rather than by analytical scientific confirmation. Therefore, emotional speculation in science, and society is nurtured to stabilize fear, insecurities, and titled superficial personas (such as outdated conservative governance). Thusly, superficially ruling and governing society from old outlandish traditions). Example," Dr. Martin L. King Jr.", "Alexander Solzhenitsyn", The Kennedy's (Robert and John), Ralph Nader, and many other creative social scientist, as opposed to natural scientists, were socially dismissed from society by ignorant, and vain governance; primarily to quince their insecurities, and to insure their antiquated (outdated) philosophical might, influence, prestige, and office. This deliberate type of governance stagnates society, politics, economics, and progressive industrialization, which is gainfully connected to the advancement of the development, framework, structure, and progression of science in the global communities.

Furthermore, *"An Interpretive Analysis of the History of Science"*, over decades and centuries of discovery has endured *Governmental* and *Religious* roadblocks, legislative roadblocks, and untimely setbacks, to the allegiance of pure ignorance, regarding civilizations endeavors to industrialize, intellectualize, and minimize insurmountable and overwhelming opaque, muddy, impervious and blinding *governmental deceptions;* which destroys progressive scientific progress to know avail. However, the catch 22 circumvents societal economic progression that is sponsored by creative pioneering industrialists (to the likes of Henry Ford), and the people for the people, that promote and validate *Sciences expanding innovations, that overcame the negation by governance to blindside creative individual's, and group innovations; which promotes their social progression and individual recognition; namely, influence and power that's disdained by zealous, fanatical, and obsessive politicians; who's power, vanity, and bastard social elitism (snobbery and selectiveness towards many), which has created their superficial social prominence, or prestige to rule, dictate, and divide themselves from select disenfranchised creative individuals; who regardless of their social status, has acquired innate innovative Scientific credibility; even though they were hampered by their humble social status.* However, many talented and proven creative innovative scientist have yet to be invested as responsible and socially privileged citizens, due to their socially inherited inability to acquire financial support or employment stability; especially in the "private infrastructure sectors" of industry. However, the crux of this matter is "*The History of Science*";which has endured prior, during, and after the Enlightenment Era and Scientific Revolution. The *Western World's 1ˢᵗ and 2ⁿᵈ Industrial Revolutions;* has enabled the emergence of a victorious *World* leading Western Industrialized *Capitalistic Powers (In the Americas and Europe); through its independent and innovative creative and cognitive acuity.*

Furthermore, antiquarian scholarly precedence (books) utilized by ancient *Scientist and Universities* (primarily in Europe, Africa, University of Timbuktu, Asia, South America and Mexico et. al.), through concise scientific precedence, from facilitated scientific data, relevant in fostering progressive creative thinker's towards scientific progression in ancient eras. Consequently, knowledge was preserved and forwarded from primary sourced data that's contributed enormously to the progress of the "History of Science". Notably, *a Universal* pledge of scholarly discipline was ordained by responsible scholar's who maintain concise accumulative scientific statistics. Thereafter, abstract scientific thinking evolved through hypothetical premise and observational research, to objective scientific reliability, emerging from factual analytical resolve to the systematic pursuit of science.

By virtue of mankind's mental spirit and temperament in observing and exploiting natural and physical scientific adaptation to their surroundings, *"The History of Science"* was born. Thusly, eradicating speculative scientific *affectations* that "pacified and appeased enlightened *artificial authoritative (government and religious)" social* norms and rules, that conjured up controlled and regulated scientific discoveries. Subsequently, limiting sciences natural relationship between mankind's discovered *academic and systematically acquired knowledge, which pertains to* natural *(inherited)* and physical *(earthly)* Universal exploitations *prior and during, "The Scientific Revolution" and "The Enlightenment Period".* However, despite bureaucratic and religious suffering during the aforementioned eras-in-time; however, the state-of-the-art inventions in the sciences embraced, capitalized, and enhanced cultural, social, economic, and political refinement through authentic scientific discoveries, which "reference the Scientific Revolution", and the emergence of contemporary science; during the premature contemporary time period in history. Thusly, energizing the advancements in physics, astronomy, biology, mathematics, chemistry, and medicines, which enhanced creative innovative ideological perspectives of individual and collective thinkers; which initially evolved from traditional accounts established by the "scientific revolution". The "scientific revolution" began in Europe near the conclusion of the Renaissance age, and persevered through the *belated* 18th century. Thusly, greatly influencing the *"intellectual social crusade" known as the "Enlightenment Period".* There are many debatable uncertainties concerning the time-and-dates of the Enlightenment era; however the *periodicals of 1543* regarding *"Nicolaus Copernicus's"* <u>*De revolutionibus orbium coelestium*</u> and <u>*Andreas Vesalius's De humani coporis fabrica,*</u> is regularly referred to as evidencing the origin of the *"Scientific Revolution". Consequently,* it's alleged that by the close of the 18th century, the *"Scientific Revolution"* ceded to the *"Age of Reflection".* Notably, the term *"Scientific Revolution"* was coined by Philosopher and Historian *"Alexandre Koyle"* in 1939 to describe and define this progressive era-in-time.

Intellectual innovative scientist's (c. 1500 – 1800's) regarded the developmental stages of the "History of Science" as a visionary phenomenon towards ingenious creative and resourceful progress associated with unimaginable inventive scientific discoveries. Notably, the *"Age of Reason"* in Europe and the "Western World", intensely advocated the use of "reason and individualism" instead of established traditional collective dogma.

"The History of Science" is / was evident of attestation, which served to either support or counter an accord with scientific methods established and structured from *newly acquired* and *established* factual scientific *methodology*. Standards for scientific evidence during the initial stages of development varied in accordance to the field of inquiry, as it's applied currently in the 21st century. The strength of *scientific evidence* is generally based on the results of "*statistical analysis"* and the strength of *scientific management, expertise, regulation, inspection, operation, control, and authenticity.* Notwithstanding, mankind embraced scientific refinement through authentic scientific discovery. Therefore, augmenting economic, political, cultural and moral social resilience. Yet, historically falling short in amalgamating *"The History of Science", as a social priority* in the initial stages of its development. Example, in the 14th-18th century's most scientific innovative endeavors combated religious, political, and traditional governance to promote social, economic, and progressive industrialization. Consequently, most early inventors were visionaries ahead of the times, based on their perceptive intellectual ingenuity, skills, and inventiveness; too emerge forward within their scientific discoveries against all traditional odds, during that aforementioned era (14th to 18th epoch). Both Western and Eastern civilizations retarded *individual scientific* discoveries if not sanctioned or approved through authoritative covenant during antiquarian era's as late as the 18th century. The

breeding of academic discipline and discovery of natural and physical science enhanced immeasurably the economic social structure of global society, academic progression and eventually global institutions; that awakened mankind's intellectual potential, and acute mental dexterity in natural and physical scientific discovery.

"Western Civilizations" awakened to the call for objective truth, as opposed to religious, and traditional beliefs regulated by the power structures that laid-down supreme ascendency over their citizens and vassals, to the extent of "social banishment, inquisition, or prison internment, to these innovative select ingenious individual scientist who questioned traditional (antiquated), and religious natural and physical scientific presumptive beliefs. Example, "the *"Copernican theory"* that the *Earth* revolved around the *Sun, which opposed* the *traditional Church's* assertion, which challenged the Church's creed, doctrine, and principles of the Universe.

Thereafter, placing him under the conviction of their first critically reprimanded scientist, regarding his *theories;* which contradicted the religious scientific natural and physical scientific doctrine, that was delegated and regulated by the Church during that era. Notably, *Copernicus and Galileo were persecuted by the Roman Catholic Church for their theories regarding their historical and brilliant Universal discoveries; however, Copernicus didn't publish his theory until his last days; therefore he was not persecuted as Galileo was regarding the infamous inquisition.* The Church labeled them both *heretics,* by spreading their scientific opinions referencing their discoveries; which contradicted the Church's *Holy Scripture.* The *Church's* traditional *Holy Bible* translated that "the earth was at the *center of the solar system, as opposed to Copernicus theory that the Sun was at the center of the solar system*, and the earth *and planets circled or revolved around it".*

Eastern Civilizations, notably *China's* scientific discoveries enabled the Western World's dominance through the advent and brilliant inventive technologies, to name a few, as follows: the compass (sustained excellent sea navigation), gunpowder, crossbow, lithography, farming equipment, and a multitude of innovative creations that fostered Western World dominance. However, it's noted historically, that Chinese scientific inventions occurred and ended through the authority of China's estimated five-hundred and fifty-two (552) imperial Emperor's reign s over its' life-span. Importantly, many questions from the West arise concerning China's remarkable head-start with regards to her brilliant innovative scientific discoveries before European and Western civilizations commenced. Question, "Why didn't China *cultivate and develop* an *"Industrial Revolution over its illustrious inventive centuries; and why did they fall behind the Western World in scientific development"? In "Jared Diamond's"* <u>Guns, Germs, and Steel</u>, the author hypothesizes that the "lack of geographical barriers within much of China's geographically enormous wide plains, with two large navigational rivers, and a relatively smooth coastline, which encompass a single government without competition; Unfortunately, at the passing impulse and inference of the Imperial Emperor's, who disliked newly innovative scientific inventions and technologies, stifled innovative Chinese science for centuries". Dissimilarly, Europe (Britain, Germany, Russia, Poland, Ireland, Italy, Sicily, Greece, Denmark, France, Spain Scandinavia, etc...) was surrounded by barriers, such as the Alps, and various peninsulas, such as the Pyrenees, and many surrounding islands, did not possess the geographical solace afforded China. Therefore, Europe was surrounded by combative aggressive neighboring countries in close proximity, and endured constant competitive challenge between each other to sustain their independent (self autonomy) and sovereignty. Thusly, as opposed to China's geographical surroundings; who possessed an opened environment, with less competitive neighbors as compared to Europe's neighboring rivalries with her aggressive neighbor Nations proximity to her (except for China's Mongolian conquest, and Japanese bandits).

Therefore, Western innovative technology was essential for scientific advancement, if they were to survive their surrounding environment against their aggressive self-sufficient neighbor Nation's. Therefore, *"The History of Science"* in the Western World, as opposed to China, was in constant mobility throughout the later centuries after China's ingenious inventions; which was advanced scientifically with advanced arsenal, which enhanced their military scientific inventions; enabling them to remain sovereign. Otherwise, if European diligence slacked in perpetual industrialization, or if assiduous neighboring European nations became deficient in scientific technology, they would have succumbed to the probability of their Nations being overthrown by their surrounding competitive self-autonomous combatant neighbor Nations. Contrarily, Western Nations never ceased their scientific industrialization of military, economic, and political scientific advancement progression; to sustain their independence, and counter or retaliate against any and all perils, and risks to their sovereignty. Noteworthy, China's historically ageless civilization, was politically, socially, economically, and militarily fragmented by their *Imperial Potentate's, and by the Mongolian invasion, which stifled "Their Scientific* progression. The Imperial Emperor's inaugurated or prevented scientific discovery, within their time-table of imperial demands; causing highly developed scientific progress to come to a halt at will; or by abruptly demanding innovative inventions to proceed at the *Imperial Ruler's* command. This aforementioned theory of China's reactionary justification, motivation, and impeding quagmire not to further the "Development of Science", was blamed on *China's Imperial Rulers ironed-fisted* governance. However, during China's earlier innovative and alluring scientific inventions, which propelled European and *Western World* dominance, China's inventions annexed unrelenting appendage to the success of both Europe and America's, *"History of Science's" with successful "Industrialization".* A vast number of China's inventions fostered Western dominance and power throughout the World, and they are as follows: *silk, lacquer, porcelain, paper, tea, gunpowder, numerous tools and farm equipment, drilling equipment, foods, medicines, printing techniques and equipment, navigational and directional compasses, zinc, explosions (firecrackers), rockets, guns, building techniques and materials, shipbuilding, and the crossbow, is* to name a few, of China's inventions that propelled the *Western World's universal, political, economic, military, and social* ascendancy to rule the World and become Empires.

Quite similar of the *Christian Church's* assertive, and dominant influence regarding *European, and the Western Worlds* suppressive dominance, over scientific discovery in the *14th to 18th* centuries, also closely relates to China's *Imperial Emperor's* authority over *scientific discovery,* in Chinese history. The Catholic Church regarded the *"Popes"* written *proclamations, decrees, and commands* as *"Directives from Heaven", within canon* and Christian doctrine (*Galileo's inquisition,* and *Copernicus innovative* scientific, and academic stagnation, curtailed his scientific discoveries; which was based on Christian Religious bureaucratic ignorance, dominance, and social and political control).

However, within both social and cultural ethnicities (Western and Oriental), scientific discovery was stifled or subdued through "Imperial domination". "The Christian Church and the Popes written proclamations maintained authoritative rule over society"; which was deep-rooted over innovative and creative scientific thinker's, on both continents during that era. *Mao Zedong's leadership was from (1945 to 1966), The Cultural Revolution commenced in (1966), and reformed China's political, economical, social, and military rule in 1945, enabling* China to become a *single party Socialist State*, which eliminated the traditional *"Imperial Emperor dictatorship laws" enacted by pasts bureaucracies.* Comparatively, in earlier years before "Mao's cultural revolution; "The Age of Enlightenment" in Europe, was a cultural movement consisting of academic scholar's such as scientist, philosopher's, and creative thinker's in the 16th to 18th centuries; and thereafter within the American colonial settlements. Noteworthy, the first "New World's" colonial settlement was located in Jamestown, Virginia. However, this "Enlightenment Era" carry over to Jamestown, which drastically revolutionized the social order and industrialization framework, by instituting intellectualism and creative innovation, which was also known as the Enlightenment Period. The *1st industrial revolution* started in Europe, and 2nd industrial revolution in the "New World". Therefore the elimination of "old" ingrained concepts and beliefs which were rooted and entrenched in the "Old World's" antiquated customs brought to the "New World; but was quickly uprooted by this new era. Thereafter, industrial progression and development enhanced creative innovative social advancements, through scientific and methodical practice, approach, interpretation, research and production of progressive utility. The Age of Enlightenment endorsed and stimulated scientific contemplation, deliberation, incredulity and scholarly exchange. Consequently, challenging antagonistic misconceptions, small-mindedness, and biasness of authority, neglect, exploitation, and abuses by supremacy of Church, and State was the major antagonists that stagnated scientific progression, during that era. The Churches control was ignored and eventually defeated over time (1890's), in the direction for an industrialized progressive society in the "New World", that ultimately, enhanced its cultures, politics, governance, and economical structural stability. The creativity of the "Age of Enlightenment" started approximately in "1650-1700", and it's alleged to have prospered until the 1800's. History holds the following Philosopher's as the initial contributors bringing into being the "Age of Enlightenment": "Pierre Bayle", "Kant", "John Locke", "Hobbes", "Rousseau", "Montesquieu", "Isaac Newton", "Kepler", "Baruch Spinoza", and "Voltaire" to name a few... However, the "Age of Enlightenment" gave way to "Romanticism Philosophy", which accentuated prominence to "Motion", with a "Counter or Contradictive-Enlightenment" which acquired force and influence.

Romanticism emphasis enabled artistic, literary, and intellectual movements that originated in Europe in approximately 1800 -1850. Its response to the "Industrial Revolution", was induced through "Aristocratic social and political norms;" of the "Age of Enlightenment", with a coincidental ramification against "The Scientific Rationalization of Nature". It personified the visual arts, music, and literature, with a predominant bearing on historiography, education and the natural sciences. Additionally, it was allied with liberalism and radicalism or extremism; however, its effect on "nationalism" was of great importance. With its position on strong emotions as an authentic and genuine resource for aesthetic experience, with great emphasis on such emotions as, horror, and terror; that confronted the sublimity of untamed nature, with its picturesque qualities of characterizations. However, It's alleged to have promoted folk art, and ancient customs to nobility, and argued for a natural epistemology of human activities, which is habituated by nature in the arrangement of language and customary practice. Romanticisms objective and prototypical was destined to promote, advance, and revive medievalism or old-fashioned origins of art and narrative, in an attempted exodus of quarantines of population growth, metropolitan breakdown, and industrialization. All the while implementing the bizarre, and unaccustomed by coupling the powers of the minds-eye (creativity) to imagine and flee (escape).

The framework structure and development establishing and instituting "The History of Science" has elevated our social, religious, economic, military, and political awareness within an industrialized global approach to a foreseeable ultramodern and space-age civilization.

"Intelligent Design," must be explicated in *"An Interpretative Analysis of the History of Science"*; due to contrasting ideology regarding "intelligent designs" explanation of the creation of the Universe by specified or unspecified "supernatural" processes; versus, the *scientific* communities *rejecting* the *extension* of science to include *supernatural* explanations, in favor of *continued acceptance of methodological naturalism*, which has rejected both tortuous complexity and precise complexity for an extensive scope of theoretical and true-life deficiencies. Briefly, "intelligent design" nurtures "certain features of the *"Universe"* and "of living things," which is alleged to be supported by an "intelligent cause", not an

undirected process such as *"natural selection"*. *Intelligent design* is a contemporaneous reworking of the traditional "study of evidences of designs in nature, which enhances a doctrine explaining phenomena by *final causes; which is an argument for the existence of "God"*. Thusly, exhibited by its supporters and believers as a "testimonial based scientific theory about *life's origin, as opposed to a "religious based idea"*. However, advocates of "Intelligent Design" believes the designer of the *Universe* and *all living things* to be none other *than Christian Deity (God)*. Importantly, *intelligent design* is viewed as a *pseudoscience* by the *scientific community,* since it lacks pragmatic and experimental sustenance, justifiable, or rational theories, premises and hypotheses.

Additionally, Europe's 18th century "Industrial Revolution" transformed human labor, consumption, family structure, and social structure through the advent of physical and natural scientific discovery.

Thereafter, *"Darwinian"* evolutionary scientific progress emerged, embracing the "Age of Enlightenment; with modern Western thinking that opened closed mines to reflect, observe, research, explore, investigate, interpret, and apply factual scientific innovation. It's alleged the *Scientific Revolution* refers to the period between Copernicus and Newton's scientific accomplishments; however, the chronological era's defining commencement and ending of the *"Scientific Revolution" prolongs* within a seventy (70) year span Prolific scholar "Immanuel Kant" (1784) defines the "Age of Enlightenment by his rendition as: "What is Enlightenment"?

"Enlightenment is a Man's leaving his self-caused immaturity. Immaturity

Is the incapacity to use one's own understanding without the guidance of

Another. Such immaturity is self-caused if it's cause is *not lack of intelligence,*

But by lack of determination and courage to use one's intelligence without

Being guided by another. The motto of "Enlightenment" is therefore:

Sapere Aude! "Have courage to use your own intelligence"!

Aforementioned earlier but with lesser pronounced detail of "The Age of Enlightenments concept; which progresses within the aphorisms of "Kant's" philosophy; which correlates rational, orderly, and comprehensive intelligence in harmony with mental liberty, to resolve natural and physical sciences innovations freely, within the context of using one's intelligence independently. "Kant" proclaims further within *metaphorical perception,* that the *maturity of man's independent intelligent* assessments regarding *"The Age of Enlightenment Revolution"* must be supported within the context and framework of "State" governance with structured management and stable laws. Thusly, networking the role of the "State" with its relationship to the individual's newly innovative 18th century philosophy, to promote a viable conceptual utility for Western World development.

From the "scientific revolution" emerged *modern science* during the early modern era, when developments of mathematics, physics, astronomy, biology, medicine, and chemistry revised perceptions of society and nature. One of the most creditable natural scientists who emerged from the concepts and intellect of the "scientific revolution" was "Charles Darwin"; an English naturalist, who originated and formulated the "theory of evolution". He speculated and propositioned that species with life over-time came from common ancestors. He then invented a branching pattern of evolution evolving from a "process he labeled "natural selection" through the survival-of-the fittest existence, which has a similar effect as the simulated selection required in "selective breeding". He published *"Origin of Species"* in 1859, over-coming many scientific put-downs of his early concepts of transmutation of species. Three (3) distinguished Darwinian accomplishments of many are as follows: *"evolutionary biology, philosophy of science, and the modern zeitgeist, ideas and spirit of time, ideas radiating more prevalent within a "period of time".*

This limited analysis of "The History of Science" and, "The Scientific Revolution" presented in stages of speculated chronology accomplished the following innovative scientific discoveries: the "chemical revolution, earth age/conservation of energy, Darwinian era, new biology, science and gender, ecology and environmentalism, medicines, genetics, human science, science and religion, (20th) century physics, science and warfare, post-cold war-fare science, revolutionizing cosmology, and science and technology etc…

The first and second "Industrial Revolutions", commencing in Europe and the American Colonies respectively, were monumental models inherited from the "History of Science" and "The Scientific Revolution". The campaign from Europe to America, initiated in 1760-1776, which traversed "The Industrial Revolutions", which cultivated and nurtured the "Western World's" influence and, super-natural global domination.

Lastly, *"An Interpretive Analysis of the History of Science"* in overall description, enlightenment, and accounts with primary objectives was to encourage readers from all fields of endeavors, to pursue further *research of this" history of science";* towards authenticating valid precedence and, chronology of these fervent scientific events and occurrences.

CHAPTER IV

The Conservation of Energy and its Development

(Analyzed and Interpreted Independently and
Histojectically By: William F. Williams)
*An Objective and Subjective Interpretation of
the Conservation of Energy Development*

A novel "Physical Science" discovery "Conservation of Energy" occurred in Europe in 1832-1854; however, Britain, France, and Germany were the three countries initially associated in this theoretical discovery. Philosopher *"Thomas Kuhn"* states in *"Peter Bowler and Iwan Rhys Morus" Making Modern Science*, that the discovery of the timing of *"Conservation of Energy"*, *"establishes concern of the object (entity), and the simultaneity (coordination) of the discovery"*. Therefore, *"Kuhn" further theorize, "that the conservation of energy is not an object discoverable, but a mere theoretical generalization"*.

This consequential analysis and viewpoint of *"The Conservation of Energy"*, is indeed a theoretical generalization at this juncture in time. Noteworthy, this theory of discovery was conducted within a thirty year period, and labeled *"Conservation of Energy"*. Properly, the question of discovery poses an additional perception of *"Conservation of Energies"* position in *Physical Science*, and *Nature* as a discovery; *due to its natural existence in physical nature,* which would nullify its discovery. Thusly, becoming a *crucial scientific study* within its *natural* existence in the

Universe as matter; and within the scope of the history of physical science. Within the field of science "conservation of energy" refers to the *"Laws" Structuring Conservation of Energy*. Additionally, one specific "Law" of the conservation of energy instructs that "energy" can transfer from one form to another and cannot be created or destroyed. However, in basic scientific terminology concerning "energy" reference it as an assertion (affirmation), and that energy from one form to another namely, e.g. nuclear, sunlight, wind, gas, coal, petroleum, kinetic, electrostatic, gravitational, chemical etc…; Consequently, the "Laws" of "conservation of energy" references that the total amount of "energy" in the Universe's isolated system never change or vacillate within its element or essence. Furthermore, in this simultaneous scientific "theoretical generalization" referred to as the "trigger factor" by many scientists, and most notable in the book titled *"Energy Conservation" as An Example of Simultaneous Discovery"*; the source and phenomenon of "simultaneous discovery" was challenged within the timetable of 1832-1854, or a twelve year scientific research conducted by Britain, France, and Germany. Coincidentally, twelve scientists were involved in this phenomenal exercise as distinguished, and are presented as follows: "Robert Mayer, James Joule, Emile Clapeyron, Ludwig Colding, Sadie Carnot, Hermann Helmholz, William Grove, and Karl F. Mohr, Clausius, Rankine, Maxwell, and Boltzmann. Each scientist grasping for themselves "the essential elements of the concepts of "energy" and its "conservation". The question arise as to why these specific scientific elements became accessible at-this-point-in-time, seeking to identify "not the innumerable prerequisites of energy conservation", but the "trigger factors"?

Significantly, the three major factors suggested for this "simultaneous research phenomena and phenomenon", relates to the development of engines, conversion process, and philosophy of nature.

> "Discovering a new sort of phenomena
> is necessarily a complex
> Event, one which involves recognizing
> both that something is and
> *What it is*. Note for example, that if
> oxygen were dephlogisticated
> Air for us, we should insist without
> hesitation that Priestley had
> Discovered it, though we would still not know quite when.
> But if observation and conceptualization,
> fact and assimilation to
> Theory, are inseparably linked in
> discovery therefore discovery is a
> Process and must take time."
> Thomas Kuhn [4]

The theoretical experience of "living force", or principles of the conservation of energy was indeed observed and conceptualized through facts and assimilation theory, "to transfer energy from one form to another within its natural creation and undisturbed nature. However, scientific argument is predicated on the *"convergence"* within the "Laws of Conservation" by the twelve (12) aforementioned scientists simultaneously, and in differing scientific experimental methods, approaches, logics, and techniques. The other pieces to the puzzle were these discoveries that originated from different locations, and *"all were in thirty year periods", how did this happen*? Additionally, the other pending scientific question concerns the legitimization of "conservation of energy" being a discovery, objective matter, entity, or theoretical generalization? Aforementioned, "conservation of energy" is claimed undiscoverable due to its natural existence in the Universe. However, as scientific ideology change and modify concerning the underlying fundamental nature of physical reality, comparably their characterizations transforms *to what it was* explicitly that expressed discovery! However, scientific discovery in (finding out progressive discovery) suggests that *discovery* requires valid authenticity, and if authentic qualifications is not met, as to an alleged discovery, then scientific discovery is without merit or fact; regarding the discovery of "Conservation of Energy". Furthermore, the process by which a discovery acquires meaning is not effectively complete until a scientific consensus has been obtained with regard to its characterization of up-to-date validity. Therefore, up-to-date meaning and qualifications for the discovery of "conservation of energy", in relative numerous physical theories validates what scientists reference "stable consensus" [6]. Example, from a mathematical assessment "the conservation of energy" is understood as a result of *"Noether Theorem,"* which identifies every *continuous symmetry of a physical theory* with *an associated conserved quantity*. However, if the theories symmetry is *time invariance* then the conserved quantity, is scientifically called "energy" [9]. The remaining question to discovery and the validity of "conservation of energy" as a discovery, is evident in fact that the word "energy" was not applied to describe the "quantity" being during its alleged discovery. Question, could this name "energy" be applied with *another* cultural language besides the English vernacular? Noteworthy, the word "energy" was coined by Thomas Young, an English physicist and physician, in the nineteenth century. Conversely, *Karl Mohr (1837)*, reciting his definition of "conservation of energy" states as follows: *"Besides the fifty-four known chemical elements in the physical world, one agent called "kraft" may appear according to circumstance as: "motion, chemical affinity, cohesion, electricity, light and magnetism; and from any one of these forms it can be transformed into any of the others"* [11]. Consequently, the German word *"kraft" translates to "energy" in the German language, and is defined as "energy, force, and power.* Noteworthy, the word "kraft" earlier in time cited by the German scientist *"Mohr"* was identifying "conservation of energy", therefore the German word "kraft" translated to the English language could now be referenced by modern-day scientists, including *"Kuhn", as an identifiable interpretation of "conservation of energy ".* Thereafter, it was determinant in *"Kuhn's" identity interpretation of its* discovery, simultaneity, objectivity, and theoretical generalizations within the "scientific genre", which he labeled *"stable consensus",* which includes *"Kuhn's" modern-day definition of* chronology of time, and conserved quantity interpretation in regards to that time-period (1832-1854).

"Conservation of Energy" reflects in its swift symmetry of time as conservation understood without being openly expressed by experiments and observations of facts that the *"laws of physics"* is constant with *"time"* within itself. Additionally, from a transparent scientific view, the physical set-of- arrangements of the "energy conservation law" is *invariant* under the *continuance symmetry*, or with reference to interrelations of parts to form a whole. Therefore, its properties are *invariant* under the *esthetic equilibrium* of time *translation*, at that point time is *conserved. Contrastingly,* non-invariant systems under time swifts do not display

"conservation of energy" without the exchange of energy with an "external system"; thereafter, reinventing invariance again. Thusly, qualifying the conservation of energies numerous characteristics in physical theory.

"The three primary factors in the "conservation of energy", as defined by *"Thomas Kuhn"* in simultaneous discovery is: *"the concern with engines, availability of the* conversion *process, and the philosophy of nature"* [12].

The *"development of engines,* through *conservation of energy, which* began almost simultaneously in *England, France, and Germany,* from 1820-1860's. Frenchman, *Leonard Sadi Carnot's* heat engine, named *"Carnot's Cycle"* was invented in 1824, and graphically expanded upon by his French counterpart, *Benoit Paul Emile Clapeyron* (1834). German physicist and mathematician, "Julius Emanuel Clausius" reinstated "Sadi Carnot's principle known as "Carnot's Cycle", and refined *the" theory of heat",* *on a" solid foundation".* One of "Clausius" most innovative Principles was the *"Mechanical Theory of Heat",* which was published in (1850). Additionally, *he initially stated the basic ideas of the "Second Law of Thermodynamics",* from which the abstract notion of "thermodynamics" developed in 1865; furthermore, he introduced the concept of *"entropy"* in 1870, and introduced *"virial theorem",* which applied to *"heat",* indeed a groundbreaking scientific innovator. *Clapeyron's* expansion from *"Sadie Carnot's"* invention, references further, the ideal *"Gas Law"* which is principled on the *"equation of state"* of a hypothetical *"ideal gas".* Being a *virtuous* approximation to the *"natural behavior"* of numerous gases under various *circumstances,* with *a number of inadequacies and restrictions,* but indeed a ground-breaking innovator.

Michael Faraday, is *respectably* one of history's most worthy scientist, an English chemist and physicist acclaimed his union between electricity and magnetism; which enabled ingenious contribution to the fields of electromagnetism and electrochemistry. His ingenious scientific breakthroughs included "electromagnetic induction", diamagnetism and electrolysis. His research in the "magnetic field" around *"conductors carrying direct current", which* enabled "Faraday's" inventive basis for the theory of the *"electromagnetic field in physics"*. Additionally, he theorized correctly that magnetism affected *"rays of light",* and that there was a causal connection between these two phenomena. He progressed scientifically to innovate the *"principles of electromagnetic induction, diamagnetism"*, and the *"laws of electrolysis"*. Most importantly, his creation of *"Electromagnetic rotary devices"*, molded the groundwork for "electric motors", and practical "electricity technology. This incredible *"mind"* (Faraday), established through chemistry the discovery of "benzene", explored, researched, and interpreted *"clathrate hydrate of chlorine",* which furthered his ingenious inclination to innovate an early form of "Bunsen burner*", and the* "oxidation numbering system, that propelled his initiative *to* propagate vocabulary terms, such as: anode, electrode, cathode, and ion. *"Michael Faraday's" scientific* contribution to the Western World, and Global Community, attributed him the honor of being appointed "Fullerian Professor of Chemistry at the Royal Institution of Great Britain". The most "Highly Honor Seat" for this incredible "Scientific Scholarly Genius". Lastly, Since our prime topic is *"<u>The Conservation of Energy and its Development</u>"*, through further research and objective data sourcing, "Faraday's" invention of the *alternator* which consists of a copper disk, that functionally rotates between the poles of a permanent magnet, which produces an electromotive force that incredibly moves and generates electricity, that required his discovery of another form of energy, that transformed from one type of energy to another type. Knowledgeably, in the field of physics "The Conservation of Energy Law", states that "energy cannot create or destroy, and therefore is a constant, endless, continuous, ceaseless, and unremitting entity. Therefore, "Faraday's" transformation of one type of energy to another, which ultimately processed and generated electricity, which confirms "Physics" and "The Law of Conservation of Energy".

"I believe that our observation thus far has shown
clearly that congruence or incongruence
Between an idea as experienced retrospectively,
and the description given by the true
Originator himself can be explained simply by
the fact that the true creator of a new idea
Is not an individual, but the thought collective,
as has been repeatedly stressed, the
Collective remodeling of an idea has the effect
that after the change in thought style, the
Earlier problem is no longer completely comprehensible"
L. Fleck [13]

"Conservation of Energy's" earlier forum presents from 1841-1854, Scientist's that sprung, soared, and elevated physical sciences introduction into modernity, and they are: English Physicist *"James Joule"*, *"German Physicist Robert Mayer"* and, *"German Physician and Physicist Hermann Helmholtz"*. On July 23, 1847, *"Helmholtz"* presented a lecture titled "Conservation of Force", at the Physical Society. He states that, *"Force [Kraft]"* is equivalent to the modern term "energy". His lecture was received with dignity, however he was forced to publish it as a pamphlet after a Physical Society member "Poggendoff" rejected it for his "Annalen", or "Annals" accountability, or chronology was speculative (hypothesized or theorized). However, *"Helmholtz" offered a* summarized conclusion modified in words, but exact in objective implication as follows:

"The inference of the submission enclosed in the thesis may be grounded on either of two tenets; either on the tenet that it is not likely by any union whatever of natural bodies to develop an unlimited amount of mechanical force, or on the theory that all behavior in nature can be eventfully referred to alluringly or from repulsive forces, the strength of which hinge on the distances between the points at which the forces are exerted". He stated that" both of his propositions were identical at the beginning of his memoirs" [15].

"James Joule, and Robert Mayer", substantiated in varying degrees, *"Helmholtz's"* theories relating to their formulated principles of the "Conservation of Energy", with affirmative results. They theorized that the "conservation of energy", or momentum, thrust, force, and the "mass of a particle", "times the square of its velocity" confirming the "Conservation of Energy" theories postulated by all three scientists. "Joule" and "Mayer's" went back and forth theorizing that heat and mechanical labor are interchangeable. From this critical discourse between *"Joule and Mayer's", "Helmholtz"* got wind-of-their intellectual encounter, and called on "Joule's" scientific discourse to put together the principles regarding the "Conservation of Kinetic Energy". "Helmholtz" does not argue that kinetic energy is conserved, rather, that the overall scalar is identifiable as a variable quantity that cannot be resolved into components, and a quantity that

has magnitude but not direction. Yet, kinetic energy may be converted into other forms of energy such as heat, but the numerical (scalar) quantity of energy will be conserved [16].

Thomas Kuhn's puzzlement concerns the timing of this scientific "Conservation of Energy" discovery between England, France, and Germany, which was conducted simultaneously, and exemplified in theoretical discourse over an approximate forty plus year period from commencement date to ending date. "Helmholtz" convergence with "Joule" and "Mayer's", and fellow peer's in Europe, bridged the gaps for valid and concrete accomplishments within the "Conservation of Energy" physical science field of study. In one of Helmholtz's essays he acknowledged previous scientists contributions that includes: "Joule, Mach, Newton, Bernoulli, and Rumford. In his "History of Mechanics", *Ernst Mach argues* that "almost all eminent scientific researchers new some form of Helmholtz's principles of "Kraft" *or "energy".* Therefore, it's obvious that these aforementioned scientist had some form of *"communication link"* or *"information diffusion"* towards the same scientific objectives and goals to master the "Conservation of Energy" principles. "It may have been through a University rumor mill" interchange during that period in time 1820-1860's; that networked a simultaneous European theory to affirm the "Conservation of Energy Law". Nonetheless, the coinciding and synchronized "Conservation of Law" theories were a pathfinder towards a new physics and physical science evolution process of innovation during that era. The availability of the *conversion process* during that era defines the connection between labor and energy. Also, the kinship and scientific manner of being connected between the two conversion processes is paramount to the conservation of energy thermodynamics. However, when brought into action in a scientific environment the calculated labor process defines a detailed account of energy or intensity of physical power enforced *"over-a given-interval"* between two points or distance:

The Equation "Work = Force x Distance".

The above equation is the mathematical symbolism of work. However, energy in scientific terminology, as it relates to the conversion process explains its' ability to perform work. Consequently, energy has a multitude of configurations, and forms. Yet, in reference to thermodynamics, energy is physically able to assign and apply kinetic energy that equates to energy connected or associated to motion or heat energy, which is associated to changes in temperature. Therefore, the leading theory of thermodynamics is the transformation of energy (conversion process) from one form to another, or from one location to another, as labor is executed or engaged. This described example explains *"Physics Work Designs",* and energies ability to perform work, through the conversion process and anything that involves moving mass.

The definitive attributes of science cognition requires research, observation, experimentation or scientific application, and rational deductions to perceive discoverable scientific postulations through a scholarly analysis. However, prognostications in the framework of science, surpasses explanations of the project, due to its manifestations of visionary and unwavering potentials to emerge successful with factual results in ones endeavor. Additionally, scientists reveal and symbolize theories in axioms, which is assumed exact, however the true discoveries of scientific axioms conceptualizations is through logic, as variables of exactitude. Yet, scientific discovery is compartmentalized into interconnected components of genuine certainty, which embraces the ultimate objectives, which is *"proven innovative thought collection".*

With the basic understanding of the attributes of science cognition, and the venture or path to *"Thomas Kuhn's", "Philosophy of Nature",* that bridges the gaps historically though earlier scientific discovery, which ultimately establishes his innovative approach to *"Conservation of Energy"* and *"Thermodynamics"* can began thusly: The first *"Law of Thermodynamics"* evolves selectively from *"James Watt's"* invention of the "steam engine", designed in the late 1800's. Most importantly, *Watt's* invention of the steam engine set-in-motions the "Industrial Revolution" in the Western World. Unfortunately, the "steam engine" had many flaws and did not work efficiently, "it's stated with authentic sourced data", that the "steam engine" caught on fire underneath its carriage", which communicated to the scientific community as far as Europe, "a flaw in Watt's cognition of "The Philosophy of Nature". The emergence of the scholarly minds of "Sadi Carnot, Rudolf Clausius, and William Thompson's" "Philosophy of Nature's" conceptualized innovative discovery was that the secondary product for "steam" is "heat"; which is essential to enable Watt's "steam engine" to work properly. Therefore, the process to create a functional efficiently running steam engine, was necessary through the principle theory of "thermodynamics.

"The Philosophy of Nature" was born through the scientific minds of "Carnot, Clausius, Faraday, Thompson and many other earlier "scientific revolutionaries", not mentioned that contributed brilliantly to enhanced the "new Physics". However, these aforementioned scientists are currently World renowned for initiating the application of the "new physics" to comprehend the "thermodynamics process and application". They diagrammatically explained the connection and kinship between "energy" and "work" through thermodynamics, as aforementioned. "Thompson" is alleged to have coined the term "thermodynamics", in approximately 1849-1854. "Clausius" essential innovation was "Mechanische Warmetheorie" or "Mechanical Theory of Heat" conducted in 1850. "Carnot's" axiom was "whatever the working substance", which emanates from "Boerhaave's Law", on the expansion and contraction of bodies due to heat, which refers to any physical body in the Universe. It alleged historically that the first of the aforementioned scientist was "Carnot" to formulate the First Laws of Thermodynamics. This 1st Law was labeled "conservation of energy", which maintains as stated numerously in this research composition project, "that energy cannot be destroyed or created, but can change into many forms". In 1850, "Thompson and Clausius" developed the *2nd* "Law of Thermodynamics"; Thompson conceptualized that heat, which is a form of energy could not convert into "work" without some "loss" of energy; while "Clausius" observed that heat could not proceed from a cold object to a hot object [19]. These two (2) valued theories pertaining to the 2nd "Laws of Thermodynamics", innovated the ideology of entropy, which conceptualizes that energy, which is inclined to scatter-in-all–directions, unless averted. It's alleged that the 3rd "law of thermodynamics" was formed in the 20th century by "Walter Nernst", expressing the nature of *"absolute zero"* that he postulates exist at zero degrees (kelvin). "James Clark Maxwell's" 19th century's contribution to the "zero law", theorize that the "state of equilibrium", balance, or stability of two objects with varied temperatures create neutrality, or noninvolvement when they interaction. The *"History of Science" scholars and peers,* highly regards "Maxwell's" *zero law* theory and propose that "its' rightful place should be selectively deemed the *"1st Law of Thermodynamics"*. However, "Nernst" refined "Maxwell's "zero law theory", and was therefore acclaimed the innovator of the "3rd Law of Thermodynamic; within the framework of the "history of science.

The *"new physics"* is labeled by *"Thomas Kuhn"* as the catalyst that advanced *"conservation of energy"*, which *"Kuhn"* defines as the *"philosophy of nature"*, from which evolves "modern physics"; consequently, within the framework of "conservation of energy", "modern physics defines itself through technological scientific innovation. However, "modern physics" has enabled deep reflective insights into the Western and Global prominence of "Industrialization". Also, the "History of Science", must give notice to the initial applications to the term "natural philosophy", to what we reference today as *"natural science"*, or *"Isaac Newton's" 1687 "scientific treatise"*, referred to as *"The Mathematical Principles of Natural Philosophy"* and "Lord Kelvin" and "Peter Tait's 1867 treatise called "Treatise on Natural Philosophy; which helped define much of "modern physics". *"Kuhn"* states from 1878-1894 in <u>*"Bowler and Morus Making Modern Science" that*</u> "modern physics" emerged from three central factors or theoretical generalizations as follows: "enterprise in the production of engines, the conversion process, and philosophy of nature".

Noteworthy, *"The Berlin School of Physics"*, was born out of the "cultural facts and scientific events" that directed the development of the "conservation of energy", to "modern physics". One of many of the co-discoverers of "kraft", or "conservation of force", was *"Hermann Helmholtz"* 1870-1878, at that time he was the "Director of the Institute of Physics at Berlin University". The following were mentored by Helmholtz: "Max Planck, Albert Einstein, Gustav R. Kirchhoff, Fredrick Kohlrausch, Emil Warburg, Walter Nernst, Max Von Laue, James Franck, Gustav Hertz, Erwin Schodinger, Peter Debye, and others" [21]. As we advance into the late 19th and 20th centuries "Albert Einstein" surface from 1879-1955, who was a German born citizen, and later an American Physicist, who discovered in 1905, "the equivalence of mass and energy". However, within the scientific environment and peer group the "equivalence of mass and energy", was referred to as "light quanta". Thusly, opening the initial stages of "Einstein's two theories for the understanding and emergence of "radiation thermodynamics" and "relativistic thermodynamics". "Einstein's statement concerning "thermodynamics" is as follows: "thermodynamics and its properties are the only physical theory of the Universal content that will never be conquered". It's acknowledged that "Einstein's" younger aged mindset from 1900-1909, was focused on the scientific process of "entropy". It's alleged that "Einstein's" first twenty – thirty published papers, over-all three hundred collectibles, focused on "thermodynamics" [22.]. Strong scientific evidence reveals that "thermodynamics" was a prominent subject matter in "Einstein's" career in his pursuit for a consolidated theory of physics. Example, "Einstein's" classmate "Max Planck", under the mentoring of "Helmholtz", as students collaborated frequently about the interpretation of "photon", and the 'photoelectric" effect, which "equation" represents the "conservation of energy" in the "photoelectric process", eventually known as "Einstein's photoelectric equation". "Einstein" was awarded the "Nobel Peace Prize" for his discovery of "The Law of the Photoelectric effect". Therefore, requiring photons with energies from a few electron volts over *1 meV*, in high atomic number elements. Additionally, the photoelectric effect led to the understanding of the "quantum" nature of light and electrons plus wave-particles, which influenced the formation of the concept of "duality". However, other phenomena where light affects the movement of electric charges includes: "photoconductive effect", "Photovoltaic effect", and "photoelectron chemical effect". "Einstein's" classmate "Max Planck" discovered "Planck's relation linking "energy and frequency", "e = hf" arising from quantization of energy; and the factor "h" is known as the "Planck" *"constant"*. Notwithstanding, before "Einstein's Nobel recognition, it's alleged that the "experimental evidence" of "photoelectric equation" was not available to him at the time; therefore, he invented it himself based on far lessor evidence, and went further to predict his findings or evidence, in published "physic books" prior. Furthermore, it's alleged that "Einstein" acquired evidence of his theoretical discoveries initially from "Planck's" theory. Aforementioned prior, in 1900's in one wall is "Planck's" theory that a "spectrum of light inside an insulated enclosure at constant temperature; notably, an insulated enclosure with *a small hole in one wall is commonly referred to as a "black body", due to its absorption of radiation flawlessly through this "black body". However, previous theories concerning the frequent distribution of "radiant-energy" in a "black body" was in violent disagreement through the "experimental research, exploration, and interpretation as non-factual.* Planck's explanation, at the time, implied that "light" was emitted and absorbed within *"energy" bundles "hv"* in size. "Einstein" pointed out a number of pieced-together evidence for the "reality" of these bundles. "Einstein" further created them in particles of light in protons, and in the same instance utilized this application to found the theory of "photochemistry", and prognosticated the results of "photoelectric experiments". "Einstein and Planck", as scientific innovators theorized the proton, in beam of "light of frequency" "v", each proton carries energy "E = hv", defined scientifically as "The Einstein-Planck" relationship. Importantly, aforementioned earlier the "proportionally constant "h" is scientifically named "Planck's constant". Speculating, that the "h" constant of Planck's, may have been selected in abbreviated reference to his mentor "Helmholtz", who initially brought-forth the conceptual gravity of both, "Einstein's and Planck's", scientific ingenious visions towards their illustrious innovations. Noteworthy, "Max Planck" originated the "quantum theory", which awarded him the *"Nobel Peace Prize" in "Physics"* in 1918. His ingenious contribution to "theoretical physics" has greatly enhanced further scientific achievements within the framework of "modern physics". "Planck and Einstein" together has revolutionized the exploration, and interpretation of "space and time"; and simultaneously with unnamed scientist worth mentioning within the framework of *The Conservation of Energy and its Development.*

Bibliography

Bowler, Peter J., and Iwan Rhys Morus, *Making Modern Science*: A History Survey. (Chicago: University of Chicago Press, 2005).

Caneval, Kenneth. *The Form and Foundation of Scientific Discoveries* / P.C.M. – Dibner Library Lectures Series, Library of - Congress Catalog-In-Publication Data (accessed Conservation of Energy – HMOLPEDIA.

Fleck, Lubwik. *Reflections on the Form and Function of Scientific Discoveries.* (Accessed April 8th, 2011).

Helmholtz, Hermann Von. United Architects-Biographies.

Kuhn, Thomas. *Stanford Encyclopedia of Philosophy*.

Kuhn, Thomas, *"Energy Conservation as an Example of Simultaneous Discovery*.

In Marshall Clagett, ed., *Critical Problems in the History of Science,* (Madison, Wisconsin Press, 1959.

The History of Thermodynamics JOURNAL http:www.ehow. com/about 5506921

History-thermodynamics.html.

Physic. 2nd ed. (*Boston: D.C. Health and Company, 1965.*

References:

Peter Bowler, J., and Iwan Rhys Morus," *Making Modern Science:* A History Survey (Chicago: University of Chicago, 2005)

Thomas Kuhn, encyclopedia of Human Thermodynamics,

Thomas Kuhn, Energy Conservation as an Example of Simultaneous discovery; In Marshall Clagett, ed., Critical Problems in the History of Science (Madison, Wisconsin: University of Wisconsin Press, 1959).

Kenneth Caneval, the Form and Function of Scientific Discoveries/P.C.M.: (Dibner Library Lecture Series) Library of Congress Cataloging-In-Publication Data.

Peter Bowler, J… and Iwan Rhy Morus, Making Modern Science

Thomas Kuhn, (Stanford: Encyclopedia of Philosophy)

Conservation of Energy-Hmolpedia. http//:www.epht.info/page/Conservation+of+energy.

Peter Bowler J., Making Modern Science.

Encyclopedia of Human Thermodynamics. Conservation of Energy-Hmolpedia

Peter Bowler J. and Iwan Rhys Morus, *Making Modern Sciences*: A History Survey (Chicago: University of Chicago Press, 2005).

Lubwik, Fleck, *Reflections on the Forms and Function of Scientific Discoveries*. (Accessed April 8, 2011, 1979), 123.

http://dannarhitect.wordpress.com/helmholtz-hermann-Von/

Conservation of Energy-encyclopedia of Human Thermodynamics

Helm Von Helmholtz, United Architects-biographies

The History of Thermodynamics Journal..

http://www.ehow.com about 5506921 history-thweromodynamics.html.

http://dannarchitect.worldpress.comhelmholtz-von

CHAPTER V

Piracy Sections

(A, B, C)

A.
Reflections of Piracy Evolution
A Global View

Evolution of Piracy: A Global Perspective
(Ran Sackers, Raiding and Despoiling
on the Mediterranean Sea)
(An Analysis by: William Williams)

"To acquire a complete history of piracy", according to "Phillipe Gosse" History of Piracy, *"Is an impossible task or undertaking, which would resemble a maritime history of the world"! [1].* "However, the analysis of *Piracy*, sections a, b, and c, presents *the conditions, geography, cultures, and sociology of Piracy".* The creation of *piracy*, and its recurring developments and deteriorations or reductions, and its varying strategies of activities over-time; to emerge resourceful and enfeebling. Additionally, the exploration of *piracies* manifestations, destinies, and acquisitions of foreign commerce on the *"high seas" illustrates their desperate nature and* systematized boldness.

Pirates through the ages has always been classified as "vague" characters in the seafaring World, and equally elusive in temporal terms. Their crafty and swift built vessels allowed these *pilfers* at sea to escape detection after raids, to their clandestine islands to salvage bounty, secure refuge, and escape unpunished by society. The Mediterranean Sea historically, was rich in piracy; however, has provided vague *factual evidence* that "corsair's or privateer's were ever a problem in the ancient world. Therefore, historians, archaeologist's, and historiographers are grateful for *"textual records"* that confer negative and positive characterization, exploits, and over-all tribulations recorded in the *earliest of times* of piracies seafaring adventures, which also involves land inhabiting or dwelling. Numerous textual sources of piracy have been recorded in the Mediterranean Sea arena since time, through dedicated sanguine archaeologist's that's identified the origin of pirates and piracy. Their character projects extreme illicit and deviant behavior that can be suppressed at the drop of a dime, if you will, depending upon *negotiating circumstances involving bounty rendered without a* skirmish or encounter. Noteworthy, the Mediterranean Sea's and its surroundings offers an idyllic *research environment* in capturing the history of piracy. In romanticized fiction conjoined with authentic historical sourced documentation of piracy, the link between pirates and their island coves or inlets, are inextricable and necessary for their survival. Pirates subsist or live as bandits of the Sea's, who like any marauders, requires vulnerable prey to compensate for their daring enterprise.

Historically, and according to ancient accountability, the "Egyptian's were lucidly preoccupied with the mysterious Sea "ran sacker's" (pirates), who were noted for their plotting and assemblage of "raider's" who consistently threatened the "Nile Delta" region throughout the "New Kingdom", until their defeat by Ramesses III. Ramesses recognized the link between piracy and land, to recuperate, evaluate, salvage, trade, sale, and store their stolen bounty. Ramesses, insightful perception regarding *"Pirate's"* sociology, geography, and maintenance of their stolen bounty enabled him to mount a successful campaign in the region and territory of the "Egyptian Kingdom"; which eradicated this seafaring menace and pilferer (piracy) from destroying "Egyptians" seafaring commercial businesses.

The success of Ramesus strategy spreads across and throughout the Mediterranean region, of his insightful perception between "piracy" and its' necessary land connection, to escape legal jurisdiction (punishment), sell or trade their goods, to recuperate, and reorganize their piracy exploits for future seafaring attacks on foreign commerce.

"Robert L. Stevenson" (1883) illustration of *"Treasure Island,* depicts a romanticized pirate, conjured-up fictionally to resemble an *"eye patched one eyed-one-legged-thief-with-a parrot-resting-on –his –shoulder-"*, and on some isolated *island or pirates ship;* which illustrates an image of what a pirate symbolizes. Also, "Pirates of the Caribbean" movie trilogy reinforce this fictional pirate imagery initiated by "Stevenson", which insures that this fictionally glamorized and decorated image of pirate's will remain for generations.

With civilizations emerging commerce and with commercial seafaring enterprise, emerged piracy. Therefore, the pirate profession herded to inconspicuous island inlets, coves, and bays. Similarly, as earlier ancient agriculturists migrated to river valleys to sustain their livelihood with fertile soil and abundant water sources. The islands surrounding the *Mediterranean Seas,* provided pirates with an established domain, with not easily seen landscape, necessary to pursue their profession of *piracy.* Although pirates were basically seafaring marauders, however, most exploited civilizations attacked by them on the high seas, didn't reflect deeply as to where their land base of necessity resided; after they were pilfered, looted and raided. Consequently, as seen by earlier *Egyptians, during Ramesses III era, "even marauders accustomed to spending the majority of their time at sea, required a ocean inlet, coves, bay's, or harbor's to use as a base after their raids on the high seas"*. Even though, coastal mainland sites could and did serve as adequate seats for pirate organizations, the inherent isolation and boundaries of these islands provided "sea-ran-sackers, thieves and bandits perfect hiding grounds for their "surprise attacks and quick getaway escapes after their seafaring raids. Pirates, harbors, coves, inlets, and bays were strategically distant from settled communities with governance near pirate's land, which nullified jurisdiction to punish these bandits. *"Corsairs and Privateers"* were also protected in the exact aforementioned strategic locations as "Pirates". *Corsairs and Privateers* used islands to their advantage, by manipulating major trade routes that always followed coastal areas, which brought forth stepping-stone islands to cross large expansive sea routes. A *privateer* is defined as a ship or body of people authorized by a specific government, through a marque or letter of assigned authenticity to attack foreign shipping during wartime. Privateering was a way of governments marshaling armed ships and sailors without having to spend government treasury resources or committing naval troops.

French Corsairs, were also privateers, sanctioned by the *"French Crown",* to raid ships of any nations at war with France. Corsairs were considered legitimate combatants in France. They seized vessels and cargo, which were sold at auction locations, with the "corsair" officers and crew entitled to a share of the proceeds from the auction thereafter. The corsair's officers conducted themselves according to existing *admiralty law, if the officer of the vessel possessed a valid letter of Marque.* The aforementioned large expansive sea routes could not be avoided, due to prevailing winds. While many of these aforementioned stepping-stone islands were not unsuitable for *major settlements of agricultural societies*, they were equally acceptable to marauders who hunted for resources in these expansive sea routed "stepping-stone" land areas. Undeniably, these stepping-stone islands and rocky promontories would naturally conceal any sea raider's, allowing them concealment, and surprise attacks to ships passing openly without notice of peril.

"Thucydides" observes that the oldest settlements were located as far inland as possible, both on the islands and the mainland to avoid the coast where the pirates lie in wait for victims (Ormerod 1924: 38). However, this strategy didn't provide sufficient security, even on the largest islands; Pirates could benefit from all sizes and varieties of islands. The same isolation that assisted pirates in their hiding could and often did bring about the end of early, as well as established settlements. Pirates would therefore exploit the benefits and burdens of island life, whereas the isolation of some islands was a disadvantage for *lawful* inhabitants; therefore, pirates would seek out such areas for their headquarters. Many of the islands of the Mediterranean are inherently isolated from the mainland, and the jurisdiction of the law. Even the most skilled seaman had to return to land at the end of the day, especially during winter months when navigation was impractical. So pirates were inclined to "lie-in-wait" in waters clustered with islands. Notably, the Cyclades along with a numerous group of islands in the "Aegean Sea" were especially favorable for pirates. The Mediterranean *"Corsair's"*, were especially successful in the area of "Tragia", lying in the *Aegean Sea*, as harboring there in amply numbers, who in *76 B.C.* captured *Julius Caesar* there, but eventually his capture cost those pirates

who captured *Caesar* their lives. Even a hasty glance at a Mediterranean and Aegean map shows and clarifies a speckled landscape of numerous small islands soared in every direction, are these numerous islands with exists and entrances with deceptively boundless islets and peninsulas. Ships carrying treasured and prized cargo, and those with far lesser valued bounty, were forced by preponderant winds and currents to cross these small islands, and on the majority of their crossings they were surrounded by waiting pirates. The most fearless sea captains gritted their teeth and braved the willpower and self-discipline to ready their men, through these snare-trapped channels, to fight these marauding pirates, to save self-respect and valued transported bounty. The *"Kythira" channels*, located in the *"Ionian" islands* had a fierce reputation for pirates throughout history. Despite the fact that the *"Mediterranean" islands* endowed pirates with the picture-perfect hunting ground, islands did not provide the only means of shelter, as the *King of Alashiya (Cyprus) was forced to remind an Egyptian Pharaoh* in one of the *"Amarma's"* correspondence (written two centuries before the inscription at *Medinet Habu*) stated, "that the Lukki, possible referring to the Lycians, were not islanders and year by year seized villages in my very own country". Additionally, the Tyrrhenian's, sheltered by the Apennines (mountain creating island-like protection on the mainland), were notorious for their pillaging by land and sea. Regardless, pirates generally sought out islands, therefore "islands" unmistakably supported their subsistence and way-of-life.

"What is a pirate"? ENEMIES ARE UPON WHOM THE ROMAN PEOPLE HAS DECLARED WAR PUBLICLY UPON, OR WHO HAVE THEMSELVES DECLARED WAR UPON OTHERS: THE OTHERS OR THE REST ARE TERMED" BANDITS OR PIRATES".

Piracy must be defined as a legitimate affirmative entity: undoubtedly, pirates came in many distinctive forms in ancient times, and of different societies, such as "corsairs and privateers". They were viewed by many in both "contrasting and similar clarity". Just as the derogatory term "terrorist" is employed in current conflicts; thusly, this word "terrorist" is unquestionably used loosely from all earthly directions, just as the word "piracy" was used to label "ran-sackers, bandits, marauders, barbarians, and pirates". Modern historians would likely refer to pirates as all of the above aforementioned, unless these terms of identity referred to ancient or modern societies who "officially declared war", thereafter, modern historiographers, historians, and governance would otherwise refer to them as "cultured and civilized". Example, in the American Indian Wars both cultures referred to each other in earlier conflicts as "barbarians" who "massacred", and ultimately if able by chance and circumstance "annihilated" each other in conflicts destined to liquidate, and emerge victorious, as "masters" in their land to enterprise. Pirates, didn't declare war, it was understood that their objective was to take what others declared their own assets and possessions; therefore, pirates were not only "ran sackers and bandit's", but also opportunistic "terrorists". However, there are dubious allegations historians used to define piracy, identifying the most fundamental definition of pirates as "armed robbers" whose *"activities involving the use of ships"*. Mind boggling, pirates never referred to themselves as pirates, however, their victims "hallmarked and pledged" them with the label pirates. Therefore, planting the "definitive and state-of-the-art" seed "pirates", which has historically unwrapped this see-through transparency of characteristic distinction, throughout global history to identify seafaring thieves that raids ships carrying cargo goods.

The English word "pirate" derives from the Latin word "pirata", and from the Greek word "peirates", which defines organized groups that overpower seafaring transport and take their cargo goods. However, pirates rob on land, air, sea, and through intellectual commerce. The Greek definition "peirates" alleged to have been used in the mid-third century B.C., in an "Attic" inscription from "Rhamnous" describing an exchange for ransoming of prisoners. Notably, this incidence of war occurred between the Macedonian and Ptolemaic armies, with a distinguishing inscription defining "peirates" as plunderer's who do so by their own conviction. Prior to the saying "peirates", Greeks used the word "leistes", which defines the modern word "outlaw, robber, or bandit". Byzantine's tenth-century lexicon "the Suda" endeavors to differentiate the word "peirates" from "leistes", even though they maintain the same meaning "robber, thief, or bandit" possibly. Yet, the differentiation of the two words refers to when they're properly used; "peirates" the earlier used word is now used in reference to "seafaring", and "leistes" refers to land bandits, robbers, or thieves possibly... Many Greek's used the two words within the same framework, with possibly alternative expressions depending on the social issues at hand. The Greek word "katapontistes" defines the Western or English word "pirate" translated it means "one who throws into the ocean"; however, this great word definition was not used often in textbooks. Noteworthy, the Greek language describes *various types* of *piracy* in the ancient Mediterranean, which distinguish between *"land and sea"* piracy. The importance of understanding that those who rob, ravish, and thieve upon coastal settlements (land) is creditable to distinguishing and observing its foundational sources, habits, origin, consequence and historical interconnection. To detach or secede *land plunderers, thieves, and* robber's from *seafaring piracy*, one must address piracy from the assessment of island archaeology, culture, sociology, and geography. This detachment or distinction derives from "the professional or practicing pirates" vs. inexperienced land dwellers who are considered temporal pirates, as oppose to seafarers for profit and bounty who *commission occupational employment* on ships to make victims for profit from enterprising commercial transporting seafarers to raid, plunder, and rob their bounty. Dissimilar in perceptive retrospection or review regarding the "temporal thieves" who illicit this type of activity upon land settlements, makes them indistinguishable from a group of ordinary impoverished, hungry or starving land people, who were established and lawful for years until catastrophes occurred, that took them to land piracy for their life sustainability; due to dire social needs. These same people, like many others in dire unsustainable need to live, and feed their families, would do just about anything to survive. Consequently, they would even offer themselves as indentures or mercenaries for profit to obtain the bare necessities to survive. Widely held belief defines "pirates" and "piracy" as those who only plunder, raid, and ran sack, for their own benefit; conversely, as aforementioned, "troubled" people would often accept any sustenance from friends, foe, or nations for profit. However, the definition of "pirates" is those who act without commission from a sovereign nation and is justifiably classified a pirate, and therefore illegally conducts piracy. Nevertheless, privateers and corsairs were not considered pirates. They were commissioned through an authentic letter are marque from a specific Nation, to conduct business on the high seas through the tenets of their sponsored Nations. The Mediterranean Sea ideally provides countless and numerous islets, coves, bays, and islands, for piracy to survive and thrive. The sea also created the perfect environment for pirates to establish their organized networks, which remained an inescapable danger throughout ancient history, as the target and bases for pirate activity and survival.

The "origin of piracy": unfortunately the further back in time we venture historically for the "origin of piracy" the more scant written source data becomes. The maturity and modernity of fact finding sophistication such as in the fields of geography, archaeology, historiography, and the social sciences, has enabled textual documentation primary and secondary data sourcing, to authenticate piracy and its historical past more fluidly. The documentation has been pieced together over the years from antiquity to the present, causing many suppositions, speculations, and further examinations of ancient historical facts.

Most historiographical documentations and recordings of piracy goes back as far as the second millennium B.C., based on substantiated Egyptian sources. Although, in many instances, Egyptian history may not explicitly describe piracy as a concept, but outlined events involving seafaring raider's plundering the coast of "Levant", as well as "Cyprus" and "Egypt" has be authentically established. Furthermore, prior to the "Amarna letters", documented evidence of piracy disappears into the cosmos and planet earth, which confirms the scattered documentation of piracy after that era. Common speculation suggest that as long as ships carrying valuable cargoes of commerce across the Mediterranean Sea, piracy must have existed in many viable arrangements. Notably, "terrestrial trade" was dangerous throughout the "Near East", due to land bandits hiding in the rugged "Wadis" and/or mountains affirms "as long as the temptation of wealth acquired by others moves unprotected by others through unknown territory, and across established trade routes on are near the Mediterranean Sea, raider's have remained a significant threat. Speculation merits common-sense analogy that piracy and robbery has been a form of livelihood from the sea's since the time people first explored oceans. This historical speculative theory of piracy and robbery in the Seas in far ancient times without textual evidence or authentic sourced data is a probable analogy only. Furthermore, the Mediterranean Sea was explored in prehistoric times, due to accountable implications of raids referenced in the "Odyssey", may be enthused by the earliest voyages into the Mediterranean Sea on the basis of archeology findings. An analysis of early settlements being constructed progressively further from the coast could very well be interpreted as an increase in the activities of pirates. From inquiry and dogmatic research archeology focus would emanate from the "largest and 1ˢᵗ colonized and developed settlements" near the Mediterranean Sea and surrounding environments. However, the hopelessness of investigating authentic documented piracy in the Mediterranean Sea before it was settled as a community, is dependent solely in divulging an authentic documented "permanent social settlement". Otherwise, our historical objective of documenting "piracy activity" before the 10ᵗʰ millennium is merely hypothesized speculation.

Recorded documentation affirms that the Mediterranean Sea was first explored in the 10ᵗʰ millennium B.C. (Broodbank 2006: 208), and it's further acknowledged that *banditry* by *land* would have proven more profitable *that sea raiding*. However, thereafter contact and trade between islands and the mainland increased, which is confirmed in the discoveries of *"Obsidian"* from the island of *"Milos of Franchthi Cave"* in the *"Argolid"*. "Horden and Purcell" (2000) states that "piracy likely increased proportionately in later periods in time, and may have on a limited scale and unclear level of activity existed during the *"Neolithic"* era, as the islands of the Mediterranean were gradually populated.

The first pirates would have been the people who failed to *find the proper resources* on which to survive beyond the mainland. The origin of piracy *was not a choice* by the *agriculturist or people* who settled the *mainland*; thusly, the need to plunder was initiated through a *survival mode* of necessity. Any people on the mainland during this era would have been forced initially to *hunt* in order to establish a society. Coincidentally, during the *"Neolithic" era* most societies turned to agriculture as a replacement for their" hunting and gathering survival". Furthermore, other settlements on the mainland choose the opposite by "following the game" from *place to place* to survive this harsh environment. Comparably, one can imagine the problems confronted by these ancient agriculturists, with crop failures and, bad weather conditions, such as droughts, flooding, and insects and indigenous animals destroying their crops. Additional, their nutritional decline would result in sicknesses and diseases, due to poor and unhealthy food intake and overall limited viable resources. Consequently, most settlements or societies would not accept the harsh difficulties that they inherited in an agricultural society.

The *Neolithic Revolution likely begun in the Levant in the 10ᵗʰ millennium B.C.; Yet, Egypt* did not become a Neolithic society until approximately, *5500 B.C.* The Neolithic Revolution had already spread to *Central Europe* (Hikade 2008). Therefore, it's quite possible that many societies may have been reluctant to relinquish the hunter-gather's life style, however those societies that gave up this life style had to secure a more reliable means of survival. Pirates then, were essentially people who had failed to maintain the "Neolithic" tradition, values, and lawlessness necessary to establish a stable settlement; and ultimately discovered *piracy on the high seas* as a means to survive. Furthermore," by land the poverty of the soil had forced societies to become hunters and brigands rather than agriculturists; therefore, the same pursuits were followed at sea" *(Ormerod 1924: 14).* Similarly, *Aristotle,* echoing *Thucydides (see also Plato, Legg. VII, 823; (Ormerod 1924: 69),* emphasizes this form of piracy as a means of productivity. Whereas, some earlier inhabitants of the Mediterranean area choose to be: … fisherman and others live by the pursuit of birds or wild beasts… Others support themselves by hunting… of different kinds. Some, for example, are brigands. [1] This image of the pirate as a hunter who had given up the agricultural ways of civilization is observed throughout the writing of ancient history.

Conclusion (a):

The hypothesis and factual "History of Piracy", and "Pirates" respectfully defined through geography, archaeology, sociology, historiography, and the social sciences expertise, which exposes the study of "ancient piracy" in a quality pursuit of factual sourced data. Some may tire in the investigation research of piracy; and only reflecting on the criminal activity that defines these ran sackers "as a stealer of cargo culture", and you are half correct to perceive as such. Nevertheless, pirates have been misunderstood, in many social instances, due to enormous social variables and barriers that stagnated and troubled mankind's survival historically on earth; that inflicted such deprivation and hardships to survive, that "piracy" was their only means of survival. Consequently, the modern image of a "pirates" is depicted on "Seas and Lands" in ancient times characterize bloodthirsty killers, plunderers, and pillagers, which was not entirely valid for all such societies in all times. Aforementioned, many pirates were impoverished settlement communities forced to survive in a world that had turned them into outcasts. Others, as documented were not even pirates in any sense of the word, only people who were unfortunate to have been in the way of larger and more successful empires. In this sense, we must reconcile that in most cases history is written by the "well feed" and "nourished" educated few. In reference to "hunger and desperate social necessities", is required to maintenance societal impoverishment and, lack of any means of economic subsistence, which ignites the existence and creation of piracies identity. To understand the complexities of the existence of "pirates", historians, historiographers, geologists, geographers, archaeologist's, students, and scholars must establish an accord on the true definition of piracy. Ancient historians are not held hostage in providing objective definitions of pirate's identity, but they are held responsible for not maintaining and recording authentic sourced data towards quality historical precedence. In modernity, the whole body of the academic historical community is answerable and on trial to uncover historic artifacts and answers through the socially scientific technological apparatus that provides answers to ancient piracy. Archaeologist's, geologists, geographers, and scientist can become dutiful by searching areas that were questionable that inhabited pirates, places such as Crete and Cilicia etc… which defines pirates through materialistic scrutiny in villages and from Mediterranean islet, coves, harbors, bays, atolls, islands, and keys. Lastly, the effects that pirates had on local and nearby Mediterranean environments and ancestral populations that continue to exist is enormous and unquestionable worthy of research, investigation, exploration, interpretation, and application into our history books. Piracy and the slave trade is another essential component in the displacement of ethnicities from countries, and islands that must be intellectually scrutinized for valid informational historical precedent. The maritime trade routes are effective natural phenomenon in the study of the social, psychological, and economic contributions piracy contributed in it historical development. The ancient Mediterranean remains a lucrative arena for scholarly tenacity, expeditions, and historical academic closure of the pirate's total range of history.

Piracy
(b)
International Politics and Geographical
Effects in the Development of Piracy

In respect to the International linkage, connection, and relationship to piracy, which is closely attached to the geographical effects of the development and elimination of piracy on seafaring or maritime enterprises, manifest essentially a *two-fold* objective. Thusly, referencing the awareness of both the *predator and prey* of the historical account of private violence within the framework of geographical, political, social, economic and infrastructural commercial combative deterrence, which promotes and facilitates an elimination of piracy. Modernity has sealed and molded the global community's governance into a "state theory" concept, to eradicate or promote respectfully, global hardships and miseries that affect political, economic, and social infrastructural economical seafaring progress; Consequently, promoting a cohesive and global sophisticated seafaring industry. Therefore, the global concept of *"state theory"* envelopes the construction of a viable international operative, namely *"state building"* that must control the global communities through the governance of *"power enforcement"; which encompass and comprise a global unilateral affirmative declaration to enhance specialized personnel to monitor, control, and eliminate "all" forms of piracy, and especially "piracy" over-trouble waters that facilitates economic instability and commercial ineptitude.* State Building recommends control over global territories in reference to piracy on land and sea. Unilaterally, States must be loyal and durable to their oaths of office regarding piracy. Consequently, "permanent institutions are required to be naturalized and autonomous" within the global decree authorized through unilateral global mandates; which operates exclusively within the framework of land, air, and seafaring piracy, that must governs and implement a Universal "monopolized deterrent" over piracy.

Historically, pirates, privateers, and corsairs in ancient times through the 16th, 17th, 18th and 19th centuries were embedded in a broad political, military and economic threat of seafaring violence; which actively promoted "private seafaring confrontations" to loot seafaring commerce, or to protect valued seafaring merchandise from looters, which qualifies the pursuit of an offensive vs. defensive seafaring confrontation to acquire (pirates) or, (merchants) to retain their maritime treasures being transported by se, respectively. Consequently, the denouncing of piracy and privateering were the consequence of numerous "interlinked political and economic trends; such as, the development of public protection of merchant shipping through the growth of centralized Navies. During earlier eras privateers services were of boundless economic assistance to government's maritime trade success by protecting merchant trade commercial enterprise from raider's (pirates). The cost for hire of privateer's in many instances, were sponsored and generated by Nations to protect their cargo; and by private investors hoping to profit from prize money earned from captured seafaring cargos or vessels. A percentage of these proceeds would be distributed among the privateer's, investors, officers, and crew. Noteworthy, privateers were part of naval warfare from the 15th to 19th centuries. Some privateer's have been prominent in the chronicles or archives of history. On many occasion privateers vessels would be commissioned into regular military service as warships. Therefore, the crew of a privateer was often times treated as a "prisoner of war" by the enemy country if captured. Furthermore, the distinction between a pirate and privateer has been nebulous, and often depending on the source labeling the type of action and circumstance. The actual occupation of a pirate and a privateer is generally the same; it is, therefore the perceived legality of the type of engagements and endorsements that materialized the distinction. Therefore, would-be authentic pirates could operate under a cover of legitimacy, if governments granted authorization of privateering to the vessels they're on. However, in reference to "French corsairs", by acting on behalf of the French Crown, if captured by the enemy, they could claim treatment as prisoners of war, instead of being considered pirates. Due to their "swashbuckling" daring and adventurous reputation; thusly, the word "corsair" is a glitzy reference to pirates. Also, there were "Turkish corsairs" representing the Ottoman and North African (Barbary) countries.

The Mediterranean's geography was the ideal location for piracy; especially to develop and organize as a viable criminal institution. The islands and islets are inherently isolated from the mainland, causing the jurisdiction and jurisprudence of the law for their marauding actions on the seas unanswerable, even if a law was imposed. It was imperative for pirates to lurk in waters that were clustered with islands. It's was extremely favorable for pirates to lurk near the "Cyclades and Tragia" near the numerous groups of islands in the "Aegean Sea"; which outlines the importance of the multitude of islands surrounding the Mediterranean Sea. Understandably, the isolated islands was a disadvantage for lawful settlement inhabitants against regulating laws against piracy.

Piracy
(C)
The Future of Piracy and Historical Problems
Affecting 21st Century Piracy
(Analysis by: William F. Williams)

The reduction and elimination of piracy by oceangoing cargo, land, airborne and through other means of economic seizures; which is essential in saving the global economies business enterprising apparatus. An advanced 21st century "global theory" concept is fundamentally vital within the framework of a transparent "mental rigorous science" in pursuit of eliminating all genres of piracy; in reality as merely criminal offenses. The advent of this *innovative Philosophy* to eliminate piracy classification (genre), is molded within the construction of a *"permanent global criminal institution of robbery";* that's structured through a *global transparent centralized-organization.* The introduction of *"The*

Philosophy of Piracy" within the *"global transparent centralized organization" (GTCO), which* qualifies and forms conceptual mechanisms specifically correlating to the categorical classifications of robbery. These representatives will have the "mental rigor" to forecast through conceptual analysis within the various types of applicable piracies confirmed, through mechanized surveillance observational apparatuses. Every global business enterprise aforementioned: seafaring, land, airborne, and intellectually inclined, will conduct an itinerary forecast months ahead of their scheduled business interchanges; that qualifies an established monetary value that warrants *moderate* or *extreme* monetary and cargo assessment; which is established through the "global transparent centralized-organization" (GTCO). Therefore, protecting, surveying, and monitoring business activities. Furthermore, business enterprising activity is confirmed and authorized prior to shipping from the shipper within two to three weeks from the original shipping dates and destination. The bank receives the business transaction receipt procurement; which records and references in-coming and, out-going completed business transactions to finalize the transactions of *speculated,* however confirmed and accountable losses.

Maritime delivery of business cargo presents an easier solution in protecting seafaring cargo and crew from piracy, due to highly structural satellite application of sophisticated monitoring surveillance mechanisms placed along seafaring transport routes; therefore, enabling transmitting warning signal alarms from the Headquarters of the "global transparent centralized organization" (GTCO). The attack helicopters or drones immediately respond to the marauding pirates, through the watchful audio visual satellite surveillance screens setup in the global (GTCO) offices located throughout strategic global seafaring route locations, to monitor, confirm and defend all valued seafaring transport cargo from unlawful raids and disruption of seafaring business enterprise, which impedes global economic growth and enterprising business stabilization.

The "Philosophy of Piracy" is an academic social science field that specializes in advanced criminology, which is fundamentally structured to analyze potential criminal piracy activities based on "actual rating analysis". This forecasting of actual rating analysis encompass poverty stressed governments, international polarized social and cultural environments, autonomous cultures, languages, religions, political stability, economic stability, proximity to water routes through harbors, inlets, islands, coves, bays, and juxtaposition to ocean routes, statistical analysis and advanced logic, and historic data sourcing to acquire precedent of past pirate seafaring attacks. An International investigative team of graduates from the "Philosophy of Piracy" will research, investigate, interpret and analysis global and colloquial ship manufacturers that sell vessels capable for seafaring to criminal syndicates and private global businesses. It's also directed at solving intellectual and white and blue collar crimes of piracy. The airborne piracy crimes will be structured analogous to the seafaring mechanism system that monitors the surveillance of airborne traffic, which correlates with "personalized criminal investigations" and "homeland security".

The piracy puzzle problems of seafaring vessels in International trade and the interchange of commerce between Nations has been restructured and reshaped within the international monetary exchange system. Piracy disrupts itinerate commercial monetary time-tables of Nations; and therefore modify and offsets an otherwise efficient and effective management of resources. Furthermore, it stagnates viable assets to govern social, political and economic infrastructure towards global progression efficiently. Consequently, business enterprises that accommodate seafaring trade of commerce is disrupted by piracy, which ultimately grind to a halt profits and managerial stability that affects the global economy. The colloquial or non-technical solution to decreasing piracy is fundamentally married to poverty. Especially, in predestined global areas that undertake this type of behavior (piracy) as a necessary sustainable endeavor for survival and profit. Third World areas are destitute for onshore industry and commerce to sustain their livelihood; which would eventually eliminate organized syndicated piracy institutions, who has acquired sophisticated monitoring systems, data sourcing and computerization to analyze and scrutinize international commercial trade routes to raid cargo for profit, within their piracy zones of attack. The second alternative in grinding piracy to a halt, is suggested for private investors, as opposed to governments, in constructing or building innovative armored proof seafaring transport cargo ships or vessels; enabling them unapproachable for boarding or destroying by artillery, and manufactured by reinforced heavy armor. This type of reinforced innovative cargo vessel for maritime commerce would be ideal for private investors owning business enterprises dealing in big business ventures.

Lastly, structure an adequate sophisticated computerized computation analysis expense ratio chart, that's mathematically designed to expertly account for monetary delivery transport expenses vs. the recommended innovative construction cost of that reinforced seafaring cargo vessel registered, and declared prior; to ascertaining a comparable analysis of the structural cost estimated to concisely determine on a long-term basis, if the monetary investment is advantageous to building this innovative cargo vessel vs. your expenditures exhausted previously in buying back your cargo losses from piracy, which is pliable in applying one expense against the other, to either build that safe cargo vessel, or continue to lose money from pirate syndicates demanding ransom for your cargo losses.

CHAPTER VI

An Insightful Analysis of China's Taoism and Taoist Religio-Philosophy

(By William F. Williams)

The sacred scripture *"TaoDejing"*, or *"Tao Te Ching"* is a religion and philosophical concept to guide, structure, and signify principles of *Taoism*. Its religion *"Tao Chiao"* is an organized or systematized "doctrine or principle", or as a verb, reference and speaks within the context of traditional Chinese philosophy and religion. It organized Chinese doctrine formalized Chinese *"Taoist"* traditions, cultural activity, and institutional leadership, which was authored and founded by *"Laozi"*.

"Laozi's" background and authentic name is somewhat of a mystery to Chinese historians. His founding or creation of *"Taoism"*, coupled with historical recorded data of *"TaoDejing"*, the *Sacred Scriptures* of *Taoism,* is also a debatable issue in the Chinese historical time-table, regarding the exact place and time of the creation of *Taoism, and Laozi's biography.* However, it's generally accepted by Chinese historians that his name was *"Li Er"* or *"Lao Tan",* and that he was born in the *State of Cho*, during the *Zhou Dynasty.* Yet, the date of his birth is another untimely mystery. Chinese historians identifies him working in the *"Zhou Court Administration",* as a keeper of *"historical archive data".* Chinese History acknowledge that while working in the *"Zhou Court",* he was approached by *"Confucius",* the *Great Sage of "Confucianism".* It's alleged that "Confucius"

consulted him on matters of ceremonies and rites during *"Lao Tze's* lifetime.

The format or edifice of the "Sacred Scriptures", *"TaoDejing"* by *"Lao Tze"*, consisting of eighty-one chapters in full recovered translated (English) text. <u>Caveat:</u> The *"Sacred Scriptures"*, titled *"TaoDejing"*, draws the texts of several popular English interpolations of *"Lao Tze"* into consistent and accessible context. However, the English version of the *"Tao De Jing"* is an interpolation from the Chinese language to the English language. This analysis from *"TaoDejing"* does not represent the original text or scriptures. Over time, the original *"TaoDejing"* is alleged by Chinese historians and scholars, to be jumbled, miss transcribed and reinterpreted over *thousands of years*. Noteworthy, the *"TaoDejing"* is a *cast-off* into the English language, incapable of presenting Chinese *poetic structure and philological connective construction* that the original *"Tao De Jing"* was comprised of, according to traditional Chinese Historians and Scholars of *"Taoism"*.

In reference to the understanding or interpolation of the *original context* and *text* of the *"TaoDejing"* doctrine quite possibly would present difficult and unapproachable meaning and translation in any language, other than *The Ancient Chinese language read and spoken during the 4-6th Chinese century BCE;* allegedly during *"Lao Tze's"* era. The analytical intent is to construct a documental understanding of *"Taoism"* that closely corresponds with the best possible understanding of *"Lao Tze's"* Sacred Scriptures (Taoism), within the ancient Chinese concept. Notably, *The Sacred Scripts* pages were *gathered* over thousands of years due to the lost, or displacement of them; and it is alleged that a huge number of loose leaf pages to the *book* were gathered piece by piece, which enabled the ancient collection and reconstruction of "Lao Tze's" Sacred Scriptures, the "Tao De Jing" to resurface in China.

Chinese history follows *"Lao Tze's"* life's journey from his alleged birth in the province of *"Honan"* about *565 B.C.;* to his place of occupation at the *"Zhou Court"*, as the keeper of archive data. It's alleged that he ventures Westward bound as a traveler, and while traveling he sees or envision a *"purple cloud"* hovering over his head, which classifies his traveling pilgrimage as the *"purple cloud of the East"*. It's alleged that on this journey he arrives at *China's Western most Outpost,* and was befriended by the guardian of the outpost, who had heard of him as *"a sage of great wisdom"*, even prior to his arrival at the *Western* outpost. The guardian of this outpost accorded *"Lao Tze"* the respect of *"student to teacher"* relationship between the two men, *Lao Tze* being the teacher and he the student. The guardian of the post ask "Lao Tze" to leave his many wisdoms about life's wisdoms of interactions between and amongst beings within this Universe in the form of writings. Chinese history alleges that "Lao Tze" wrote a five-thousand word scriptures entitled *"TaoDejing"*. After writing these sacred scriptures and leaving them with the Western guardian of the post, *"Lao Tze"* journeyed onward *never to be seen again"*.

The sacred scriptures of *"TaoDejing"* became popular during the early part of the *"Han Dynasty"*. The principle concept delegate or signify "the *way"*, *"path"*, *"route"*, or as a verb, *speak*. It's contained by traditional Chinese Philosophy and Religion, as a metaphysical concept that gave rise to *"Tao"* or *"Taoism"*. Notably, the "Tao" concept is shared with *"Confucianism"*, *"Chan"* and *"Zen Buddhism"*. However, it's shared more broadly throughout *East Asian philosophy and religions* in general. Within the aforementioned concepts of

"Tao", it represents the archaic *lifeblood* or *spiritual soul* and nature of the universe. *Lao Tze* emphasized or stressed that *"Tao"* represents *no name* for *a "thing,"* but is the *"causal"* or *"pivotal" natural order* of the *"universe"*, whose definitive quintessence embodiment or *spiritual soul* is *incomprehensible, unintelligible, and impenetrable* to delineate. Thusly, *"Tao"* is *immortally, infinitely, and ceaselessly "nameless"*; as to be separated from the immeasurable or numerous *"named" things* which are deemed or regarded as its *endorsements or testimonials (manifestations)*. Furthermore, Taoism, Chinese Buddhism, and Confucianism, is the ideology of spiritual preparations to become *"one with the Tao"*, or to *harmonize one's will with nature or the universe in order to achieve" effortless action"*. The *"Tao's"* historical attributes and objectives was to establish harmony and peace amongst the Chinese population during and after the turmoil erupted between the *warring states*; and especially after the *"Han and Qin's"* civil war. Hundreds of years thereafter, Chinese history asserts that when the "Taoist and Buddhist" were competing for followers "Taoism" emerged as the canon, or majority system of philosophy and religion amongst Chinese civilization during that era. Thereafter, "Lao Tze" was honored and venerated as the founder of "Taoism"; which predicated on his writing and concept of the "sacred scriptures", or *"TaoDejing"*, namely titled *"The Way"*. Additionally, Chinese scholars of *"Taoism"* assert that during the *"Tang" dynasty "Taoist"* followers multiplied in great numbers throughout China; Notably, during the latter period of the *"Han Dynasty"*. Furthermore, *"Lao Tze or Laozi"*, was revered as a deity in most religious forms of Taoist philosophy, which often refers to *"Laozi (Tao Tze) or/as Taishang Laojun"*, or *"One of* the *Three Pure Ones"*. Furthermore, it's alleged by Chinese tradition that he lived

in the 6th century BCE. Whereas other historians contend that he lived in the fifth to fourth century BCE parallel with the one hundred schools of thought and Warring State era. Coincidentally, other Chinese sources argue that "Lao Tze" is a mock of multiple historic notables or that he is a mythical figure. Notwithstanding, he is a central figure in Chinese culture, being that both ordinary and aristocratic people claimed "Tao Tze" in their lineage. It's noted that he was honored as an ancestor of the Tang Imperial Family, and was accorded the designation "Supreme Mysterious and Primordial Emperor", or (without the Chinese assents) "Taishang xuanyuan huangdi".

Most importantly "Taoism" is the only original Chinese religion that evolved from Chinese culture and its civilization's. During one era in China's historical societies, aristocratic or noble clan membership were the only requirement to acquire a high ranking civil position in government; while bureaucratic leaders ignored skilled qualified and capable persons seeking high ranking government positions. However, noble clan membership lineage to acquire high ranking government positions ceased during the emergence of the "Tang" dynasty. The "Tang Royal Rulers" and family members were aware of their mixed or amalgamated blood lineage and immediately claimed direct ancestral descendants or lineage to "Lao Tze" inheritance. This acclaimed blood lineage to "Tao Tze" by the "Tang Royal Family Rulers' during this era instantaneously established "Taoism" as China's national religion during that specific era.

The principle ideology of "TaoDejing" and the utility of the sacred scriptures establishes a model for living standards for its followers to spiritual and social covenant. One of the scriptures requests to its "Taoist" believers is to focus on the universe and the world around them, to comprehend inner harmonies with the universe. Taoism aforementioned is the "way, path, or principle", which enunciates something that is both the source of power and impelling cause, and powerhouse behind all "matter", or "everything" that exist in the universe. The "Tao" is in the end imperceptible, indescribable, and indefinite. The "Tao" that can be told is not the eternal or infinite "Tao". "Lao Tze or Laozi, and "Zhuangzi", together wrote the texts that built the *philosophy* of "Taoism"; which is individualistic by nature, and is not institutionalized. Notably, institutional forms, however, evolved over time in the guise of materialization of a numerous count of Chinese schools of doctrine, thoughts, and principles. Often integrating beliefs or principles and practices that even predated the theories of the "School of Naturalists"; which synthesized or fused the concepts of "yin and yang" and the "five elements". Taoist schools traditionally feature devotion to "Tao Tze or Laozi's" immortals or ancestors, and numerous varieties of divination and exorcism rituals, and practices for achieving ecstasy, longevity or immortality. Additionally, structured through its religious system, which requires profound focus, concentration, and contemplation of rituals with required patterns of social observation.

The *"Tao's" cosmic* and *spiritual connection* to the universe and the World is defined as simply *"The Way"*, which unites all living matter with the creator of the universe or *"God"*. Therefore, *metaphorically and symbolically* creating a *sacred bond* between the universally undefinable symbolic *"ten thousand things"*, or *"all existence* in the universe". The *"ten thousand things"* are expressionistic symbolic qualities of the *"five elements"* combined to produce all universal matter. The *"Tao's" cosmic* and *spiritual forces* establishes the "five phases of transformations, and five elements of changes", which represents: *metal, water, wood, fire,* and *earth*. These five energies or patterns of movement supports and controls each elements transformational changes. Therefore, each elements compatible energy or universal forces relates to seasons of the *universe, air, wind, direction, color, taste, internal forces, spiritual energies, sense organs, sound, internal organs,* and all universal elements that *constitute cosmic* or *interplanetary existence*. Thusly, *"Taoist's"* followers must master and develop *"sense cognizance"* that heightens their spiritual and *inner soul* consciousness to the supreme level of *usefulness* vs. *uselessness*, to *"come and go as one pleases (mental transitions)",* through cosmic principles directed by energy forces. This *"sense emergence"* to *"the way or path"* derives from *within the self-conscious state* that transcends beyond *earthly range and boundaries*. The infinite *cosmos* within "Tao" structures *"energy sensitivity"* that *enlightens* the path to infinity or *supreme nothingness*. "Taoism" completes and returns to this earthly journey through its inheritance or marriage to *"quanzhen"* (complete reality), *"lingbao"* (numerous treasures), *"shangging"* (highest clarity), and *"tianshi dao"* (way of the celestial masters). The sacred scriptures suggests that "understanding and interaction" is a cosmic foundation of perceptive social modifications and simplifications, that transcends a focal analysis of "life" into simpler levels and stages towards an organized system of "sensibility" and "reflection" on the path to "Taoist" principles and doctrine interpretations, that releases one's self to cosmology and humankind in earthly interactions within the universe or "Tao". The Sacred Scriptures transmits a mystery of cosmic universal relevance, because it cannot be defined, spoken, or known on earthly terms within the *context and transcendental range* of *"Taoism"*.

However, *"the way"* or *TaoDejing* can be read by numerous *"Tao"* followers who's subconsciously and consciously absorbing varied and undefinable interpretations of the *Sacred Scripture in different spiritual perceptions.* Thusly, each follower that reads the scriptures of *"Taoism"* has a different interpretation that can be expressed intuitively through their *personal range* of *spiritual comprehension* and *submission* to the *"way".* Subsequently, after follower's read scriptural verses of "The *TaoDejing" their understanding of "Tao" becomes an individual spiritual journey,* through "Tao's" guided forces of cultural *mysticism,* which enhances universal wisdoms that guides a *conscious submission* into an *enlightening path* of spiritual, principled, and *canon focus* of "the way"; which, represents the tenets of "Taoism" within individualistic *dimensional* perceptions of *"life's energies"* from the *wisdom* of an ancient traveling sage *"Laozi",* who's known as the *"Father of Taoism".*

The forceful expressions and *turn of phrases within ancient Chinese spiritual, religious, and cultural languages* founded "Taoism" that exemplifies philosophy and religion within the scriptures of "The TaoDejing"; which has cultivated insightful non-tangible faith through consciousness within and throughout the souls of beings; and from a *transcendental supernatural meditation* and *earthly* assistance within a *natural* and absolute *living relevance.* An Example of earthly assistance references "inner alchemy" (experimentation, transformation, and "pseudoscience"), or "qigong forms" which are Chinese traditional practices within "Taoism" that focus awareness of breathing and the flow of "life-forces" through human physical forms, practices, methods of procedures, and through "Taoist" rituals. Also, the practice that connects "Taoist" with conveying inner feelings and thoughts within the natural souls of nature initiates guidelines through inbuilt healing forms, or practices via the "Yuan's methodology".

The "sacred scriptures" contradicts some *Confucian* concepts of "individual moral duties", "community standards (the caste system)", and his concept on "government responsibilities". "Taoist", belief propose doctrine is as follows: "The government of the people for the people", which disproves Confucian's "caste system". The formers beliefs (Taoist) is that it is "fair and unbiased to qualify the best capable people of the communities or provinces, to acquire quality leadership in the social infrastructure, and in governance from the best minds and aptitude in Chinese society". Contrarily, to Confucian beliefs, that governance and society should be ruled by, *select families*, that descend from aristocratic and noble lineage.

The most universally shared *"symbolic"* and *"emblematic"* philosophy and concept from "Taoism" is the *"yin and yang"; which* ostensibly describes *"contradictory* or *opposite forces"*, which are interdependent and interconnecting in the natural world, and at the same time, give rise to each other as they interrelate to one another. Scores of natural dualities are conceptualized or thought of, as physical materializations or manifestations of the *"Yin and Yang"*. The concept lies at the origins of "Taoism", and other numerous divisions and subdivisions of "ancient classical Chinese and Oriental Sciences and Philosophies. The "Yin and Yang" is also a vital contributing factor and guideline of ancient and (modern) traditional Chinese and Oriental medicines; and is also a central principle of different forms of "Chinese and Oriental" martial arts and exercises, which includes "Baguazhang", "Taijiquan", "qigong", and "I Ching" etc… The forces or energies of "Yin and Yang" are complementary forces, as opposed to opposites, which interacts to bring into being a whole greater than "either" separate part; in effect it manifest a vividly brilliant and dynamic system. Therefore, in that "everything" has either "yin and yang" attributes, which either of the two major aspects, may well reveal or manifest more strongly in one or the other particular objects, which strongly rest on decisive factors of the observation at hand. The "yin and yang" is the symbolic ancient Chinese masculine and feminine energies representational of *"all"* diametrically oppositions of minds which brings into being our total experiences of the World. The interlink or interconnection of the "yin and yang" categorically constitutes natural interrelationships within family, life, earthly experiences, the Universe and World occurrences as mutually affected by each interrelationship simultaneously, whereas one cannot and will not exist without the other. Example, if one side of your person is in a shaded area and the other side of your person is in the sun, one is the yin and the other side of your person is the yang; however, you may *identify either* as the "yin or yang". Consequently, within every human body lies both the "yin and yang" (energy and forces). Noteworthy, all eighty-one plus verses of the sacred scriptures "TaoDejing" substantiates the balance of opposites in the existence (experiences and life's forces) in the Universe. When the "yin and yang" are equally present *all is calm, harmonious, and peaceful.* Contrastingly, when one is outweighed by the other they manifest turmoil, confusion, and disarray. The "yin and yang" is the "sacred scriptures" support system; and the "sacred scriptures" or "TaoDejing" is also the "yin and yang's" sustenance; because one is a transcendental supernatural universal roamer (yin and yang), the other is its dwelling (TaoDejing). The "sacred scriptures" assists the "Taoist followers" to faithfully envision, explore, and ingest the principles of "Tao" doctrine, and faithfully retain its tenets within one's *mortal soul*, and to elevate as close as possible, to the eternal "Tao's" *spiritual awakening* to *"immortality or an everlasting life"*.

The sacred scriptures convey *"Taoism"* as incorporating within ones principles both a *philosophical* Chinese tradition *"tao-chia"*, which is linked to *"Lao Tze"*, *"Chuang Tzu"*, and *"Lieh Tzu"*; which constitute the three (3) historically recorded founders of the Chinese *"Taoist" religious traditions*. However, "Tao Chiao's" organized doctrines formats "Tao's" cultural worship activities, and spiritual reflections within institutionalized Chinese traditions, that qualifies its "objective, subjective, and transcendental" mystical universal human experiences; however, its *spiritual transition* to the human soul is *permeated only within the individual's human range of acquired scriptural cogniz*ance. Thusly, "Tao" follower's *spiritually incorporate* both the *earthly* and *transcendenta*l concept of "Taoism" *simultaneously;* which transitions (mentality and spiritually) the "way or path" to reach and transcend "Tao"; and thereafter, to seek immortality or everlasting life; *before and after* departure from this earth. The construct of "Laozi's TaoDejing", brings forth numerous dimensions of compassion; yet, I will cite two of many compassionate principled forces of energy referenced in the sacred scriptures; and they being enjoined and infused with earthly activities shepherded through *"empathy and objectivity"*, or "Taoism (heaven) vs. earthly turmoil". "The Way's" impartiality, independence, and detachment from earthly things is deduced to "supreme nothingness"; and the compassion or *empathy* that nurses "earthly turmoil" is understanding the *"way" or "path"* that *spiritualizes principled* detachments from earthly problems. However also, by continually separating the mind and spiritual soul from earthly *confusion, instability,* and *chaos*; which emanates through rigid preparation and *focused spiritual* practices of *"Taoism"*. "Lao Tze's" empathy or compassion referenced through the scriptures was prompted from Ancient China's social, political, and ruling class's governance that administrated civil turmoil. This ruling administration unlawfully enacted anarchy, which prompted civil disorder, which was experienced by Chinese society, and especially by the working class population, before/during the Han's dynasty, or Chinese civil war. "Lao Tze's" keen intelligence, innate perception, and compassion for his people ignited the fuse that enabled him, and his aforementioned counterparts or founders of the "Taoist" doctrine, to acquire the honors of "The Fathers of Taoism". His "bedrock" work of literature in "Taoism" is the "TaoDejing", a concise and ambiguous book containing his teachings, which many social scientist acknowledge derives from the aforementioned cruelty of Chinese civic legislation and rule of governance against its people in ancient China. "Zhuangzi" has not been mentioned as one of "Laozi's" or Tao Tze's" counterparts or equals, in writing and of founding the "Tao Te Ching"; which constructs the philosophical foundation of "Taoism". Noteworthy, evolving over years in the *nature, form, and model* of varying Chinese institutions was *"naturalism"*, which often integrated beliefs and practices that even *predated* the *root-sources* of "Taoism". The philosophy, concepts, ideas, principles, and theories of the school of "naturalists" synthesized the "yin and yang" concept, coupled with the advent of the "five elements". Also, aforementioned previously, is the "Taoist" schools which traditionally featured reverence for "Laozi's" immortals or ancestors along with numerous divinations, exorcisms rituals, and practices for achieving or acquiring ecstasy, longevity, or immortality through rigorous "Taoist" practices and exercises.

"The Way", was written by "Laozi and Zhuangzi", who communicates forthright, transcendental and earthly internal experiences directed philosophically, and stupendously in the direction of cosmic or celestial vs. earthly materialism in constructing the "TaoDejing". Their physical vs. mental philosophy between mankind's objective contradictions on earth, is somewhat resolved by utilizing the philosophy of "subjective" cosmic emptiness or universal space to create the concept "nothingness"; within their mental wisdom, knowledge, and analysis of the "transcendental" approach to "an untouchable source of meditation"; which is undefinable with comprehensive structural reflection of a mystical nature, to establish a logical universal rebuttal to "earthly divergences". Thusly, baptizing ancient Chinese Philosophy and Religion into the universe as "the way" or "Taoism". Consequently, the "Tao's" mysticism of intuitive spiritual revelations is philosophized in social and religious revelations, as the "purest" form of undefinable representation of the divine order in representing the founding concepts of "Taoism". Naturally, the correlation of the supernatural unknown mysticisms in "Taoist" doctrines vs. earthly experiences within the covenant of governance and social survival, often conflicts with human consciousness and earthly expectations; within the scope of civil integrity, honesty, and unselfish dogma. Therefore, the human conscious and subconscious seek questions regarding their salvation and human existence or purpose on earth. Thusly, Philosophy and Religion are founded to *"inject supernatural potencies"* into the lives of people earthly bound (past, present, and future), who are obligated to strengthen societies challenging survival obligation within the scope of humanity. Therefore, "Taoism" religions and philosophies, "inject this transcendental supernatural potency" (spiritually) into the lives of follower's seeking to capacitate and facilitate their personal spiritual growth, which will develop and prepare their mortal soul's to an immortal earthly departure. The "sacred scriptures" of "TaoDejing" calms and breaths harmony into the conscious and subconscious spiritual soul, along with tolerance, humility, honesty, truth, goodness, and unyielding integrity that bends to know unjust social cause. Therefore, "Tao" has the dimensional capacities to balance the natural order of life's forces of negative energies into positive forces, through universal divine reason, virtue, and from highly accountable ethic embrace, through the "path or way". Consequently, "Taoism's" objective capacity is to heighten its follower's supernatural mental spiritualistic aptitude, through the sacred scriptures, the five elements, and through the yin and yang; as their foundational sources to place and position earthly experiences into submission, isolation, temporal separation, and into a universal transcendental framework that adjust "all matter" into its proper metaphysical concept of "nothingness" or the "ten thousand things". Taoism signifies the essence of the fundamental nature of the universe. "Laozi's", primary message explains that "Tao" is not a name for a thing, but the underlying natural order of the universe, whose ultimate essence is difficult to impossible to define. Thusly, "Tao" is eternally nameless, and is to be distinguished from the countless "named things" on earth, which are deliberated to be "Taoism's" materializations, symptoms, expressions, and manifestations". Tao's faithful followers are able to replace earthly "trials and tribulations" that's within "Tao's" loyal principled systems of beliefs, conceptualized through trust, and the purest "Taoist" sacraments; which acknowledge, bless, and untangles the negative human experiences on this earth; by defining its objectives, purpose, and intentions; through the sacred scriptures of the "Tao De Jing".

The infinite "Tao, Universe, and Solar System" are ultimately one within themselves; however, both lives within the "Tao" (heaven, infinity, and eternity), which is defined as "nothingness" (action without action), or "The Supreme Being". The "Tao and the Universe" is the cosmic air we breathe, feel, and live to exist from; through an undefinable evaluation or imagination of its undefined identity. Consequently, the "Taoist" mysticism of "nothingness", "Supreme Being and Existence", is "Taoist" objective and subjective principled belief pilgrimage, or journey to reach and achieve the goals of "nothingness", in acquiring "immortality or everlasting life" through "Taoism". The "Tao De Jing" (sacred scriptures) presents "Tao" or "God" as the "Unbroken and Undivided Interactive Forces within Itself". Who could ever contradict or untangle this mystic creation of the universe? This original modeled supernatural "heaven" envelopes our *before and after lives* eternally through our existence. Our measured life's existence on earth is spiritualized through "Tao's" elements, which is all-encompassing universal matter or composition again, that completes the universes eternal reprocessing from its original source of infinite existence occurring over and over again within its infinite eternity. Subsequently, a "pure and unchallenged cosmic universe", is absolute, empty, useless, useful, and unlimited within undefined and immeasurable space" (Universe). The "Taoist's" sensory capacity must continually perpetuate highly realistic "Taoistic" principled doctrine preparation standards, through the "TaoDejing's" reflective verses, founded by "Laozi" and counterpart's;

that exemplifies a model "Taoist" following of believer's, for student's of "Taoism" to solidify an "immortal and everlasting life"; before and after earthly departure. However, each "Taoist" student's interpretation of "TaoDejing" is received, assessed, calculated, and time-honored *differently*, within one's *personal spiritual perceptive analysis* of the "sacred scriptures", through their *personal earthly* experiences, and cognition of perceiving "Taoism".

The symbolic interpretation of "God" is the "Tao"; that figuratively represents the "Master of the Universe", through the "sacred scriptures" of *TaoDejing*; which is exactly exemplary to the "Christian beliefs that represent "God" "The Master of the Universe", through the scriptures in the "Holy Bible". In essence, the macro or Universal factors that unites both religions definition of "God" evolves from similar religious and philosophical principles, which is to acquire "everlasting life" in the hereafter. Example, scriptural verse # 40 from "The Tao De Jing": *The motion of the "way" is to return, the use of the "way" is to accept, all things come from the "way", and the "way comes from nothing"*. Therefore, one interprets "nothingness" as "The Supreme Master", therefore all things is under the umbrella of "God", and infinity is eternal space undefinable and mystical, which must be embraced by *faith*, and not by "sight or name", which qualifies "The Supreme Existence of God'. Thusly, each "Tao" believer must develop, acquire, and display their "sense acuity consciousness, and sub-consciousness between transcendental and earthly material relevance, to fully interpret, transition, convert, and modify the "way" or "path" to "Tao's" ultimate "immortality and everlasting life".

The "Tao's" *ten thousand things,* refer to its "tenet" that "everything that exist in the universe is *Tao*". Central to this conceptual belief resides in *"Qi",* life's-energy forces in the World that *stimulates all things and forms* in the Universe. Identified as the *pulse (*happenings) of all natural and unnatural phenomena in the universe. The Egyptians identify this phenomenal entity as "Ka", Christians "The Holy Ghost", Africa "Ashe", Hawaiians "Mana or Ha", American Indians "Great Spirit", Greeks "Pneuma", Japan "ki", and India "Prana or Shakti" et. Al,. All the above *"Qi"* or *energy forces* in their respective philosophies and religions is reflected and principled by "Taoist" as its manifestations or materializations from "Taoist" eternal, and infinite existence. However, the range of the "sacred scriptures" development never fulfills its *infinite subjective or objective* impossible end result. However, when "Taoist" followers reach the pinnacle of their "path or way" (euphoria and exaltation), their range of "Taoist" *transcendental reflective introspection is revealed,* that transmits a state of spiritual and mental exaltation that displays to the believers the "infinite forces of energy which radiates as visible, touchable, and approachable assessments of their spiritual dedication and aptitude; through the *"subjective and objective"* mental phenomena of "Taoism". Subsequently, the "divine way" is revealed through the spiritually sublime universal cosmic motion of energies that transitions its infinite rotation through the "Taoist" doctrine and practices, and surpasses through its follower's physical life forces which reveals to the "Taoist" the *"divine way".*

Religions breeds *objective* and *subjective devotion* that's permeated by "faith factors", and therefore is principled through "religious piety, devotion, loyalty, systems of canon dogmas, and codes and articles of beliefs etc... The contradiction to *faith perception (belief) is objectivity, which contradicts the subjective religious dogma* "to walk or live by faith", which exalts religious faith believers. Thusly, "faith belief" is an intangible, elusive, indefinable, vague, and elusive devotion. However, "faith healing" reinvigorates, revives, strengthens, and sustains the sacred spiritual, physical, and nonphysical *devout religious* believer's human souls. Notably, the subjective minds of religious followers parallel their subjective "faith belief" membership acceptance, conviction, loyalty, and credibility, through a mental process; which is attached to a "cause and effect" psychological or conscious process that develops its outcome, which is the "faith healing" process thereafter. Nonetheless, slices of the objectivity pie is revived after the "faith healing" of followers from varied religions secures positive feelings of physical and mental relief through their psychological beliefs in "faith healing"; which stimulated support, comfort, solace, and "healing" through "faith"; which thereafter, converts from an intangible "faith belief" psychological process, into a tangible "faith healing" cause and effect process, which derives from the subjective mind-set of "faith belief".

The religions popular to China as actual practicing and historically acknowledged religions includes: Confucianism, Hinduism, Jainism, Buddhism, Islam, Animism, and Taoism etc… However, Taoism is the only authentic indigenous Chinese religion founded by Chinese civilization. Taoism's has structured and organized the development of Chinese culture through many attributes, from philosophy, religion, science, medicine, hygiene, to political and social theories of social and moral conduct throughout Chinese history. The practical and personal societal circumstances of Chinese culture that allowed the growth of "Taoism", was implemented through the experiences that shaped and developed "Taoism", and its growth as a philosophy and religion. Thusly, its foundation is directly related to the social experiences of the Chinese civilization; which includes their history, and other observable factors relevant to "Tao Tze or Laozi's" concerns for the survival, and social upheaval detrimental to Chinese society. It's alleged that "Taoism" emerged or was founded during the Eastern "Han" dynasty, which also relates to the Chinese ethnic group, namely the "Han's". The Eastern "Han's" totaled approximately ninety-three (93%) percent of the Chinese population. The Eastern "Han" dynasty ruled from 206 B.C. to A.D. 220, and was accountable and liable for organizing Confucianism as a viable system of governance, that established the official process of systematic bureaucracy, during this era in Chinese history. Initially, "Laozi" along with his counterparts and founders of "Taoism", witnessed the social and political conditions falling on the Eastern "Han's" deteriorating ruling government. The Confucian philosophy ignited discontent between the ruling class and the majority populous, due to bureaucratic injudicious negligence of the needs, concerns, and social stagnation of the people, especially the working class. All viable infrastructural facilities and control was in the hands of the ruling class structure or bureaucracy, which upheld Confucianism as its principle set of guidelines. "Laozi and founders" of "Taoism", witnessed that a newly innovative order of philosophy and religion was necessary to refute the ruling classes guided by "Confucian" dogma; which upheld the cast systems fundamental right to rule Chinese civilization at will. During the Eastern Han's dynasty, social and political instability resulted in unruly and immoral political behavior, judicial injustices, and instability to rule the people justly; albeit, crop failure was caused by a severe drought during this era in Chinese history, which added to the negative ruling government's troubles during the Han dynasty. Furthermore, excessive economic exploitation of the populous created enormous social and political pressures on the citizens making it almost impossible for them to lead stable and decent lives. Accordingly, the conflict between the aristocratic ruling class and the general population was intense during that era of the Eastern Han dynasties Imperial rule in China. Peasant uprisings were occurring frequently, during this era according to China's historical records. Furthermore, economic and political unrest was paramount, which initiated political unrest and spiritual and moral decay throughout Chinese civilization, during this era; thusly, opening the door for *"Laozi's Taoist philosophy and religion"* to reform and restore China's decaying society. Political, social and economic turbulence historically in "all" societies, causes severe hardships that eventually requires social structuring, and political transformations or reforms to restore social order. Consequently, when working class societies and, the underprivileged populous becomes desperate for social change, they tend to hinge their hopes for a better society on prayers, protests and spiritual support.

Therefore, the direction and route ancient Chinese protester's utilized to reconcile or resolve their "deprived social, political, and economical reality, was to form "survival groups", throughout their communities that specifically dealt with their social deprivations. Noteworthy, during this era of "Laozi", most of China's poorer class population embraced and gravitated to "Taoism"; which inspired hope and social opportunities towards a "Taoist" interpretation in acquiring philosophical and religious gravity; to combat their oppressed conditions in China. Without question, the deteriorating and inefficient governance of the populous administered near the end of the "Han Dynasty" facilitated and enabled "Taoism" to become known as a viable "Philosophy and

Religion" for Chinese society; which welcomed *all* social classes in Chinese society. Notably, the peasant and lower class structure in China provided outstanding membership, with the majority of the people following "Taoism", during this era in Chinese history... Furthermore, the cause of "Tao's" rapid growth and development during this specific era examines the contrasting "Confucian" philosophy, ideology and religion, which adapted its principles towards establishing a "unified feudal system", society, and dogma for the aristocratic ruling class in China. Although religion played a significant role in Chinese society, it never became an overpowering force to be reckoned with compared to "Taoism's" innovative concept for China's troubled society during this time in Chinese history. It's historically alleged in Chinese records that "Confucianism did not become a religion during the Han dynasty for the simple reason that it attempted to *materialize* the ideals of governing the states, and to pacify China. Following the decline of the Han dynasty, Confucian ideology not only fell short of becoming a religion to *feudal* ideology for the ruling class, it witnessed the decline of Confucianism and the rise of Taoism. Notwithstanding, history always repeats itself whenever the dominant ideology of the ruling class lose its power to govern, due to an escalation and ascendancy of a counteracting power, ideology, and influence, against a harmful burdening force of governance, against its people. Although Confucianism had declined in influence, near the end of the Eastern Han's dynasty, many aspects of its ideology, creed, and dogma were absorbed and enveloped into "Taoism". Example, one of many Confucian principles that absorbed in "Taoist" conception *"is the ultimate peace in the unity of heaven, earth, and man"*. Consequently, this specific Confucian concept was dutifully engaged in the political reality and notion of "sanci" which relates to the three endowments mentioned in *"Yi Zhuan"*; that *"the sky and universe were formed by breathe or Qi"*. However, this concept allegedly may have derived from the "Chinese philosophy of the *"World Creation"*, *"Yin and Yang"* principles, and the five elements cited in the concept, *"being of questionable authority"; which closely relates and connects to "Eastern Han and Confucian thought"*.

The translation of the "Tao De Jing" from Chinese to English categorizes each page in scriptural paragraphs from one to eighty-one verses, which differ in spiritual definition or "spiritual verse interpretation, through metaphorical representations", of life's many personal contradictional issues endured by mankind, which confronts mankind within his temporal earthly experiences. Yet, Taoism guides its followers and believer's to embrace their "God", the "Tao", or *"the eternal infinite Universe"*, that *"all"* worldly matter derives from. Therefore, "The Tao's foundation is transcendental with the objective and subjective models of symbolic directives from the "yin and yang", TaoDejing or sacred scriptures. Consequently, conceptualized through the philosophy and religious canon of "Taoism". The sacred scriptures objectively defines the perceptive teachings and guidelines of "Taoism" that motivates subjective transcendental super- natural spirituality necessary for believers to ascend from the mortal state of being, to the immortal existence, to ultimately acquire an "everlasting life" during and after death. This model philosophy and religion of "Taoism" is in direct likeness to Western Religions follower's doctrinal origins, that aspire to attain their supernatural faith through subjective belief, to ultimately ascend to "Heaven" to acquire "everlasting life" in the hereafter. Additionally, "The Tao's" earthly and cosmic interrelationship and interaction with mortal and immortal conceptualism is substantiated through the *sacred scriptures,* and through mortal definitions of recorded documentation of "Laozi's" spiritual "Taoist" word-based creation of the "Tao De Jing"; which also represents "The Way" or infinite "Universe", that opens the door to total enlightenment as a true believer in "Taoism". Both "Taoism" and other religions of the world requires its believer's to acquire spiritual transformation or faith-ridden conversion to their religious or philosophical beliefs... Numerous worldly religious characteristics that transcends spiritual subliminal expressions to reach "The Tao" or "Heavens Everlasting-life", is conducted through "chants, burned incense, candles, trance states of uncontrollable bodily physical movements, while speaking in tongues", and/or through prayers.

The historical problematic issues concerning the study of Taoism evolves from Ancient Chinese theory that "it is an impossible task for "Taoist" believers to mentally retain the "twelve-hundred plus Taoist verses, or textual guidelines, that structure "Taoist" rules, principles, actions and interactions, that dictates the purest form of "Taoist" character; which leads to "The Way", an infinite Universe, and Everlasting life. "Taoist Priest" countered the problematic issues of the numerous readings required by followers of "Taoism", to retain the many verses and guidelines in becoming committed, and devout "Taoist", by stating the following: "If Taoist followers retain and absorb *"one"* "Taoist scripture or verse *earnestly and intensely,* out of twelve-hundred plus scriptural guidelines and principles, they've become devout "Taoist".

CHAPTER VII

The Comparative Similarities between "Taoism and Christianity"

(Analysis by William F. Williams)

Western Religions and Beliefs, is the cornerstone to cleansing mankind's mortal sins, from earthly confusion, which eliminates their sins through prayer and repentance, which qualifies faithful worship. Christians absorbs tenets in written word from their respective religions to cleanse the mind, body, soul, and spirit, from the *"Holly Bible's"* guidelines and principles from informative ancient historical chapters. Thereby, absorbing reflective and revealing historical ethical reliance; through biblical values, concepts and principles, on the road to religious convictions (generally speaking). Additionally, the Christians *"Holy Bible"* is their ethical imperative from the Commandments of the "holy scriptures", established through the practices and teachings of *"Jesus Christ",* and his *disciples.* The initial principles of Christianity is to embrace the principles of *"Love".* For it states in three prominent phrases "Love thy brother as thyself", and "To love thy God in Heaven, and place no-other God before him". Also, "love" is the pivotal force necessary to enter the "Kingdom of Heaven"; Additionally, in (John 15:12) which states, *"Love one another as I have "loved" you".* Subsequently, the principle of active spiritual "love" rests in the "inherent hearts and souls of "Christian's through their fundamental upbringing and nurturing". The descriptive analysis aforementioned "love thy brother as thyself" refers to "love" towards all of mankind in this Universe which validates Christian sanctification. These tenets of *love* manifest the basic preliminary inaugurated guidelines for followers of the Christian faith. Additionally, these tenets are the initial entrance of conceptualizing the historical suffering, humility, degradation, torture, and crucifixion of "Jesus Christ" from the "Holly Bible's" historical teachings and interpretations of his journey on earth, before he ascended to heaven, after his crucifixion. Thusly, "Jesus" to Christian followers is regarded as the "Son" of "God", or as the "almighty" savior of mankind and creator of the Universe. "Jesus the Son of (infinite) God", reinforces Christian "faith" in the conceptual context and framework of the divine and supernatural spiritual embodiment of Christian life's expectancy; and in the belief of obtaining an *"everlasting life"* in the hereafter. Therefore, the Christian's submission to the principles of "the Bible's historical divine chapters, scriptures, verses, phrases, and the teachings of "Jesus Christ's" earthly suffering, is the directory or reference to establishing the spiritual foundation to "walk by faith and not by sight". Thusly, obtaining immortality is to acquire "Everlasting life in Heaven", through biblical doctrine. However, during "Jesus Christ's" crucifixion, he reveals to his following (disciples) before his earthly demise inflicted upon him by Roman and Jewish exccutor's the following statement: "forgive them father (God) for they know not what they do"; thusly, substantiating and reviving the Christian faith, through this "love" *initiator*; and through his forgiveness to his crucifier's, prior to his ascend to "Heaven". Notably, translating his mortal presents on earth as a human being, tood a spiritually transposed embodied immortal state, prior to his ascend to the *"Kingdom of God"*. The historical experiences of *"Jesus Christ* symbolizes to his Christian followers a *Supreme Being's* exodus from earthly suffering as a (mortal) *human being,* to an immortal supernatural *"God..."* Therefore, the Christian ideology of "walk by faith, not by sight" reveals insightful transcendental deliberation through religious fervor necessary as a religious paradigm, to elevate spiritual and faithful believer's communion and fellowship through "Jesus Christ's" experience. Christian *ethical behavior* is idealistically structured through ceremony, rituals, consecration and services open to its follower's, similarly to Taoism.

Comparatively, the "Christian Bible's guidelines and canons", express explicitly, subconsciously and consciously, a factual religious conceptual tenet linkage and continuity in numerous respects, to the "Tao's" *TaoDejing's,* sacred scriptural concepts of "Universal decree". Example, both religions, be it "Christian or "Taoism" relinquishes and exonerates its follower's earthly transgressions through sacred ritualization's, to cleanse their earthly sins through their physical and spiritual humility and remorse. Therefore, all sinful earthly acts conducted by followers of both religions must transmit their acts of transgression through transcendental meditation (prayer), through their respective religious spiritual systems, principles of dogmas or specified religious doctrines. However, contrastingly to "Taoism", the "Christian" creed or belief refers to reincarnation, which continuously recreates the Christian's persona to an elevated character in the direction of the purest form of "Holy" or "sacred behavior" attainable in his or her earthly experiences; which incorporates, and absorbs the mental reflections between Christian believers or followers; within Christian guidelines constructively facilitated from the "Holy Bible's" biblical collective histories of "Christ and his

Disciples" earthly experiences. Consequently, his followers suffered from the constant assimilation and conversion, from pagan and animist influences too Christianity; however, in time converted faithfully to the teachings of the Christian "God", through "Jesus" and his devout "Disciples" historical journey's. In the books that constitute the "Bible", followers of "Christ" endured intrinsic suffering, and social humility; but sustained their faith through forgiveness and love towards their oppressors, in the same way "Christ" endured suffering and forgiveness to his tormentors; which supported Christian belief through Jesus teaching principles of faith conversion, such as: "walk by faith, and not by sight" epics, which sustains Christian followers belief in the guidelines of the "Christian Bible". Consequently, Taoist scriptures were also structured as philosophical / religious guidelines for its faithful followers to secure "ethical reverence", and virtuous principles from the sacred "Tao De Jing". The "Tao De Jing" directs the principle guidelines to Taoist followers through its conceptual deliverance that the "Tao" is nameless (Godly), and cannot be labeled or defined in its encounter within the Universe, due to its unnameable equation to "nothingness". Contrastingly, Christian beliefs are nameable with definite labels and earthly definitions, as it relates to mortal minds, that sustains human transgressions within earthly boundaries, to repent all sins and acquire an eternal everlasting immortal life after death. However, within the aforementioned Christian example of its religious guidelines to define and identify all religious meaning through names and labels of definitive credence; however, the Tao's undefined and nameless identity is contrastingly different than Christian identity guidelines in this instance. However, in Taoism the "Tao-chiao" is created in concept by the "Tao De Jing" or sacred scriptures, through unassertive energetic actions, within the eighty-one plus verses of the sacred scriptural principles. It elevates within Taoism the purest forms of spiritual attainment as "The Three Jewels of Taoism": compassion, moderation, and humility, or (pinyin, sanbao, and sanpao), translated meaning kindness, simplicity, and modesty. Furthermore, if this translation of "The Three Jewels of Taoism" is deciphered into Christian ideology, the comparative defined religious/philosophy analysis would translate to: love, humility, forgiveness, and suffering. Thusly, both religious concepts (Tao and Christianity) in this definitive regards associates with both "Jesus and Lao Tzu's" teaching philosophies. Furthermore, "the Way, Road, or Path" associated in Taoism is to obtain "hsien"; which connotes religious immortality prior to death on earth and ascend to heaven after death, which denotes a comparative Christian destiny, to manifest an "everlasting life". However, after a mortal existence on earth in Christian tenets, thereafter, both "Taoist and Christians" ascend to heaven immortally. Furthermore, the Taoist spiritual attainment of immortality is the Universality of "all earthly matter" (hsien) obtained by Taoist through the "way" or "path", which refers to the transcendental belief that the mortal soul of Taoist immediately "transforms" from mortality to immortality during one's earthly experiences. Thusly, obtaining the purest form of Taoism; which refers to the concept of the "ten thousand things", implying that all matter within the Universe, or the "way" symbolize or manifest "Tao's divinity, mysticism, and holiness. Notwithstanding, Christian theological philosophy cleans the mortal soul through repentance prior to death, which transforms the soul or physical being too the "immortal" state of being (to acquire an everlasting life in the hereafter), in order to transcend to heaven, which qualifies the Christian soul to pass through the holy gates of heaven.

The sage's and disciple's in both religions who administered their teachings; both, Lao Tzu and Jesus respectively, converted non-believers to their religious and philosophical practices in both Taoism and Christianity. Ethical behavior and earthly fulfillment is the theme of both religions, which is to purify and manifest an everlasting oneness to coincide with a temporal earthly experience; however, both doctrines are structured in principle and designed through both the "Tao De Jing, and the Holy Bible.

Individual sages or followers of Lao Tze who made exemplary contributions to the sacred scriptures "Tao De Jing", is mentioned briefly in the history of Taoism; however, one notable individual of many contributors to this masterpiece is "Zhuangzi", who enabled the "philosophical" foundation of Taoism; which is individualistic by nature. Consequently, "philosophical Taoism" is not institutionalized. Yet, institutionalized forms of the philosophy of Taoism, evolved over time in the context and establishment of numerous schools or institutions, often integrating their newly founded beliefs and practices that predated the basic texts. Such as, the general principles of the schools of "naturalism", which synthesized and composed the concepts of the "yin and yang" and the "five elements". Notably, Taoist schools traditionally featured reverence to "Laozi" or "Lao Tze's", immortals or ancestors along with a multitude of varying divination and exorcism rituals and practices for achieving ecstasy, longevity and immortality. Noteworthy, "Zhuangzi or Chuang Tzu" wrote resplendent and penetrating "Taoist" religious literature propelling the Taoist philosophy; sacred text, and formatting the chin te=power techniques that realized the effects flowing from "Tao's" "way or path" within universal infinity; which is created within Taoism from earthly conception of "all" generations from birth, and from person to person, because "extended life is matter that's eternal infinitely, through the "way or path" from the "Tao" to initial mortality and ultimately to immortality. Therefore, all matter within the universe is immortal and is continuous in its existence as matter, of infinite substance through the "way or path" of Taoism. Definable, all existent human and materialistic creation is infinite from creation to eternity through the "Tao". Zhuangzi, (philosophical creator of the Tao) is considered with Lao Tze, and "Taishang Laojun" as one of the creators of "Taoism; which is translated as "One of the Three Pure One's"; Notably, evolving in the 5th-4th century, and concurrent in time with the "Hundred Schools of Thought", and the "Warring States Period" in ancient China. Also, others argue that "Lao Tze" was a synthesis of multiple historical figures or, a mythical figure, which has not to this date-in-time been authenticated as a factual historical person (here-say). However, he is authenticated as a central figure in Chinese culture, with both nobility and common Chinese claim him (Lao Tze or Laozi) in their lineage. Aforementioned previously in earlier paragraphs is his honor as an ancestor of the "Tang Imperial Family", and was granted the supreme title "Taishang Xuanyuan Huangdi" (absent of Chinese accents and symbols), translated meaning "Supreme Mysterious and Primordial Emperor". Importantly, "The Three Pure One's" accomplishments and creation of the Tao philosophy/religion, has been embraced by "various anti-authoritarian movements" arising throughout Chinese history. As referred to earlier, Taoism is a metaphysical concept (relating to the transcendency or to a reality beyond what is perceptible to the senses; and labeled or marked by unconventional imagery); originating with "Lao Tze" that gave rise to a religion and philosophy referred to in the Western World, with the singular term "Taoism". The concept of Tao was shared with Confucianism, Chan, and Zen Buddhism; however, more broadly throughout East Asia. Within these contexts Tao signifies the primordial essence of the fundamental nature of the Universe.

Notably, in the construction and initial foundation of Taoism, referencing the "Tao De Jing" or sacred scriptures, "all things" is explained by Lao Tze as "Nameless", because the underlying "natural order of our Universe's ultimate essence is difficult to circumscribe. Thusly, Tao is "eternally nameless", and is to be distinguished from the countless "named things" which are considered to be its manifestations. Furthermore, in Taoism, Chinese Buddhism, and Confucianism, the object of spiritual practice is to "become one with the Tao or to harmonize one's will with "Universal Nature" in order to achieve "effortless action", which involves meditative and moral practices which translated to the Tao's concept of "De". Functional historical dissimilarities of the two religions (Taoism and Christianity), is that the disciples of "Jesus Christ" is categorically and historically featured in their individual and group participation in spreading the Christian faith which is paramount in the "Holy Bible". Example, the chapters of Matthew, Mark, Luke, and John et al... Thusly, justifying their contributions to the Christian faith as "Jesus Christ" disciples. Dissimilarly, the Taoist "sages" who accommodated "Lao Tze's contributions, creation and formulation of the "Tao De Jing" or "sacred scripture", historically appear vague in identity (name); also they are ambiguous, obscure, and unclear in regards to their specific religious teachings, philosophical contributions regarding their assertiveness, and their resounding and dedicated participation in the creation of Taoism. Furthermore, the Tao's religious and philosophical conceptual principles are predicated on the tenets and teaching "not to supplement the natural through "human acknowledgements" or categorically by name, because the Tao is "nameless": as the following concept states, "unconcerned they came and unconcerned they went"; therefore, to name Universal matter would contradict the principle teaching of "not to lead the heart astray from "Taoism" (Daojiao).

The religious and philosophical nature of both religions qualifies the similarity of both's ethical dogma, which is to excel in earthly patterns, practices, and principles of earthly morality and ultimately to immortality. Which constitutes the cultivation of character to the highest endeavor to obtain "everlasting life" (immortality), and thereafter ascend to heaven after death on earth, which references Christian tenet; However, Taoist tenets retain "everlasting life" while living on earth", and upon their final physical transition of matter or death, one merely returns to Universal matter. Taoist believers remain "the same constant matter", and remain as "Cosmic or Unlimited Universal" matter, which saturates within the "way or path" of Tao through "everlasting life". The Christians sacrament or rite of passage for an everlasting life is sanctioned after death. Tao, "the way or path" is a "nameless universal cosmic matter", which is infinite within the cycles of Universal infinity, thusly transitions between life, death, birth, etc... remaining "The Ten Thousand Things", or everlasting and unchanging, and does not promote the Christian's transcendental faith process structure in the deliverance of an immortal soul through scripture, ritual, or prayer in the hereafter.

Christianity	Taoism
Biblical deliverance and healing	Tao De Jing deliverance and healing
Biblical deliverance= Truth	Sacred Scripture Guide =Truth
Scripture Guidance	The Nature of Taoism
Connecting with "Jesus Christ	Tao = immortal souls = In Life
Overcoming "mortal existence"	Death + EVERLASTING LIFE
Death = Immortality	Continue as Universal Matter
EVERLASTING LIFE	TAO'S "Way = Path = Infinity
Ascend to Heaven	Universal Cosmic Matter

Christian deliverance epitomize historical biblical events of "Jesus Christ" rescuing both his follower's and disbeliever's of his faith from bondage, oppression, hardships and evil etc... Christianity, through the Holy Bible depict "Jesus Christ's" social degradation and ultimate crucifixion, that canonized biblical scriptures definitive principles of "repentance and redemption"; through spiritually healing the mortal wounds of mankind; which faithfully and spiritually elevates the true nature, practice, and teachings of the sacred Biblical objective and subjective (faith) canon through the "Holy Bible".

Conversely, the Taoist "rituals" and "libations" of deliverance and earthly healing is through immortal sanctity and salvation, that explores the Taoist's "islands of the immortal" alchemy, through ceremony and ritualistic herbs and chemical compound intake that ensures their earthly immortality. Traditionally, Taoist exude great interest in personal health and vitality rituals conducted through herbal and pharmacology medicines. Additionally, Taoist ritualistically explore, develop, and exploit principles of ancient Chinese traditional cooking, along with other ambrosial diets structured through Taoist tenets, guidelines, and principles. Fundamentally, novel Taoist research and developmental principles of biotic (organic) cooking is a vital solution to a healthy diet; which enhances the natural order of the "Ten Thousand Things" or Universally infinite materialistic essence of "all matter" sustained in the creation of the macrocosm = "Tao".

Taoist belief's is that the "spirits" pervaded nature, which includes both the "natural world" (universe), and the internal elements composing the human body; Therefore, enable these myriad or endless spirits manifestations of the" Tao, The Way, or Path", which constitutes the "Ten Thousand Things" Universal Materialism), or "God", who cannot be represented by an image or name; However, contrastingly to "Christian" doctrine, "Jesus Christ the son of "God" is visualized and supported by name and by viewing photo imagery.

Transcendentally, the Tao represents the "spiritual way" and "universal cosmos", which equates to infinite "nothingness", that's regarded through "Taoist" tenets as the "Purest Form" of existence within the infinite boundaries of Universal continuation, which never ends... Christian tenets is "faith" bound or pledged in the belief's that "walking by faith and not by sight" strengthens the mortal being to become that everlasting immortal after death, in order to manifest divination, and forecast the provisions in the hereafter of "an everlasting life", and ascend to "Heavens"; contradictory, to the "Tao's" infinite eternal pathway or ascent back to the infinite Universal matter (Heaven). Principally, ritualistically, and theoretically Christianity supports and promotes "Supernatural" images of "God's" life like presence to its follower's. Thusly, uniting the mortal healing stages within the universe through a "transcendental faith belief" akin to the "Taoist" transcendental infinite concept of immortality; in acquiring an infinite "everlasting life" from converted mortal's to becoming immortal's; and thereafter, within the concept of the "Tao's" tenets of "nothingness and endlessness" by comprising immortality that composes nothingness, through universal continued or revolving infinity of "all matter" past, present, and future. The "Tao's" conceptualized phenomenality consistently promotes the immortal healing stages through refined Taoist rituals, and by way of the essential (natural) energies of life; which is the mandate that enables "all matter" inclusive of all thing's and being's, to be themselves in harmony with the "Tao". The physical body in "Taoist" tenets "is the universe", that remained within the supernatural transcendental essence in "solidifying a submissive immortal presence"; which is ritualistically and scripturally embodied from both the "Tao De Jing and Yin and Yang", which is enabled from the "ch'i" or cosmic flow of energy linking Taoist's to the Universe.

The role of the Christian clergy is to baptize, and purify the soul's through holy communion, and prophesize to his Christian follower's the tenets of the teachings of "Jesus Christ", through the Holy Bible. Most importantly, he must interpret the Christian principles and guidelines of Christianity in both principle and ritual. Also, Christian's take sacred vows and commit themselves to a communal life through honor and holy sacrament, therefore, qualifying for the commission of becoming "Christian missionaries". The tenets or principles, rituals, and Holy Scriptures (from the Bible) are analogously equipped for Christian's to piously embrace the decree and institutional religious directives from the historical journey through "Jesus Christ's" sufferings and dogmatic Christian faith belief. However, his "crucifixion on the cross" established faith binding and unequivocal strength to his Christian disciples, follower's, and convert's as a viable testimony for the "faithful" to witness and embrace the "Holy Christian" devotion to "Christ" their savior.

Only consolidated relationships bound faithfully with "Christ's" tenets that authenticate Christian deliverance, correlated with earnest ethical responsibilities which consolidates the status of a faithful Christian "soldier".

The Taoist Priest view numerous "god's" as the ritualistic manifestations of the "Way", "Path", or "Principles" that validates the supernatural universe. These select Priest's have been ritualistically trained to understand the inner relationships of Tao, through ancient identity (name), rank (status to universal immortality), and the correlating factors relative to the powers of various spirits associated with Taoism. Therefore, they ritually connect and direct these viable rituals through meditations and visualizations. "Daoshi" refers to a Taoist Priest's", and these recluse Priest's in earlier times practiced alchemy and austerity in the mountains, with the objectives of becoming "xiam", or immortal beings. The activities and principled guidelines for these Priest's were written in the ancient "Daozang", which is the Taoist canon. Nevertheless, each individual "Daoshi" either inherited or was permitted to select a specific text; which was passed down generations after generations from Priest to Student in unpublished doctrines. These "Daoshi" practices would include various ritualistic ceremonies. Importantly, the two dominant "Priesthoods" are the "Quanzhen" and the "Zhengyi Dao". The former is located in the Northern half of the "People's Republic of China"; who closely resemble "Buddhist Monk's" in their moral character as follows: celibate, reside in temples, and are vegetarian's.

The most renowned temple is the "White Cloud" temple in Beijing, China. However, the latter "Priesthood" (Zhengyi Dao) respectfully can marry, non-vegetarian, and reside in their homes. Noteworthy, they are considered part-time Priest's, and many hold outside occupations. They are noted to reside all over China, although they have varying lineage identities; Example, in the North of China the "yin yang masters of the Lingboa sub-tradition is present and so on...

The Daoshi (Priest's) exercise extensively in their teaching doctrines the principles of one of their most precious ancient traditional beliefs, which is "The Three Treasures"= Jing, Qi, and Shen. These are "universal energies" Daoshi cultivate within themselves to qualify immorality, which they also rigorously teach to students of Taoism; however, these principles are testaments within the concept of "qigong and inner alchemy". Notably, "Jing, Qi, and Shen" does not have a translated "English" equivalence, however, they can be translated to "essence, vitality, and spirit". "The Three Treasures" are often referred to as "Three Frequencies" or existing along a perpetuity of recurrencies.

The Daoshi master's transforms "Jing into Qi into Shen", also referred to as the "path of metamorphosis", and transforms "Shen into Qi into Jing", which is ascribed as the "path of generations or manifestations". When "Daoshi's" acclimate "Inner Alchemy", it's speculated that they harmonize their consciousness along a pulsating progression and select their frequency within their conscious level. "Jing" is linked to our physical body, that radiates a concentrated vibrating energy. It's also associated to the "dantian" or "kidney organ system", the reproductive energy of the sperm and ovum, and the root of human vitality. Notably, "Jing" is lost from the human body through stress and worry; however, restored through dietary and herbal additives and "gigong" exercise practices. "Qi" is our life force energy, and it produces a varieties of movements such as: movement of breath in and out of our lungs, movement of blood through our blood vessels, and the functioning of numerous organ systems. Its resides in the "middle dantian", and affiliates the "liver and spleen" organ system. "Qi" can be associated with the flame, engine, and the "main device or essence of the "Qi" that enables the objects to produce its goals or outcome. The "Shen" is our "Mind and Spirit", which resides in the "upper dantian", associated with the "Heart Organ System". It projects or discharges "Universal Kindness, passion, forgiveness, generosity, radiance, luminosity, glow, and shine of enlightening power of a heart brimming with the wisdoms of the world. A Healthy "Shen" is totally dependent upon the cultivation of the "Jing and Qi"; and it is only through the aestheticism and sanctuary of a healthy and powerfully balanced body that a beaming and lustrous "Spirit" can glow.

The ancient Chinese term "neidan" is esthetically attached to "inner alchemy", which attaches its metaphysical concept to "qigong". Its significance relates to the "art and science" of storage, accumulation or assemblage, that enables the constant flow of energies through and within the human anatomy; which constitutes the "Taoist" ritualistic art form. Thusly, this aforementioned interchange of inner alchemy cultivates the "Three Treasures" jing, qi, and shen; which balances the Taoist's physical, mental, and demonstrative feelings, or emotional stability to unite with the "Tao's" Universal immortal acceptance.

The word "dantain" is reflective and emulative to the "chakra's" of the Hindu Yogic System, which identifies the region or locale of the delicate parts of the human body to collect and assemblage the metamorphosis of "qi and prana" in the Taoist interpretation of inner alchemy. Consequently, the "lower dantian", in the "inner alchemy", as instructed by the Daoshi masters is the primary home of the "Immortal Fetus".

The embodiment of the Tao is to accomplish ritualistic secondary immortality, that's sanctioned through inner alchemy, which is dependent on the ritualistic manifestations of the "Eight Extraordinary Meridians" resulting in a healthy Taoist.

The sacred scriptures "Tao De Jing" enforces the principled guidelines (tenets), and is the sacred directive towards the spiritual embodiment of nature and its relationships between humanity and the infinite Universe; through the Taoist concept of "Wu Wei" (action through inaction), which produces the ultimate "harmony" with the Universe or "Tao". The reinforced Taoist "faith" process is prevalent in the sacred verses that heals earthly wounds through the immortal universal harmony and "ancestor spirits"; which protects the "way, path, and principles of the "infinite" immortal soul embedded in the "Tao".

Contradictory to the "Daoshi or Taoist Priest's", the "Christian Clergy" does not worship idle "God's"! They perform ritual's of confession, baptism, communion, matrimony, burials, unction of the sick, worship through the Holy Bible, celebration, ceremony, confirmation, exorcism, blessings of the Holy Water, and numerous sacraments through established consecrations. Thusly, validating "Christ's" empowerment and canonization through "faithful" belief that his presence on earth is omnipresent in all Christian endeavors. Therefore, the "Christian Clergy's" instructs his follower's, through the "Holy Bible scriptures" to strive towards an "immortal life", to receive the blessing to ascend to "Heaven", from being awarded an "Everlasting Life" upon their death on earth.

The Daoshi masters worship numerous God's, which are "idle" or "worthless" to the Christian faith belief; However, significant and necessary for Taoist Priest's and their follow's, within their tenets and principles of their religious faith. Furthermore, "ancestor worship" is a treasured example of the transcending concept embodied in "Taoism" that completes the transition of Universal matter continually present or infinite, from the past, present, and future, which derives from the "Immortal Fetus", through the Taoist ritualistic practice of "inner alchemy'. Similarly, "Christian's" also worship their "ancestor's; however as a sacred lineage that enabled their mortal being to survive the "trials and tribulations" mankind bequest historically to them through an enabling inheritance of social, civil, and inherited "rite de passage". Additionally, Christians also have a "spiritual ancestor worship", through their "sacramental celebration oath divinity", that's incorporated in the remembrance and celebration of ancestral birthdays, deeds, and rituals through parades and elaborate or decorated ceremonies conducted by communities, townships, counties, states, and country leader's that compliment and embellish the "Christian Faith". In the Eastern concept of Taoism there is know dichotomy in names, ranks, or procession order status, merely a calculated exactness of the ritualistic practices within the pantheon of Taoism. Aforementioned previously, Tao does not have a "God" similar to the "Abrahamic" faith. The Taoist "God" is without name or personal identity, because its' supernatural divinity is bound to Universal infinity or unmeasured "nothingness", which envelopes "all matter". The Universe originates from the "way or path" with its conceptual boundaries of "Wei Wu", which is the

Taoist ideal to fulfill that which is naturally structured through the principles of the "Tao De Jing". However, this doesn't prevent a person from living a zealous life, but their life must fit into the natural patterns of the Universe, which conveys detachment and disinterest in ego-driven emotional behavior. Example, "perfect activity leaves no tracks behind it, perfect speech is reflective of a apathetic worker whose tools leave no mark". Secondly, "wu wei" identifies Taoist character "living by or going along with the ideal nature of the universe, by not obstructing the "Tao" by letting things take their natural course of action in this world. The "Tao" is lacking human traits, while anonymously within the "path and way" of the "Ten Thousand Things", that's Universal "matter" encompassing "all things" in the cosmos; and journeying along their natural paths in harmony with "nothingness" towards absolute purity". Yet, the ritualistically ridden "Tao" is and was at rest in open mystery, and far beyond spoken wretchedness, while mingling in secretive infinity. Strangely enough to the non Taoist, to here Taoist prayers, and meditation in words, one would refer to this type of communication as "God-talk", seeking spiritual acknowledgement, and fulfillment through symbolic and sacred ancient Chinese artifacts, that guides and generates their present and future immortality that's already embedded in their "Taoist" body system.

Lastly, both religions chore is to direct their origin and nucleus to their respective tenets, origins, rules, and canons, which teach these ethical moralistic aphorisms to their dedicated follower's. Contrastingly, Christianities beliefs/tenets resides in one God and Savior; Taoism's tenets reside in the Universal and natural cosmos energies and forces of life that finds the "way or path" which enables "matter and things" to be in accord with the "Tao" in complete harmony.

Tao is both the "source and living force" or the driving vehicle all- encompassing and exclusive that umbrella's the infinite universe, which defines the "Tao". Additionally, unlike Christianity, Taoism is both a philosophy and a religion;Thusly, the Tao religion (sacred scriptures) followed in time its originating and authored philosophy, "which is to conduct ones' person simple and natural to derive and evolve a virtuous humanity". Nevertheless, both religions are embodied, formed, created and molded by different cultural and historical environments. Similarly, Christian and Ancient Chinese Taoism was structured to inject social, ethic, and moralistic standards to control and structure civilizations newly formed social guidelines, or to correct straying adrift leaders ignoring civilized social equality, humanity, legitimacy, modernity, and/or governmental duty to protect and serve the citizenry equitably.

Bibliography

Kohn, Livia and Michael LaFargue. *Lao Tzu and the Tao De Jing.* New York: Sny Brook Press, 1998.

Martin, William. *A Path and A Practice: Using Lao Tzu's Tao De Jing as a guide to an Awakened Spiritual Life. Marlowe & Company, 2005. ISBN 1-56924-390-5*

Moore, Charles A. *The Chinese Mind: Essentials of Chinese Philosophy and Culture.* Hawaii University Press, 1967.

Carr, David T. and Canhul Zhang. *Space Time and Culture.* Springer, 2004, ISBN 1-4020-2823-7.

Hansen, Chad. *"Taoism"*. Stanford Encyclopedia of Philosophy (Metaphysic Research Lab). Calif.: Stanford University Press, 2008.

Kim, Ha Poong. *Reading Lao Tzu. Companion to the Tao De Jing with a New Translation. New Jersey: Xlibris Corporation, 2003. ISBN 1-4010-8316-1.*

Markham, Ian S. and Tina Ruparell. *Encountered Religion: An Introduction to the Religions of the World. Blackwell Publishing, 2001.*

CHAPTER VIII

A Brief Synopsis of The Mongolian Empire's Inventive Contributions to Ancient China and World Civilizations

(By William F. Williams)
(Synopsis of Genghis and Kublai Khan)

The Mongolian era in China is remembered from the Mongol's invasion of China, lead by Kublai Khan in approximately 1271. He was the son of Genghis Khan known as the World's most peerless conquistador. Genghis was fathered by a secondary (minor) Mongolian Chief in the eastern part of Mongolia in the year (approximately) 1167. His birthright (inherited) name is alleged to be "Temujin"; however his loyal army (followers) named him "Genghis Khan" translated in Mongolian it means "Universal Ruler". Although he was illiterate, he mastered the art of unifying all the nomadic Mongolian tribes in a military state with extraordinary discipline and loyalty in his command. It's alleged that he was responsible for the butchery of "millions of people" he besieged in the Mongol's conquering blood invasions. It's alleged historically that his military skills as a ruler hailed or derived from his superhuman ability to mobilize, strategize, and organize the Mongolian army into a superior (historically world renowned) killing machine.

Kublai Khan and his massively organized and structured army invaded and conquered China in the year (approx.) 1271, and after the invasion of China moved the capital to the city now known as Beijing. Even though the Chinese language was foreign to his culture, it is not known historically if he spoke Chinese; however, upon his conquest of China he acquired the name "Yuan" for his dynasty, which ruled all of China. Consequently, the "Yuan" dynasty went down in history as the only "foreign" empire to rule China. Additionally, at the pinnacle of the Mongolian empire's many conquests, it's alleged to have spanned from Hungary to Korea, and as far south as Vietnam. Therefore, it was historically recorded as the largest and greatest empire in the history of mankind to date. However, coupled with their unparalleled military ferocity they developed and promoted trade throughout the empire, which included Europe. Furthermore, the Mongolian empire constructed a road system linking China to Russia facilitating enormous trade within that geographical annexation.

Upon the death of "The Great Kublai Khan" in approximately 1294, the Mongolian might, power, and authority lessened in China. However, while conqueror's of China they were accorded the social, and bureaucratic status of the elite during their China rule. Naturally, over a period of time the Chinese citizenry resented their privileged status, especially the tax exempt status that the Chinese citizen's had to adhere to. Following Kublai Khan's death numerous "natural disasters" fell upon the Mongolian authorities governance that they were unable to manage; such as "peasant rebellions", and the rise of Buddhism. Thereafter, a strong-willed and tenacious young peasant organizer and leader by the name "Hung Wu" and his wife, and industrious inventor comrade created firing armament, rifles that shot bullets or lead balls ignited by the very Mongolian ruled Chinese invention that enabled the Western World to emerge as World conqueror's, with the advent of "gunpowder". Hung Wu and his peasant Buddhist army defeated the Mongols; thereafter, expelling thousands from China, which ended more than one hundred years of Mongolian rule in China and established the newly formed "Ming dynasty".

The Mongolian Empires Inventive Contributions to China and The World
(Critique by William F. Williams)

Aforementioned in the synopsis, the Mongolian era in China is remembered primarily from the Kublai Khan invasion and ultimate rule. Many historians refer to the Yuan dynasty as China's golden age. It's estimated that the Yuan dynasty existed from 1271-1365. The Mongol's initially opened and expanded over land trade routes linking China to Central Asia as far south as Vietnam, westerly as Europe, north easterly as Russia, and the Mediterranean et al... After further expansion by the Mongol's, it's historically documented that they expedited trade and travel through a full-fledged systematic road construction, that enveloped one-sixth of the "Old World's" land mass. One of the primary historical trade routes in history is the renowned "Silk Road" established by the Mongol Empire. This was the famous caravan route linking China to the West (Europe). Three essentially established cities were: Bokar, Merv, and Samarkand, in naming these few, along the caravan trade route that provided necessary provisions for trade, travel, and extensive or large-scale accomodation's for wary, frugal, and prudent tradesmen. The "Silk Road" enterprise insured the Mongolian Empire tremendous economic success and impending and forthright control over its many participating vassal's (conquered inhabitant's). The Mongol's ferocious aggression in its military invasions and offensive crusades insured their success in establishing the "trade routes", because their conquered vassals welcomed this life saving alternative of economic enterprise over instant death, which would have been their fate administered by the Mongol's if they opposed this opportunity to become established tradesman for the Mongolian Empire's economic prosperity.

Importantly, it's alleged historically that the "Venetian Marco Polo" linked the East and Western World's through his stunning journey and written account of the Mongolian Empires rule in China during his expeditious trek there; from approximately 1275-1291. He provided creditable accounts of the Mongolian's governance in China, persona, and leadership within the administrative and cultural entities he witnessed there. He especially rendered to the Western World detailed accounts of the "Great Khan's" leadership and personal extravagance, while working in "Kublai Khan's" administrative court as a linguist. Marco Polo was distinguished in the "Khan's" court as being an extraordinary linguist who spoke four languages, and immediately became a welcomed necessity and favorite ally or colleague to "Kublai Khan", and his administration. He was later appointed by the ruler to a high court post in the administration and sent on special commissions within the vast range of China, Burma, and India.

Unfortunately, comparing many historical events contradicted by unauthenticated sourced data, Marco Polo's accountability and credibility of his "Far Eastern" experience in China during the "Yuan" dynasty under the rule of Kublai Khan is questionable by a prison inmate in a Genoese Jail during "Marco's" alleged incarceration there, by a fellow inmate named "Rusticello". Rusticello is alleged to have been a writer from the City of "Pisa" and disclosed his journey to China to

"Marco Polo" while both men were interned. Thereafter, when "Marco Polo" was released from internment he published the book with two titles, "The Description of the World" or "The Travels of Marco Polo"; which elaborated his personal account of the treasured wealth of China, the might of the "Mongol" Empire, and the exotic, bizarre, and colorful customs and cultures of India and Africa during his travels in the East, which illuminated imaginations. His published book with two titles became one of the most popular editions in "Medieval Europe", during "Marco's era in Europe, that gravitated tremendous merit, attraction, and distinction; until the word was out publically, academically, and socially (colloquially) that this published book by Marco Polo was fabrication, fiction, and contrived concoction. Eventually thereafter, his book was known as "II Million" translated meaning "The Million Lies"; Consequently, Marco Polo was designated the nickname "Marco Million", meaning "Marco the Lie", throughout his native birthright and medieval Europe.

Whether "Marco Polo's" book was fact or fiction, he was either the most brilliant fictional publisher, or the most proliferate or abound historian of Far Eastern cultures (China's Mongolian Empire); that illuminated and illustrated factual depth and remoteness of one of the most militant, warmongering, aggressive, and productive Empires ever to assemble in the history of the Universe, lead by both father and son; "Genghis and Kublai Khan respectively".

History uncovers the journey of two alleged Jesuit priest's and "Westerner's, who journeyed to The Far East and enter the Mongolian Empire. They were "Giovanni di Piano Carpini, in 1245, and Guillaume de Rubrouck, in 1253. They are believed to have arrived in the Karakorum, Pakistan area; coincidentally, during this era of "Genghis Khan" in 1220 who established this City (Karakorum) as the "capital of the Mongolian Empire". Furthermore, in its best years it was a multicultural and cosmopolitan City, filled with traders from all over the World. However, after the two priest's stay in Karakorum, they safely returned to their Western monasteries to reveal their journeys to their peer's, in witnessing of the "great Mongolian Empire's cultural and military might", according to secondary source historiography.

Importantly, "Marco Polo's journey to China and his experience working in the "Mongolian Empires" administration is recorded data (researched as factual by Hans Ulrich Vogel); and reliable enough as written, to confirm that he traversed from his home in Europe to China, and returned to his European residence. We must take into account China's printing advancements, as it relates to chronological historical events and historical documentation, that did not clarified and substantiated Marco Polo's visit to China.

Notably, prior to the Mongolian invasion in China, their World enterprise fostered a completely new innovative commercial World; which was the advent of paper money, jade, bronze, ceramics, compass, printing (Mongol's added new innovations to printing, and other inventions in China prior to their rule), silk, domestication of animals, porcelain, magnet, building roads and trade routes (Mongol's), literature (Mongols created advanced literary additions), navigation (Mongol's further advanced China's inventive navigation skills), turtle boat (Mongols), yurt housing construction and architecture (Mongol's), gunpowder bombs (Mongol's), landmines (Mongol's), shopping malls (mongol's), canon's (Mongol's), mail system (Mongol's), fire arrows (Mongol's), trade routes for commerce (Mongol's), rack and pinion steering (Mongol's & Chinese), the phags-pa script

(Mongol's, unified the system of writing in both Chinese and Mongolian languages), dominoes and dice (Mongol's), horse saddle, Mongolian alphabet, calendar, postal service networking, newly innovative system of warfare (Mongol's), trade routes uniting Asia, Middle East, Europe, and Russia, curved shooting bow, soap, glass, ink, irrigation canals, map making, oars, kite, crossbow, mirror, ice cream, the wheel barrel, canal locks, windmill, magnetic compass, and many more inventions such as farming and medical tools etc... The Song dynasty and Yung dynasty merged; however, were separated after Mongolian rule, and the new Yung dynasty emerged. Chinese prosperity created new demands for a literature that did not confine itself to the classical models alone, but also produced a colloquial literary style, which was far less demanding than the elaborately structured classical Chinese literature; because it was only understood by the minority elite class structure; who were the minority within the populous count. Nonetheless, China's literary life gradually secured a marginal literary alternative to its official culture; due to Chinese society becoming literate within its official administrative culture; Therefore, enabling Chinese society and foreigner's to acquire access to authenticated historically informed eventful sourced accountability; Thusly, reassuring historians up to date recorded historical events, such as "Marco Polo's" and other's visits to China. Unfortunately, "Marco Polo's validity in evidence of his travel's to China and experiencing a Mongolian Empire presence is not found in historical archive print, or in manuscript referencing his journeying to China during the Mongolian Empire's rule. Nonetheless, this doesn't completely nullify his storytelling events of his journey to China; because the newly acquired (dynasty) administrative take-over after exiling and defeating the Mongol's, may have destroyed all factual evidence of historical records pertaining to the Mongolian Empire within the context of what's substantially valuable to them.

The Mongolian Empire's most awe-inspiring contribution to the World at large, is their inventions and trades in firearms and firepower. The "Western World's" would not have emerged as "World Power's", without Chinese and Mongolian military inventions, which also includes the "seafaring navigation equipment" such as the magnetic compass, boat oars, horse saddle, trade routes, gunpowder, dominoes and dice games, postal service network, expansive trade routes, landmines, gunpowder bombs, shopping malls, yurt homes and architecture, fire arrows, rack and pinion steering, Phags-pa script (unified the system of writing), large crossbow, large canon, and many other viable innovative tools and mechanisms that sprung world power dominating activity.

Lastly, the Mongol's invention of the "two stage rocket" launched an unbelievable seafaring trade in firearms to the "West and Middle East", which enabled their armies to emerge victorious against other adversaries. Eventually, the spread of trade rumors echoed in trade for "Mongolian large canon supplies, along with gunpowder", under the "Genghis Khan" era in the fourteenth century during China's "Yuan" dynasty. Following the trades for firecrackers, which enhanced the advent of rockets which also advanced global military weaponries progressive mechanization, especially in the "West" which elevated further the precision of military armament industrialization.

Reference:

Roberts, J. M. *A Short History of the World,* Oxford University Press

CHAPTER IX

The British Industrialization in Global Perspective

(The Industrial Revolution and
Modern Economic Growth)
(Analysis and Interpretation By: William F. Williams)

(America and England Eighteenth
and Nineteenth Century)
(1733-1870)
<u>The First and Second Industrial Revolutions:</u>

(Analysis and Interpretation By: William F. Williams)

<u>The First and Second Industrial Revolutions</u>

This essay critiques the economical, political, and social events that motivated both industrial revolutions in Europe and America (The New World). The industrial revolution's cultivated western world technology, social productivity, and commercialism et.al... The historical events that activated the first industrial revolution into the second industrial revolution is evaluated in this research thesis... (By William F. Williams)

The theme of this research thesis characterizes the motivation and innovative perpetuation of the necessary industrial development and motivation of the "first industrial revolution"; which established and enhanced the "second industrial revolution" in North America.

The following events were preeminent in the innovative industrial construction and development of both the "first and second industrial revolution's which were initiated between the" seventeenth and eighteenth centuries (17th & 18th) that generated the "enlightenment" or "age of reason" era, approximating to have come into being between the years sixteen-eighty five to eighteen-fifteen (1685-1815). The enlightenment era's consist of variable ideologies within cultures and time frames. Thusly conceptualized within the aforementioned year's of its'culturation, development, and progress. In Europe, there existed individual "Enlightenment" thinkers, which included the English, French, German, Swiss, Italian, Scottish, Spanish and other visionaries et, al... There was no specific consolidated "Age of Reason". Consequently, respective or sole thinker's to this movement had contrasting pursuits in defining the philosophy, intellectual and cultural movement within this creative social application. It accentuated the science of rational and reason to syllogistic empirical observations. By incorporating a "worldview" that examined the truth concerning "human society", self, and the Universe. Therefore, it grasped that there could be a science of mankind, which was progressive in nature, which could be endless and uninterruptedly accompanied with the correct contemplating intellectual and objective reflections. The "Age of Reason" contemplated that the Universe intellectualized by philosopher's (thinker's) could be a mechanism or functioning machine, which could also be modified and transformed. The enlightenment produced an abundant and diverse number of books, scientific discoveries, inventions, laws, essays, and its share of revolutions. Notably, the American and French revolution's were precisely galvanized by the enlightenment creative intellectualism, goals, ethics, and values; therefore, designating the pinnacle of its authority, prestige, and the beginning of its' recession, by bending to nineteenth century "Romanticism".

Between the years sixteen-eighty five and seventeen-thirty (1685-1730) "Bacon and Hobbes (England)", "Descartes (France), and the primary instinctive and essential philosopher's of the "scientific revolution", included "Galileo, Kepler, and Leibniz". However, if we backtrack to sixteen-eighty (England) "Sir Isaac Newton" published his "Principia Mathematica" in sixteen-eighty six (1686); and "John Locke" published his "Essay concerning Human Understanding" sixteen-eighty nine (1689). Importantly, these two masterpieces (books) administered and arranged the mathematical and philosophical mechanism for the Enlightenment's extensive prelation. Newton's systematic method of treating problems by a special system of algebraic notations, as differential or integral calculus; coupled with his optical theories that implemented and supported the dynamic and vigorous Enlightenment concept, essentially implied comparisons for accurately consistent, systematic, and deliberate measured change and illumination. Respectively, "Locke's" theoretical approach to "Human Nature" reflected the capabilities of change in form and nature, whether frequently or constant; and that "learning was achieved or acquired through an increased attainment of empiricism"; as opposed to procuring external hearsay or unsubstantiated truths.

Between the years 1730-1780, radical intellectual stimulus focalized on the intense discourse and printing of written publications of the "Age of Reason", during the initial "Enlightenments" time period in history. The primary actor's and delegation's was initiated by French theory, doctrine, ideology, and reason; inaugurated by "Voltaire, Rousseau,

Montesquieu, Buffon, and Diderot", with the likes of other lesser theorist and logicians. However, this "Enlightenment" period can best be epitomized by "Voltaire's "Philosophical Dictionary": "a chaos of clear ideas"; which stimulated the concept, perception, and thought "that all in the Universe could be appropriately or judiciously unmasked, revealed, and documented". Notably, the hallmark and acclaimed proclamation during this era was "Diderot's "Encyclopedie" (1751-1777), congregated prominent thinker's and writers to construct avid and resourceful assemblage of anthropological understanding and knowledge

It was the "Age of Enlightenment" for "Absolute Rulers", prospective revolutionaries; namely, "Frederick the Great" who modernized, unified, and rationalized Prussia; and influenced "Thomas Paine and Thomas Jefferson's", "Declaration of Independence" (1776) respectively; which blue printed the "American Revolution" in qualifying its' mandate and ordinance from "Locke's" inventive and inspirational "essay". It also galvanized religious innovation and changes in altering believer's religious faith within logical and rational concepts of "God and the creation of the Universe". The "Freemasons, Rosicrucians, Bavarian Illuminati, et. Al... developed and multiplied in Europe.

Consequently, establishing fresh state-of-the-art approaches to religious alliances. Establishing pliant venues to circulate innovative ideas to communicate, publicize, exchange, disseminate, divulge, and pass on valued information during this Enlightenment era. Its goal was to establish "open and rational" mental dexterity in the pursuit of freedom, liberation, and self sustaining ascendancy to full social, political, and economic equality. Therefore, "The Age of Reason" and "Enlightenment" influenced the overthrow, revisions, and sovereignty of governments, such as the "American and French" revolution's, "Haitian's War of Independence, and South America's "Paraguay's self determination against radical racial Inclusivism". Consequently, all emerged out of the "Common Enlightenment" themes of rational questioning and opinions making headway or advancements through positive discourse and social exchange of rational ideology.

Aforementioned, the incredible "European philosophical movement" was profoundly characterized by the reliance on astute calculating and insightful "reason"; which enthralled empirical, practical, experimental, observational and factual discourse amongst these selective thinker's and philosopher's in the "Enlightenment era". Astonishingly, great interest emphasized humanitarian social, political, economical, and educational objective goals that catalyzed, organized, and activated the "first industrial revolution" inaugurated and launched in "Europe". The question asking the great German Philosopher "Immanuel Kant" during this "this Age of Reason" era was as followers: What is the Enlightenment? and was answered by him thusly: Sapere Aude! [Dare to Know]" Have courage to use your own Understanding". Additionally, he states that the "Enlightenment is man's emergence from his self imposed immaturity. Immaturity is the inability to use one's understanding without guidance from another. This immaturity is self imposed when its' cause lies not in lack of understanding, but in lack of resolve and courage to use it without guidance from another". "Laziness and cowardice are the reasons why so great a proportion of men, long after nature has released them from alien guidance (natura-liter maiorennes), nonetheless gladly remain in lifelong immaturity, and why it is so easy for others to establish themselves as their guardians" etc... Consequently, these innovative philosopher's and thinker's who advocated the "Enlightenment or Age of Reason", were convinced that they were emerging from centuries of "Ages of Darkness and Ignorance", into a newly innovative and creative "Age of Reason".

Initially, such thinker's were referred too and labeled "Philosopher's" in France. Notably, elite and well-bred Women in France who perceived this great "Enlightenment" challenge would organize discourse sessions for these "Philosopher's"; which cultivated and fostered the first beginning of the "Scientific Revolution". Coexistently, in England organized discussion groups were empowered by "English" academia in the likes of "John Locke's" essay "Concerning Humanitarian Understanding". He states that the "individual is a blank slate at birth, thusly a quality education would redirect the individual mind to think freely and progressively independently of "old traditional dogma". "Voltaire and Rousseau" were at the forefront of the "Enlightenment" era in France. Additionally, back in England "Adam Smith's" proposal emphasized a newly innovative "economical reform for "Great Britain". Representing French thinker's, "Voltaire's (1694-1778) dilemma centered on his hatred, disdain, and derision of the "Jesuit Catholic Church, where he received his primary education"; which motivated and fostered his "Enlightenment" beliefs stating through his "deist" attitude, or state of mind that "God creates everything, and then steps back to see how it evolves on its own". Also, his famous quote regarding the Catholic Church is "crush the horrible thing" [Ecrasez I infime]. However, his most famous work is "Candide" (1756), which summarized a quote of his that "one must cultivate his own garden". Nonetheless, "Voltaire's legacy emphasized to the individual to "struggle for or towards religious tolerance". "Voltaire's countryman, "Charles Louis de Secondant's", and Baron de Montesquieu (1689-1755), authored the "Spirit of the Laws", which was a valued concept in the "Enlightenment" era. "Baron de Montesquieu", was a distinguished member of the French aristocracy; Yet, he was intellectually inspired by the "political system" of Great Britain. Notably, the connection, association and network in Frances Enlightenment era was extremely extrusive, and rendered a palpable presence in fueling "Britain's" Enlightenment ideology, principles and knowledge (philosophy), towards innovative scientific expediency and recourse. In "Charles Louis de Secondant's" published document (book) "Spirit of the Laws", he advocated a "separation of powers" between the branches of government, which creditably inspired the "system of checks and balances", that represents two key elements in the "Constitution of the United States". These two noticeable elements are as follows: "Politics requires a Document or Instrument and Statute outlining the Basic Laws or Principles by which a Country or Organization is Governed". "Secondant's" countryman "Denis Didot" (1713-1784) is acclaimed the most prolific and demiurgic achiever in the Enlightenment era for his publishing masterpiece "The Encyclopedia" (1751). Notably, "Baron de Montesquieu" influenced the likes of "Rousseau and Voltaire", who contributed greatly with articles written in "Didot's" book "The Encyclopedia". This ingenious publication enlightened and enhanced the progression and success during the "Enlightenment period or The Age of Reason", throughout the "European Global Communities", and "The New World's" (Atlantis). This book "The Encyclopedia" was disseminated, propagated, and diffused amongst the "Thinking Intellects" in "Russia, Scandinavia, Germany, Belgium, Scotland, Ireland, and throughout Europe and The America's. Thomas Jefferson and Benjamin Franklin were ardent and passionate students of this ingenious published "masterpiece", which liberated their mental reflections towards a viable and stable United States governance. Importantly, the profoundly ingenious "intellectual and brilliant mental acuity" of German Philosopher "Immanuel Kant's", "Critique of Pure Reason" was extremely instrumental in shaping, structuring, and institutionalizing the "Enlightenment" philosophy and scientific movement; which was one of the front- runner's and "pacesetters" in connecting the framework of "The Enlightenment" into an iron-clad coalition across oceans and continents. Consequently, a newly innovative rational and ideologically movement relished a Universal birth, the "Age of Reason".

The "despot's" that were enlightened by the "Enlightenment", which inspired their perspective ideology towards a stronger and pliable governance over their subject's in their respective countries; however, adamantly envisioned that this "Enlightenment" intellect would augment their futuristic influence, longevity, and jurisdiction of their kingdom's.

The timespan of the Enlightenment is often thought to envelope much of the seventeenth (17th) century; and the previous year's or era's labeled the "Age of Reason". Nonetheless, its approximated historically that these two eras of the "Enlightenment" and "Age of Reason" are divided or breached; Yet, it's historically acceptable to "hold the opinion" that these two historical philosophies conjoined together as "one lengthy period in time". The "Enlightenment" followed the philosophical ideology of notable scientist's, thinker's, and philosopher's such as "Pascal, Keppler, Leibnitz, Galileo, Copernicus and others not mentioned", who paid humiliating dues for their creative and inventive discoveries opposed to traditional conceptual dogma and theism. Most importantly, scientist and mathematician "Sir Isaac Newton" brilliantly blazed a newly innovative "aftershock" in his extraordinarily ingenious "natural scientific transformational discoveries" in fusing axiomatic proof through empirical observation into a consistent, comprehensible logical system that validated authentic predictions enabling him to publish his "Philosophiae Naturalis Principia Mathematica", "Laws of Gravity", "Co-Founder of Calculus", and discovered the "Laws of Light and Color". Additionally, "Newton" arranged "Keppler's" "Reality of Planetary Motion and Optics, which he diagramed and explained the mechanism of optic lenses theory and performance. Historically, many scientific believer's approximate that the "Scientific Revolution" structured the necessary social, economic, and political endeavor that fostered the advent of "commercial enterprise". Lastly, the "Scientific Revolution" and "Industrial Revolution" coalesced to establish the most powerful industrialized "Nations in the History of the eighteenth, nineteenth, and twentieth centuries..."

The First and Second Industrial Revolutions
(Analysis and Interpretation By: William F. Williams)

The first Industrial Revolution (18th – 19th centuries) begun in England (Britain), which took place due to a predominantly agrarian rural society. Additionally, Britain's colonies in America were experiencing the effects of their "Mother-Countries" Industrialization; which is categorized or designated as the second industrial revolution. However, the industrial revolution which initiated in Britain expanded, developed and advanced throughout "Europe"; and was predominant in Belgium, France, and Germany. The asian nation of Japan was absorbed in this industrial revolution which initiated on the European continent.

Preceding the industrial revolution in Britain, mass-production (manufacturing) was accomplished in rural community homes using basic hand tools and machinery. However, be mindful that earlier civilizations evolved due to the "agricultural revolution" in England that culminated in food "de trop" or excess in the 18th century. This emancipated countless inhabitancy from farming land owned largely by wealthy and aristocratic landowners. Notably, this property was leased to "tenant farmer's" who paid for their land lease's in "real goods", such as food, clothing, furniture and tools, that they produced on these farm's. However, during this transitional era leading to the "industrial revolution", the overabundance of "food surplus" enabled approximately half the population to leave the farm's and settle in the cities; where employment activity in this newly found "industrial economy" became obtainable.

An instrumental sum of determinants were the results of "Britain" establishing the role as the "birthplace" of the industrial revolution. Primarily, it had great wealth through deposits in coal and iron ore, which firmly established its capacity for industrialization. Additionally, "Great Britain" was the World's dominant colonel "might and enforcer"; which used its colonies as providers of "natural resources from raw materials"; that developed economical marketplaces for "manufactured goods". Thusly, as the insistence and appeal for British merchandise heightened, broker's, vendor's, dealer's and exporter's required profitable mechanisms for manufacturing. Leading to the acceleration and surge of industrialization and the factory-system. During the 18th century, numerous innovations actuated increasing productivity, which required less human energy to produce manufactured products. Example: John Kay(1733) invented the flying shuttle which increased the weaving process; James Hargreaves (1722-1778) invented the "spinning jennie/jenny", which capacitated individual's to manufacture or produce "numerous spools of threads concurrently. Between 1764-1776, there were approximately 18,000 to 22,000 "spinning jennies" which were utilized across Britain. Thereafter, British inventor "Samuel Compton" (1753-1827), invented the more powerful "spinning mule". Richard Arkwright and Edmund Cartwright, English inventor's (1743-1823), invented the "power loom", which was another pivotal machine that enhanced further industrialization in textiles, that mechanized the process of "weaving cloth" in approximately 1780's, taking fabric-weaving out of the homes and manufactured at sites where water-power was bountiful. Thereafter, a ceaseless, relentless, and boundless array of innovative developments occurred in fostering the first "industrial revolution" in Britain which can be chronicled as follows: "Abraham Darby" (1678-1717) innovated an economical process to manufacture "cast iron". Afterwards, Henry Bessemer (1813-1898) discovered an ingenious and low-cost method to mass-produce steel. Thusly, these innovator's were the primary developers in the "iron and steel industry", in the first "Industrial Revolution"; Consequently, they along with many other unnamed contributor's, were the vital patron's in the discovery of the varying processes, to develop ways to utilize "iron and steel" materials in Britain's industrial revolution. Importantly, these two ingredients produced and contributed to Britain's infrastructure, construction of buildings, ship industry, the manufacturing of tools and machines, and varying appliances, et al.

Furthermore, in approximately 1712 the "steam engine" was another indispensable innovative discovery by Englishman "Thomas Newcomen" (1664-1729). However, grape-vine "hearsayer's" disclosed that "Newcomen's" invention was relegated to pumping out water from mines. Nonetheless, this invention prompted Scottish innovator "James Watt" (1736-1819), to desperately improved the functionality of "Newcomen's" creation from "pumping water from mines", to powering average to massive equipment such as "machinery", locomotives, and ocean-faring ships respectively, during the first industrial revolution. However, let's not overlook "Eli Whitney's" (1793) ingenious invention of the "cotton gin" which generated enormous amounts of "cotton" to be processed in America or the Americas, and exported to "Europe"; which eliminated the "textile industry" from operating in homes and into the "textile mills" exclusively.

From the aforementioned discoveries, the "transportation and commerce" industries filtered from "Great Britain to its Colonies in America", which substantially revamped and transposed the first "industrial revolution". In the newly transformed and innovative transportation and commercial industries, it was know longer necessary to haul "raw materials" and finished manufacturing in horse drawn buggies, or by vessal's through waterways (rivers or canals). However, the primary reason that the transportation industry progressed and enabled commerce to advance during the first industrial revolution, is credited to American inventor "Robert Fulton" an engineer, inventor, and painter (1765-1815). However, he was an American British subject. Therefore, we're still within the era of the first industrial revolution. Yet, "Robert Fulton" is continually regarded as an American who invented the first rewarding and acknowledged "commercial steamship" in 1807. Consequently, in the aftermath of "Fulton's" successful invention of the "steamship" numerous steamships were transporting commercial and other types of freight crossed the "Atlantic Ocean" by the middle nineteenth century. Notably, the first "Steam-Powered Locomotive Engine for Rails" was invented by British engineer Richard Trevithick (1771-1833) in 1830. Importantly, George Stephenson & Son capitalized on Trevithick's invention and lead the way for a more progressively advanced "Steam-Powered Locomotive" in 1820. Thusly, enabling the British Empire and America to rapidly Industrialize, due to their enormous supply of coal; which powers the steam engine. However, it's historically recorded that "Trevithick's" creation of the "Steam-Powered Locomotive's" power to haul coal a long distance is based on his designs and implementation on its engine designed pressurized coal process; which to this day is the basis for all steam engines to run more efficiently and productively, which enabled rapid industrialized expansion throughout that era. What transpires during and after a century elapsed is a miracle of massive innovations, communication, travel, industrialization, and banking enterprises.

The Industrial Revolution at this point in time conjoin both the first and second "Industrialization", which consolidate and incorporate colossal innovative inventions on both continents of Europe and America, respectively. On both continents the Telegraph machine was invented by "Samuel Morse" 1837 (American), and "William Cooke" (1806-1879) and "Charles Wheatstone" (1802-1875) (British); However, the two aforementioned British inventor's are alleged to have obtained the "first" patent for the "commercial electrical Telegraph mechanism, and "Samuel Morse" patent was received in 1847. Historical credence authenticate that in 1840 railways incorporated the "Cooke-Wheatstone Telegraph" system. Furthermore, in 1866 a Telegraph cable was laid across the Atlantic Ocean, which further substantiates "the Telegraph time-table of "Cooke and Wheatstone" being the "first" before "Morse" to invent the Telegraph machine. Notwithstanding, the tremendous impact of the Industrial Revolution on both continents is by far the most progressively advanced innovations of renowned "World" achievements. The following is a limited American time-table of credible inventions, which excludes many other inventions, that changed the World from rural agrarian in-house manufacturing to urban "factory industrialization systems": The Telegraph -1847, Samuel Morse; The Telephone -1876 Thomas Graham Bell; The Light Bulb- 1879 Thomas Edison; The Internal Combustion Engine -1885 Gottlieb Daimler; The Radio- 1890's (approximately) Marconi Guglielmo; and The Airplane- 1903 Orville and Wilbur Wright. However, let's not forget the tremendous advancements in "medicine and science", Pasteurization, X-rays, and vaccinations were imminently within this time frame. Most Importantly, "Charles Darwin" the "Father of The Evolutionary Process Through Natural Selection" was the stepping stone for progressive scientific modernity. The "Whitney" system was developed through the newly innovative "Factory System", which were responsible for advancing "interchangeable parts" to expedite the necessity of broken down machine parts" uniformly if immediate replacements are needed. Let's not overlook, "Mr. Henry Ford's" ingenious assembly-line creation which allowed each individual worker to be responsible for "one" part of the finished product (automobile parts), where consistency, efficiency, and quality of the finished product constituted an assembly-line team as opposed to individuality.

The Industrial Revolution changed the "Families" social and economic status in two distinctively different era's. Initially "Women and Children" worked in factories for "low wages, long hours", and in dangerous factory conditions. In many circumstances worker's were required to live in boarding houses with total dependence on companies for personal items, and food. However, these new living arrangements opened up social independence away from their respective homes and fostered new "Laws", which insured their income management skills, and a more permissive leisure social atmosphere; which progressively enhanced a "new cosmopolitan and urban working class".

Thusly, prompting the entrance of an emerging "middle class", which afforded progressive changes to the family structure. Home and the work environment were separated by "time, place, and space. The middle class found leisure in travel, and vacations, which expanded their outlook of the World. Splurging, consumption, and extravagance was emerging in urban society, due to the advent of mass produced products, and higher wages, that fostered a "new economic" social class.

We must evaluate the "Scientific and Industrial Revolution" which supported each other in application, theory, and financial management. The "Scientific Revolution" activated the process of exploration, discovery, academia (learning), evaluation (analysis, and synthesizing), and mastering the "natural world" from traditional reflectiveness to empirical application. The "Industrialization" process promoted, advanced, and cultivated cognizance through an intelligent and practical end result. Consequently, innovative learning developed progressive social, ethic, and analytical functionality, that circumvented the globe throughout academia, that resulted in ingenious and creative minded innovative industrial and scientific inventions.

I've excluded many major factors that enhance and reinforced war's during the "first" (England, Europe, and Japan), and "second" (America's) "Industrial Revolution's. Yet, we're encouraged to highlight events that commenced due to these revolutions, such as "Laws" passed as creditable accomplishments such as Britain's "Factory Act of 1883", "The Free Market System (Capitalism)", "The New Economic and Social Philosophies"; fostered from individual's like "Adam Smith, The Wealth of Nations", "Karl Marx' and Engel's, The Communist Manifesto (Marxism)", European Imperialism and Colonialism, Political Developments (The American Revolution), The French Revolution, Independent Movements (Political): Latin America, Haiti, Mexico, Brazil, Africa, Russia, Ottoman Empire, and the U.S. Foreign Policies: (Monroe Doctrine, Roosevelt's Corollary, Panama Canal, Spanish American War); Consequently, America was manifesting "World Power" that eventually came to fruition. The advent of intellectual and technological progression rapidly grew within one hundred and fifty years, which firmly established economic, political, and social changes throughout the Universe.

CHAPTER X

The Nigerian and Biafra Civil War and Foreign Oil Interest (1967-1970)

(Analysis By: W. F. Williams)

The Nigerian Civil War is also known as The Biafran War (1967-1970); which was unmerited on ethnic, political, economic, and social origin. The primary foundation for "conflict" was predicated on the attempted "secession" by the Ibo nation's located in the Eastern and Southeastern regions of the Nigerian Federation. The "Ibo's" under the leadership of Lt Col. "Ojukwu" governor of the Eastern region promptly established a declaration for the "secession of The Republic of Biafra"; which was/is predominantly administered and populated by the "Ibo" population.

Nigeria's economic, political, social, and ethnic issues were predetermined before it was established as a nation. Fate or destiny predetermined the journey of "Lugard" from Europe to the African continents geographical location in "West Africa", when it was ripe for plucking (colonialism). He arrived in Nigeria in approximately 1894 with an emphatic unequivocal, smooth and calculating aptitude for economical mastery of the land for "whatever" will produce treasured wealth, with a "union jack" rehearsal, which fostered a tactful colonial objective. He surveyed the vast pictorial optics of the "The Great Spirit's", "Allah's", or God's, beautiful, beautiful "African Landscape". In that instance "African People of varied Nationalities" were immediately excluded from his administrative arrangements to impose a calculating imperialistic expansionism foreseen by him and associates with rapid managerial fortitude; Nonetheless, he even witnessed "Benin" to the west, "Chad and Cameroon" to the east, and "Niger" to the North. He lavishly reflected as an eyewitness to the coastal regions of the "Gulf of Guinea" to the South, "Lake Chad" to the Northeast, which also radiated an optical illumination of the majestic "Adamawa Highlands", "Mambilla Plateau", "Jos Plateau", and the "Obudu Plateau". Lugard's enterprising adventuring industrial aggression heightened when he laid his eyes on the transportation water routes of the "Niger, Benue, and Niger Delta's"; that propelled his mental dexterities towards an industrialized monetary enterprising foreplay, which he attached to this "extraordinary land mass" yet to be named.

The Nigerian and Biafran Civil War and Foreign Oil Interest (1967-1970)

It's alleged that on "Lugard's" arrival to this West African country he was in the employment of "companies" as opposed to the British government. Consecutively, these companies were the "East Indian", "Royal East African", and the "Royal Niger" respectively. "Lugard" transferred to the employment of the British government from the "Royal Niger Company". Importantly, approximately four (4) years after transferring to the employment of the British government he formed the "West African Frontier Forces", which was estimated to total approximately two-three thousand "Northern" and "Middle Belt" Muslim troops. Thusly, "imperialism", "expansionism", and ultimately "neo-colonialism" commenced. "Lugard" thereafter was designated by the British government the title "Lord". The advent of British economic interest in present day Nigeria was launched between 1898 and 1914. "Lugard" conveyed expeditious communication between "London and himself", in regards to the "amalgamation 1914" declaration, which was approved and signed in 1913 by the "order-in-council" a year prior, but enacted officially January, 1914. "Lugard's" business venture objectives and overall economic and political value for Britain became exceedingly worthy and forthright in obtaining British goals in cashing in on present day Nigerian wealth.

Lugard's operational mandate was organized through British authorities foreseeably need to construct a "railway from Northern Nigeria to the coast", to secure economic business exchange between this vast geographical area. Therefore, the "amalgamation 1914" act was enforced to unite North and South Nigeria. Notably, Southern Nigeria came into existence in approximately the 1900's; however, one-hundred plus years after the "fall of Benin". Importantly, history reveals that the conquest of "Benin" in approximately 1896, by the United Kingdom, completed British occupation of Southwestern Nigeria. Consequently, initiating the creation of the "Southern Nigeria Protectorate" in approximately 1900's. Noteworthy, in order to utilize the "amalgamation 1914" declaration, Northern Nigeria had to be conquered; Thusly, the conquest and annexation of Sakwato or Sokoto was achieved in 1903; which enabled the creation of the "Northern Nigeria Protectorate". Now, the British could "amalgamate" Northern and Southern protectorates" administrations, which was designed to open business (trade) access between these two vast regions. The (1914) amalgamation of the Southern Nigeria protectorate and Northern Nigeria protectorate is now mandated, decreed, assigned, and authenticated British established *"administrative"* business, that's unites "these two aforementioned *region's,* as opposed to uniting the *numerous (people) or ethnic group's* occupying this vast area between North and South Nigeria.

Lugard's business resource appraisal of the South and North was intensely examined, and determined that the "protectorate North was void of resources and therefore unable to fund and finance its administrative obligations". He cited many reasons why the North was incapable of administering its own region, and they were as follows: The people were *uneducated and poor*; and they were *landlocked* and *cut-off from the sea*. Therefore, he convinced the British government that the people of the North were a disenfranchised and ineffective lot to govern themselves. Conversely, The South of Nigeria was capable of financing its administration due to the highly educated "Ibo" people (the first group to be colonized, and to come in contact with European's in present day Nigeria), coupled with the South's many viable resources ably transported by sea and/or by water routes for commercial trade, which would enhanced the British amalgamated Southern protectorates financial administrative sustainability to manage itself. Therefore, the root cause of the "Nigeria Biafra War" tragedy is evident in the "amalgamation act of 1914" that United the *Northern and Southern Administration's* "only" for British business purposes, *without uniting the vast majority of ethnic Nigerian's* from the "(1914) *amalgamation decree".* Furthermore, the plight or prospective burden to sustain and finance the *"Northern Nigeria Administration's" defunct protectorate,* that the *"British and Lugard"* established, was the optimum and infinite issue at hand of finding and creating the *financial resources* necessary to sustain its' *Northern Nigeria protectorate;* after the *amalgamation declaration* was finalized in *1914.* The common-sense issue evolved in question was as to, *"who will finance the Northern protectorates defunct administrative financial sustainability to operate exact and rigorously with the amalgamated Southern protectorate"?* The British administration or Order-in-Counsel "relished and luxuriated in" constructing a "railway system" uniting the North and South regions, to establish an *"Administrative Economic and Prosperous Dominion's",* by uniting these two vastly distinct and diverse religious, cultural, and ethnically region's, to in the construct of a "railway system" or "jirgi-jirgi". Notably, when the amalgamation initially actualized in 1914 it extended forty-six years to 1960; Consequently, the British government closed the North and South borders to prevent the "Ibo (Southern) and Fulani-Hausa (Northern)" people from assimilating or forming any type of mutually social or bilateral bond of affiliation. Thusly, securing the "business interest" of Britain, by keeping these two regions and people separated for 46 years; which restricted any political, social, and economic engagement between these two intentionally designed commandeered regions from each other. Therefore, the fundamental comprehensible social, political and economic analysis of Britain's historical actions in separating these aforementioned regions initiated *Nigeria's 1960 independence from Britain;* and the *"Nigeria Biafra War (1967-1970),* was also historically predicated and instigated from the *"amalgamation 1914"* protectorate mandate; which was fraudulently imposed on the North and South regions of Nigeria, for British "interest" through "Lugard and his British" counterparts geographical annexation of the two regions in the 1913 authenticated deliberations by the "order-in-council" signing of the decree.

The "Nigeria Biafra War" commenced in 1967 due to the withdrawal of the Eastern region from the Nigerian Federation, and ultimately seceded from the Nigerian

Federation to establish the "Republic of Biafra". This secession by the "Republic of Biafra", was led by "Colonel Ojukwu" an Ibo officer with prideful determination to establish the "Republic of Biafra" in the Eastern region from the Nigerian Federation. Notably, the climatic development of Nigeria's oil industry was nothing more than "absolute" unforeseeable opportunity for Eastern Nigeria to revenge for Northern historical financial dependence on the Eastern region; which financed the North's protectorate "amalgamation 1914 declaration", through defraying the Northern regions administrative sustainability for 46 years, by usurping and exhausting protectorate Eastern Nigeria's resources. Therefore, there was deep-seeded political tensions and habitual social and economic antagonism that fostered the motivation of the "War" which was initiated by the "protectorate amalgamation action of 1914"; which separated the two regions from historical bilateral affiliation, that created ignorance of each others historical intent, jealousy, and hateful rivalry between these two diverse cultures; Muslims of the North and Christians and Animist of the Eastern region. However, the petroleum industries discoveries in Eastern Nigeria accelerated the secession of the Eastern region from the Federation of Nigeria. Consequently, the countries oil explorations and progress of discovering an abundance of oil reserves in the Eastern region initiated the essential elemental justification and legal grounds for "conflict"; which fostered considerable international industrial reflective concerns. The issues concerning this conflict involves deeply, the domestic origin and the involvement of international nation's decisive roles in endorsing a Nigerian victory over the newly formed "Republic of Biafran" state.

The protectorate amalgamation which was activated in 1914 United Northern and Southern Nigeria regional administrative, British controlled governance, between these two regions, is once again referred to for Nigeria's historical precedence, that validates forty-six years of separation of the two regions. Furthermore, thereafter the time-table confirms that from 1946 approximately, the commencement of Nigeria's geological reconnaissance, exploration, and surveillance of "dry test holes" by (BP) Shell-British Petroleum, for nine additional years, which concluded a fifty-fifty joint petroleum venture with Nigeria in 1956; which was still a British colonial subject. Even through, BP recorded progressively successful findings of numerous "oil reserves", they didn't reveal the magnitude of their explorations for political reasons a number of years. However, it's documented that Shell-BP spent approximately one hundred and fifty million pounds in the exploration of oil discovery by 1967; the year the "War" started between the "Nigerian Federation and The Republic of Biafra". During this era in time (1967), essentially most of the major oil companies acquire an interest in Nigeria's petroleum industrial potential. The oil quality was excellent with relative low infernal content, coupled with a high fuel yield, and quality blending ingredients, and sold at an exceptionally low price. Nigeria's infrastructure for oil exports and exploration towards quality development was firmly established in the mid-60's; and its' oil productions reached a respectable overly achieved growth. From 1958 to 1966 Nigeria's "petroleum exports" reached approximately 92 million pounds; with a 43.4 million pounds net output to the Nigeria balance of payments. Furthermore, Nigeria was allotted stipends for "net capital influx and service payments" for persistent progress and development of its oil industry. Importantly, its estimated that during the years 1958 to 1967 oil exports increased approximately 30 percent. Consequently, just prior to the "Nigeria War", oil production and development became the focal point and major factors in Nigeria's social, political and economic "interests"; as well as "World-Wide" international "interests".

The political prosperity from oil development enterprising merged socially with incessant internal tension of wretched proportion between historical ethnic rivalries; which developed among the three major ethnic groups in 1914, under the "amalgamation protectorate" declaration between the North and South regions, which was established through adamant British leadership. The Nigerian people were never involved in the protectorate amalgamation of 1914, only the two British administrations were endorsed to promote or resolve political, economic, and social matters that arose concerning the British Commonwealth's colony "Nigeria". Therefore, ethnic division resulted in distrust, envy, fear, hatred, and ignorance; which further promoted political, economic, and social ethnic insecurities between ethnicities in Nigeria. However, Nigeria's Federal structural governance set-in-motion the process of establishing a stable economic and political infrastructure to balance political power of authority between all Nigerian citizen's. Nonetheless, it's quite obvious that the groundwork for "one" unified Nigerian principality "was not acknowledged or generally agreed upon" by an enormous number of Nigerian citizen's; due to its *historical experience of population demarcation,* resulting in distinct ethnic separation initiated by "Lugard and the British" protectorate amalgamation decree of 1914. Nevertheless, the cry-out for self autonomy and welfare from inter-regional ethnic groups deepened the quest for their collective and individual ethnic cultural identity to control their destiny in Nigeria.

An Army revolt occurred in 1966 that seated a majority "Ibo" government to power in the Capital of "Lagos, Nigeria ". However, presently "Abuja" is The Federation of Nigeria's current Capital, since 1976. This "army revolt" widen the already existing fragile gap between ethnic Fulana's-Hausa's, Yoruba's, Ibo's, and lesser populated sub-cultures; politically, economically, and socially, which disrupted their balance of an equitable distribution of wealth, and cultural stability that historically *imbued* from the *protectorate amalgamation of 1914 declaration. Thusly, implementing the cultural divide, between* Nigeria's ethnic groups, *which was initiated* by the British, between the Northern and Eastern Nigerian regions. However, this 1966 military take-over by "Ibo military officers" provoked rekindled Hausa's fears of relinquishing political, and economic domination to the exclusively elite educated Ibo's; who at once declared that regional subdivisions in Nigeria would be eradicated to unify Nigeria.

Due to this "Military Army Coup" in 1966 led by Ibo officers predominately, caused the Hausa's in the North, and Yoruba in the West to respond to this abrupt coup with "violent attack's" on most Easterner's living in the North, and other regions respectively. Thusly, initiating a calculating surge-of- Northern military force's that implemented a victorious "counter-coup" led by a Northern Army Major General "Y. Gowon", in July of 1966; who also loomed as the conciliate, and selective choice for "Nigeria's Military Head of State". Gowon's adversary was an Eastern "Army Lt. Col. C. O. Ojukwu", a former military governor, who rebuffed disdainfully and blatantly "Federal ascendancy, rules, and Northern domination over Eastern and South Eastern "Ibo" people. Notwithstanding, "Ojukwu" suggested with ardent and stoic sophistication "a temporary detachment" between the regions as a panacea regarding the "initial Army coup by predominately Ibo officers, and the counter-coup by Northern led General Gowon". Unfortunately, in September 1966 an estimated 30,000 plus "Ibo's" living and working in Northern Nigeria were massacred; which caused stagnating disunion between "Ojukwu and the Federal Administration in Lagos; which was led by the governance of Gowon's military to resolve this turbulence".

Nigeria's were engaging in newly found oil resources and economic prosperity during "Gowon's (Northern) and Ojukwu's (Eastern)" politically exsistent ethnic rivalries. Importantly, two of Nigeria's four regions comprised abundant petroleum reserves; which incessantly expanded the political divide that invigorated the Eastern region to secession from the Nigerian Federation. The two productive oil fields were in the Eastern and Middle West (Yoruba) region's, which were comprising between 50 to 70 percent of petroleum revenues annually. Consequently, the political, economic and social conflict escalated, due to "Federal policies requiring revenues coming from Eastern and Middle West oil reserves to be allocated between the regions". Due to this mandated "Federal Policy" of dividing oil revenues between the regions, which comes from the predominant "Ibo" majority regions, which further ignited "Ibo" leadership to oppose the redistribution of oil revenues from their regions. Nonetheless, ethnic groups residing in regions without oil fields that produced revenues concurred with the "Federal Government's" policy of redistribution of oil revenues to their ethnic regions, further infuriated the "Eastern and South Eastern Ibo leadership, and the majority of its'people" to secede from the Nigerian

Federation and establish the "Republic of Biafra". In May of 1967 "Gowon" and his Federal Administration disclosed strategic political and geographical procedures to revise Nigeria's four administrative regions into twelve separate states. The realignment of Nigeria's geography was as follows: the former Eastern region was divided into three states: (1) East Central, Rivers, and South-Eastern; Thusly, mandating "only" the landlocked and overly-populated East Central Region to the majority "Ibo populated". Consequently, *denying* the "Ibo" people legal geographical sovereign authority and preeminence over "Port Harcourt" and "major oil fields" concentrated within the boundaries of the "River States". They were also excluded from oil wells in the regions historically and legally classified by the Nigerian Federation, as the "Ibo's" domain. However, Port Harcourt accumulates a 90% Ibo population. This newly established proposal seriously eradicated and demolished "Ibo's" 95% oil revenues conjoined with losing 60% of its agricultural revenues, and virtually cutting off these aforementioned regions heavily populated by the Ibo culture, and its subcultures at "Calabar, Ogoja, and Port Harcourt"; which would seriously impoverish "Ibo" peoples of these three regions. All "Ibo" hopes and dreams of a "Gowon" administration being sensitive to "Ibo" interests is thrown out the window, through this newly decreed "State Structural" demarcation established by "Gowon's" Federal Administration to eradicate the "Ibo's" control of vital and major oil rich environments in Eastern, South-Eastern, and the vital Port Harcourt area. By the end of May 1967, "Ojukwu" proposed the formal secession of the Eastern region from the Nigerian Federation. "The question remains, "if there were no petroleum discoveries in large reserves in Eastern and Mid-Western Nigeria regions would there have been a "War or Secessionist conflict of interest in Nigeria" between the Federal Governance (Gowon) and the 'Ibo" ethnic group and its leadership (Ojukwu)"? There would have been some type of ethnic conflict, due to the protectorate amalgamation decree of 1914, initiated by "Lugard and the British Government", that isolated major and subtle ethnic groups within the protectorate Northern and Southern Nigeria regions. "Isolation of ethnic groups breeds suspicions, fear, hate, and unstable governmental supervision and respect for country policy and ethnicities; which fosters "conflicts" of varying proportions within ethnic quests for political, economic, and social control of their respective cultures regions. However, the major objectives of collective cultural groups in Nigeria historically, is to acquire, maintain and sustain, social dominance within their respective regions, and ultimately their Nations.

Ojukwu and his Biafran counterparts official seceded from the "Nigerian Federation", on May 30, 1967. They hastily and instantaneously established vital geographical "Biafran" boundaries that controlled oil reserves, and commandeered export terminals for petroleum "exports", and viable imports that would fortify their cause. The paramount areas were "Port Harcourt", the channel island of Bonny (Nigeria's only export terminal), and the essentially indispensable "swampy and soggy creeks" that produced an excellent high-grade crude oil. However, *"Ojukwu's"* subjective calculations speculated that Biafra's "international" acclaim and official legal affirmation", as a legitimate sovereign "Nation", with total control over the petroleum reserves, and oil fields in the lucrative River State environment, would suffice for total "international recognition"; assistance, business affiliation, and unification, within their global communities at large. However, due to Biafra's (Ibo's) newly acquired "petroleum bargaining power" they were politically assured within this succession framework, that they would emerge victorious in their designs for a concrete succession from the Federation of Nigeria. Biafra had seceded from the Nigerian Federation with effortless maintenance and authority over the oil export facilities. Consequently, Ojukwu requested through legal demand and framework "all earnings from oil sales" to defray military expense and the thousands of "Ibo" and "Eastern" refugees fleeing Northern Nigeria back to Ibo regions, who were caught up in horrible massacres imposed by ethnic Fulani/Hausa's (Northerner's) against them. He insisted on payment from Shell-BP of approximately seventy-eight million pounds in taxes and royalties from the production and exportation of oil from the Eastern (Ibo) regions; however, the payment was never transacted, or sent to "Ojukwu" from Shell-BP as demanded by him. Notwithstanding, whether the "Ibo" leadership was aware or not, that the Federal Government responded hastily to Biafran secession by implementing stringent and rigorous blockades of all export revenues to Biafra.

Notably, the Federal Government's acted hastily and imposed austere economic sanctions on Biafra as well. Furthermore, "Gowon" ordered Federal Nigerian troop's on "Bonney" in the latter half of July 1967; which systematically corroded decisively "Ojukwu's" bargaining power. Consequently, exports were stopped immediately and Biafra lost the majority control over their newly occupied regions petroleum manufacturing and production capabilities. Thereafter, in August of the same year, Gowon authorized a full scale military operation against Biafra; as they advanced into the Mid-Western (Yoruba) states that comprised approximately 39% of oil-resources. However, during this military campaign, the Federal troops military might, bountiful supplies and aggressive manpower monopolized Biafra's ill-equipped, and wretched dis-enfranchised army. Notably, at the beginning of 1968 the Federal army captured and took full control of Biafra's major towns: "Calabar. Nsukka, and Enugu; thereafter, reducing Biafra's state dominions to approximately 65 miles by 35 miles in total area. Importantly, International intervention and assistance was "Ojukwu's trump card to even the conflict; however, his strategic calculations failed to bring forth international assistance to the Biafran cause. Furthermore, "Lagos" was functionally cognizant, and two-steps ahead of "Ojukwu's military objectives (trump cards), and rationalized that a successful and sovereign Biafran Nation would forfeit more than two-thirds of the Federal Government's oil wells and its petroleum processing installations. Therefore, Nigeria's Federation was aggressively fighting for a sustainable economic and politically progressive future.

January 1970, the pursuit for an independent Biafran State was crushed, and the Federal Nigerian forces defeated the entire Ibo regions of Eastern and Southeastern Nigeria. The Biafran Army fought with valor and courage, to know avail, in their pursuit to secede from the Nigerian Federation. Thusly, they fall victim to defeat, which resulted in the unconditional surrender of "Ojukwu and his Ibo military commander's" military campaign; which ended the thirty (30) month long "War". The "Oil Rich Eastern Regions", which account for approximately 70% of oil revenue was once again United with the Nigerian Federation Government.

NOTEWORTHY

The suffering and sacrifices of the predominant "Ibo" people and their vassals (sub-cultural ethnic groups living in the East and South Eastern Ibo states) experienced gross deteriorating and unimaginable decay and poverty in this "war", due to their quest to secede from the Nigerian Federation. Additionally, their telecommunication, postal services, and Air Flights to Southeastern Nigeria was extinguished, which promptly limited Biafra's internal and external mobility, and overall infrastructure. Consequently, the entire Southeastern infrastructure was destroyed, coupled with severe food shortages, which caused severe mass starvation, malnutrition, and rampant diseases that drastically affected both military combatants and non-combatants (innocent women and children). Additionally, it's estimated that more than 25 million Biafran's were displaced and homeless near the end of the conflict. However, Biafra's sympathizer's declared inhumane genocide to the International World Body, which includes the French Government, American Government, and many African and Foreign Countries sympathetic to the Biafran cause. Sympathy for the plight of the fallen Biafran people fueled international sympathy as opposed to military support. Frankly, an attempt by any outsider's to enable the Biafran military, and "Ibo" occupied territories were meet with fierce aggression from the Nigerian Federal Army, who had strategically surrounded "all" Ibo territory. Importantly, it's "factual" that the Nigerian Federal Government allowed teams of "International Observers" inside the war-torn Biafran regions who immediately reported to the outside World concrete evidence of severe and insurmountable famine, starvation, and multitudes of unnecessary deaths inflicted on innocent women and children. However, it's reported that this same "International Observation Team" stated "that their observations resulted in no genocide or systematic destruction of property in the war-torn Ibo regions"; However, Ibo leadership declared to the "International World Body" that mass deliberate genocide was imposed on the entire Ibo ethnic group's and its' vassals, who resided in Eastern and Southeastern Nigeria. Contrary, to the proposed findings of the "International Observers" who were allowed in war-torn Nigerian regions, the "(ICRC) International Committee of the Red Cross, estimated that during the 30 month war, approximately upwards of 14 thousand non-combatant's (civilians, women and children) were dying on a daily basis in Eastern and Southeastern Biafra as a result of the war. Nonetheless, it's also documented that many survivor's after the official surrender of Biafra in defeat to the Nigerian Federal Military, died from unnecessary starvation, diseases, and malnutrition et. Al... It's emphatically observed by many ethnic groups residing in the war-torn regions of Nigeria, that the Nigerian Federal Government with unflappable Military assistance, "obstructed directly and indirectly access of International Relief Agencies (NGO's), to help severely inflicted casualties in the war-torn regions after the war. It's also alleged and documented in many instances that the Federal Government's rational for obstructing "NGO" relief agencies access to helping the defeated Biafran's, was based on the possibility that they would resupply the Biafran's with concealed "arm shipments", in an attempt to resume the "war". War is what it is, "a determined opposition to defeat one's opponent at any cost". Unfortunately, the articles in the: 1949 Geneva Conference cite on August 12, 1949 "Protocol II", "The protection of victims of non-international armed conflicts"… In acceding to Protocol I of 1977, article 44, paragraphs 2, 3 and 4… Please acknowledge the International Geneva Conference signings of this article by numerous Global Nation's, which includes the Nigerian Federation.

Conclusion

Hindsight reflects the arduous possibility that international military and economic support would have been at the disposal of "Col. Ojukwu's" Biafra forces; imminently, if they had gained and maintained full control of key oil facilities and installations; which would have enhanced the consistent progressive exportation of oil trade abroad. Thusly, if the aforementioned circumstance had occurred, the possibility of the "Nigerian Federation" seeking a negotiable forum with Biafra might have ensued. Furthermore, the stability and organized preparation required by Biafra's military was incumbent on forging a negotiable pact with the Federation to maintain and govern Biafra as a sovereign state by "Ibo" leadership; in the Southeastern and Eastern regions. Notwithstanding, "Ojukwu's" intelligence was extremely keen and pious; however, his negotiating scheme of "tit for tat" tilted when his needed revenues for petroleum was denied disbursement from Shell BP. Therefore, the foreign exchange revenues necessary to defray expenses for military assistance, including arms, food, equipment, and clothing, shattered the expectations of a determinant sovereign and independent Biafran statehood. Contrastingly, Nigeria's Federal Governance was accorded full recognition by the World International Communities, as the legitimate Nation between the two, who successfully negotiate and receive decisive resources from oil revenue, which enabled it to bear sophisticated armament to win the War against Biafra's unequipped military.

Bibliography

Primary Sources

British High Commission to Secretary of State for Commonwealth Affairs. 27 July 1967, (Pro/FCO/38112).

Chibuike, Uche. Petrole, Internet's Britanniques ET LA Guerre Civile Nigeriane. Cambridge: University Press, 2008, Journal of African History A. 2008, vol. 49, n 1, pp. 111-35 [25 pages].

Graham-Douglas, N. Ojukwu's Rebellion and World Opinion: London, 1969.

Madiebo, A. The Nigerian Revolution and the Biafran War. Enugu, 1980.

Obasanjo, O. My command: An Account of the Nigerian Civil War, 1967-1970. London, 1980.

Ojukwu, Biafra, vol. 1; selective Speeches with Journal of Events. New York: 1969.

Permanent secretary, Ministry of Finance, Enugu to Shell BP, 21 July 1967 (PRO/FCO/38/112).

See Estrange to Davies, 2 August 1968. Public Records Office [PRO/38/321.fo.54]

Stewart, Michael. The Secretary of State for Foreign Affairs "To the British Parliament on 12 June 1968 (FCO/156).

Stremlay, John F. The International Policies of the Nigerian Civil War, 1967-1970. Princeton University Press, 1977.

CHAPTER XI

A Historiography of the "Removal of the Cherokee Nation" and the "Five Labeled Civilized Tribes to Oklahoma" (THE TRAIL OF TEARS)

An Analysis of the Cherokee's and Native American's Exile from their sacred land (1814-1858) (An Analysis and Interpretation By: William Williams)

The Dispute of Controversy

The United States vs. Cherokee Indians

Arranging to access Indian lands, Georgia broadens her laws throughout Amer.-Indian territories: "An be it decreed, that after June 1ˢᵗ next, all "Laws": legislation, mandates, statutes, applications, executions of decrees, treaties, and declarations of any type, in form or credence of whatsoever made or applied for, whether passed, or... enacted by the Cherokee Nation in the State of Georgia... are hereby asserted, affirmed, pledged, and declared nullified and void, and of no consequence, as if the same had never existed, happened, endured, or occurred.

The Cherokee Protest

"We as a Nation aspire and wish to continue to reside on this land of our "Fathers", and "Fathers", "Father's", and ancestors. Our sacred, original, and authentic rights to reside and remain on our "forefathers" land without interruption or molestation is our "Constitutional Rights" by American Law. The treaties we present this day are enacted canonicals Effected through the laws of this United States of America, and is authenticated in pursuance and ramification of signed treaties; which lawfully guarantees our residence and privileges, that secures our unanimity and identity with our "Forefathers" land against all intruder's.

The Supreme Court Upholds the Rights of the Cherokee Nation

The Cherokee Nation... is a distinct community, which occupies its'own territories... with boundaries accurately described, in which laws of Georgia can have no force, and which the citizens of Georgia have no conceivable right to enter..."

(Histojectic Phraseology: By William F. Williams)

----- John Marshall

"However", as a companion to President Jackson's implicit approval, the Governor of the State of Georgia disregard and challenge the "Supreme Court's ruling to uphold the Cherokee Nation's land possession". "The dexterity, genius, brilliance, and shrewdness of man might be disputed, questioned, and challenged to interpret, demonstrate or exhibit one single sentence of the United States Constitution relinquishing capacity and power, either explicit or implicit, to the common or general Government... to nullify the laws of a State... or compel and browbeat submissiveness, by force, to the decree or order of the Judges of the Union".

_____ Wilson Lumpkin

The Native American Indians are removed from Georgia, and a New Englander writes in condemnation, disapproval, and damnation of this genocide:" In our entire and whole history of our Government's transactions and dealings with the Indian Nation's, there is no account of events or proceedings so "black, bleached, and tattered" as the record of its treachery or perfidy to the Cherokee Nation, and to the entire body of American Indian'residing under our newly structured United States Constitution, and Bill of Rights.

_____ Helen Jackson

"But a Southerner historian justifies the policy of American Indian removal. The threat of being deprived of a great part of the United States domain by an alien and semi-barbarous people appeared intolerable and unthinkable to Georgians...I personally forbade the Native American Indians to play with their *make-belief* American Government. With this crude savage finally out-of-the-way, the State of Georgia in her first time in historical existence, is the master of her own territorial destiny", by removing the Indian from her sight.

<u>The Expulsion of the Cherokee Nation, and the labeled "Five Civilized Indian Tribe's"</u>

At the beginning of the American Revolution the "happy hunting grounds" of the Cherokee Nation's were lawfully conceded to extend from the neighboring "Mississippi River to the Eastern Slopes of the Blue Ridge Mountains; and from the Ohio River as far South as Central Georgia. However, there was European-American settlement's sprouting up on lawful treaty mandated and ancestral Cherokee land. These Euro-American immigrant settler's to America, experienced very little Cherokee resistance to the acquisition of Cherokee land; and the Indian's adapted and acclimated themselves to respect these extremely self reliant greed-ridden immigrant's as neighbor's. Notably, these Euro-American's found identity as Cherokee Indians, due to their lost British or European identity; therefore, through rape and inner-marriage within the American Indian Nation's... Consequently, this is why many "Whites" today in this 21st century claim to be Cherokee Indian's, because their nationality (identity) after the American Revolution was tainted and dismantled in many instances. Nevertheless, the Euro-American immigrant's with strong families and national identity who lived in Cherokee and Indian territories, and within these aforementioned borders, strongly embraced their European identities such as: the French, German, Scottish, English, Irish, etc... However, the aggressive nature of the American Government and its newly arrived immigrant's spiritual insistence and faith - ridden beliefs of obtaining Indian land through the declaration of "Manifest Destiny" resulted in the Cherokee's and other Indian Nations in this region of America, either selling, surrendering, or abandoning their land, depending on the variable circumstantial encounters of settler's; who confronted the American Indian's for their lawfully treaty-procured "forefathers lands" either violently, persuasively, or through "underpaid" transitional acquisition (monetary purchase).

The symbolic title "Trail of Tears" reference the specific removal or forced migration of *all* Native American Indian's from their rich and fertile Southern lands. The designated five civilized tribes refer to the Cherokee, Choctaw, Creek, Seminole and Chickasaw Nations; however, the Federal U.S. Governments symbolic reference to their forced migration was labeled "The Death March". The land of the Cherokee Nation's extended from Tennessee, Alabama, North and South Carolina, and Georgia primarily.

From approximately 1780 to 1830's, immigration from Europe increased by an unaccountable body-count or census to the "New World", resulting in newly arrived European freedom seeker's, with bottomless opportunities to steal fertile lands, possessed with mineral rich soil, gold, and natural earthly bounty. Farming of cotton, rice, tobacco, animal husbandry, and other valuable commodities brought about lucrative industry from county to county and State to State, by these Euro-American settlers. However, at the expense of removing Native Americans from their ancestral lands, to land west of the Mississippi, against their will, principles, and humanity, which psychologically destroyed Indian cultures, families, and ancestral folklore. Furthermore, in these southern states, immigrant owner's, and mixed blood Indians benefited tremendously from African slave-labor. Nonetheless, the endless arrival of European's sought after rich bottom fertile land, while non-slave owner's confiscated "cheap fertile land" from the Native American's, to better compete economically with their slave-owning neighbor's who dominated the South's commercial industries. The Cherokee's and Choctaw's ancestral lands were in the SouthEastern part of the "New World". However, geographically their land was in the original 13 colonie's regions. Notably, American Native land was occupied by individual Native American ethnic group's or tribe's stretching miles and miles apart from other Indian

Nations. Historically, recorded data from "immigrant white settler's" who illegally confiscated Native American Indian lands, used the excuse that the Native American's were not utilizing their lands properly, "by not operating large scale farms"; thusly, white settler's across the boards opinion's were that the Indian was guilty of stagnating economic and social progress, in this aforementioned southern region of Georgia, Alabama, Tennessee, Mississippi and North and South Carolina.

The Cherokees were the last Nation to leave until they were forced to leave their lands by the Federal U.S. Government's deployment of Militia and Federal Military Soldier's. Yet, between 1777-1830's the Cherokee's began to cede or relinquish their "hunting ground lands", while firmly holding on tenaciously to the land surrounding their towns. However, in the very early stages of the Cherokee land invasion during the 2nd Cherokee's War of 1776-1777, and at the beginning of the "American Revolution", which commenced in 1776. A large body of militia from the southern states made a successful attack on the eastern villages of the Cherokee Nation; however, during that period the Cherokee's were in alliance with the British Commonwealth. Thereafter, the attack by the militia on the Cherokee's forced them to seek a legitimate peace treaty with the Commissioner's of Georgia and South Carolina respectively administered at *"Dewitts Corner" May 20th 1777, which officially ended the Cherokee War of 1776-1777* against British American subjects (American Colonist's). After reconciling defeat at the hands of the British American colonial subjects, the Cherokee yielded their "American Titled Land Deeds" in South Carolina proper to the immigrant settler's.

Cherokee families which had lived on the predominant South Carolina property, that was confiscated by relinquishing heir American Land Titles to immigrant settlers; and moved westward, extending their settlements along the Tennessee River. Nevertheless, during this time frame five new villages were built by the more "warlike" Cherokee groups in the Nation on the "Chickamauga Creek", and in the neighboring district southeast of "Lookout Mountain, Tennessee". Before the end of the American Revolution the Cherokee's were again at war with the American's. General Elijah Clark led an expedition against the Cherokee settlement on Chickamauga Creek. This sudden raid by Clark caused such terror in the Indian Villages that the inhabitant's eagerly promised secession and relinquishment of their "ancestral lands" to the squatting settlers already occupying Indian lands, and hoping that Clark would stop this brutal military terror imposed on them. Clark immediately proposed a treaty with the Cherokee's, which was historically labeled "The Long Swamp" treaty. This treaty arranged by Clark was not authorized nor followed-up by the proper authorities, so claimed the Military Commands; Thusly, Clark's campaign was regarded as fraudulent, unethical, and insignificant. Therefore, General Elijah Clark was deprived of honor in his campaign of 1794. His objective was to benefit the white immigrant settler's (land grabber's) to this specific Cherokee Indian land after their defeat, and his victory was declared unauthorized by the U.S, Government. Consequently, Clark's brutal military campaign of 1794 for immigrant settler's to homestead on Chickamauga Creek land was denied by the Government. Keep in mind that in 1763 prior to Clark's campaign, the American Colonist Government decreed a "Proclamation Line", which was designated to prohibit "White Settler's" from entering Cherokee Lands. Also, be mindful that the Cherokee's Nation's had ceded or surrendered more than 50,000 square miles of their land to White settler's; and the Indian Nation's had surrendered 25 million acres or more to White immigrant settler's. Notwithstanding, between 1785 and 1800's, major Cherokee and Native land was forcibly taken by immigrant settler's in North and South Carolina, Alabama, Mississippi, Georgia, Tennessee and other Southern States, at the close of the "American Revolution"; while forcibly uprooting Native American's Westward.

Importantly, the first (1ˢᵗ) treaty of "Hopewell" (1785), was signed by the Cherokees; however, all three Nation's were coerced, browbeat, and strong-armed to sign; which included the Chickasaw, and Choctaw Nation's, who signed their treaties in (1786). Thusly, three (3) unrelated tribal "Hopewell" treaties were signed in different years and dates; Notwithstanding, all three "Hopewell treaties" were signed at the same location "Hopewell Plantation", owned by Andrew Pickens; on the Seneca River in Northwestern South Carolina. Interestingly, the treaties were signed between the "Confederation Congress of the U.S. of America with the aforementioned Indian Nations. The "Hopewell" treaty strategized a western boundary for American and newly arrived immigrant's settler's. The Cherokee's signing delegation's of this treaty included the Chickamauga/ lower Cherokee from the town of Chickamauga proper, and one delegation signer from "Lookout Mountain Town. During the signing the Cherokee's angrily stated" that in excess of 3–4,000 white settler's in the physical, or were in the *"de facto" State* of Franklin, were already squatting on the Cherokee side of their agreed (treaty) land illegally.

The Cherokee's continued to feud about whites illegally settling on their land, until a new border was designated by the *"1791 treaty of Holston". Furthermore, for the historical record,* the 1785 treaty of "Hopewell" coerced the Cherokee Nation's to place themselves under the protection of the "American Government"; agreeing as mentioned prior, to stipulate boundaries for their geographical territories; Yet, made no "order of authority" or mandated Cherokee privileges in the "State of Georgia". Notably, the treaty of "Hopewell" was belatedly confirmed at the convention at "Holston River", in 1791, and again in "Philadelphia" 1793. Noteworthy, it's alleged that Euro-American settler's major complaints during this era in history was that "Native American's occupied choice fertile land that they wanted, and that they would seize this prime fertile land by any means necessary, and at any cost".

The "invention of the cotton gin in 1793", caused White settler's "stressful panic" to acquire Native American lands; Consequently, they took their land request to their respective State land commissioner's to illegally confiscate prime fertile lands owned and occupied ancestrally by both the "Cherokee and Creek" nation's during this era. Thereafter, the Creek's lands were immediately taken by force, and gainfully secured by White settler's. A few years thereafter, they proceeded to illegally confiscate the Creek Nation's neighboring Cherokee lands, and began conducting *strenuous, exhausting, and laborious militia attacks* on the Cherokee Nation's, conjoined with *legal efforts* for the expulsion of the Cherokee's from their ancestral land and ultimately from the State of Georgia. Importantly, the *Indian expulsion era seeded outraged evil atrocities against the labeled Five Civilized Tribes; and was deeply ingrained and related to "Cotton and Slavery". History data concerning*

Native American expulsion from their lands cite the reasons as "Gold on Cherokee land, which was discovered". However, white settler's used the excuse, that the "Creek's were driven out of Alabama because their temperaments, attitudes, and over-all mentality towards White settler's was threatening"; and therefore they couldn't get along with their White settler neighbor's.

Notably, history denotes that there were very *"few real"* Cherokees living in the "Georgia Gold Belt" within their boundaries, when gold was re-discovered in the "Nacoochee Valley". However, the State of Georgia seized the gold fields nevertheless, and proceeded to arbitrarily redraw fraudulent boundaries, which enveloped or surrounded the gold fields. The vast majority of genuine (full-blooded) Cherokees were "always" concentrated in Northwest Georgia. However, for the history records, "they were sanctioned Northwest and North Central Georgia by the Federal government in 1793; Consequently, the Cherokee avoided the mountainous areas to the eastern region, and were permitted temporarily to reside in the outlying "Upper Creek ", in small villages" in that region. Importantly, the Upper Creeks had given the Cherokees sanctuary during the "Chickamauga War". The "myths" that the Cherokees conquered Northern Georgia in extended Wars with the Creeks, was *actualized* by the U.S. legal system, when the Cherokees were fighting eviction in the Georgia Supreme Court. Nevertheless, "Georgia's initial legal grounds for the Cherokees eviction from Georgia, was stated that *"they were not indigenous to the State of Georgia". Cherokee lawyer's* utilized *"English Common law rights of possession"* to counter Georgia's legal system to evict the Cherokees from their land. History witnessed that the majority of people who claimed "Native American Ancestry", whether calling themselves Creeks or

Cherokees did so during that era to claim rich and expansive lands, according to the American Governments census in the 20th century. However, decendent's of these "inherited claimed Indian's decendent's", who recently in the 21st century, took DNA tests revealed from their bloodlines, that most of these so called Cherokees, or Indians, who inherited these lands illegally were decendant's of European immigrant settler's; with a limited few possessing mixed ancestral Native American Indian blood-lines. However, many married into Indian heritage thereafter; and many Indians women were victimized to numerous rapes over the past centuries, which is documented data during America's historic Indian campaigns.

What historiographer's discovered in extensive research is that White settlement farmer's (agronomists) purposely delineated on maps prime fertile cotton growing soil, so that "Andrew Jackson" could steal 24-30 million acres from the Creek Nation; and also delineate the areas in Northwest Georgia that calculated below 1,000 feet in elevation for more than suitable cotton industrialization. Notably, from 1814 onward the late President Andrew Jackson systematically schemed and stole "Northwest Georgia from the Cherokees", so his slave owning White settler's could develop palatial plantations from free slave labor. Furthermore, a real estate consortium from Virginia and South Carolina, who were mainly planter's, exposed the bottomlands of the Cherokee Nation instantly and promptly, after the Cherokees were "locked up inside timber forts", as the U.S. government was preparing for their exodus westward.

The Creek Nation's endured untruths, deceit, and dishonesty in "Alabama's history books by stating that" in 1832 the U. S. government affably gave allotments to Creek families, who choose to reside in Alabama. "Claiming that the cantankerous and bad-tempered Creeks just couldn't get along with their civilized immigrant white settler neighbor's". Furthermore, stating that "the Creeks caused trouble and eventually started another war". Therefore, U.S. militia and volunteer's gathered as many Creek's as possible and marched them at gunpoint in 1836 westward, because whites alleged that their hostile disposition required constant military supervision. The historical contradictory truth found that the Creeks were diversified successful Alabama farmers, before and during the U.S. governments takeover, and were far more productive than their white neighbor's. Notably, the Creek farmer's in Western Georgia and East Central Alabama were enormously affluent by selling livestock and produce to their white settlement neighbor's in Georgia and Alabama. The truth is that "during this era in history", white immigrant settler's preferred to invest in cotton and slaves in Western Georgia and East Alabama. It was very natural for the Creek's to get unruly in Alabama; because real estate speculators hired rowdy thugs and volunteer gangs to debouch on their farm-land, and demanded the Creek farmers at gunpoint to exit their own land. However, history cites that any Creek farmer who resisted were fired upon and killed at will, if not immediately, and eventually they were ambushed and killed like animals if seen in their settlement tribal regions by immigrant settlers. Importantly, the secrets omitted out of the Alabama and Georgia history books, is that the Georgia Gold Belt extended southwest through the "original"

Muskogee Creek homeland in west-central Georgia, to east central Alabama. History revealed that when "William McIntosh" relinquished all of the Creek lands remaining in Georgia, which was delegated by the "Treaty of Indian Springs" in 1825, he acknowledged thereafter that gold deposits abounded in that location. However, it's historically noted that he kept a substantial square mile of gold reserves for himself in "Carroll County, Ga. where the gold is said to have been in abundance". Gold prospectors are alleged to have literally swarmed into west Georgia as soon as the treaty signing ink had dried. This treaty however, was null and void by Georgia's Congressional authority; to know avail, due to the tremendous flow of white immigrant squatters residing illegally on the Creek Nations land.

The "Treaty of Cusseta" (1832) signing, preceded the "gold rush in Central Alabama; in the locations of Randolph, Chambers, and Lee Counties Alabama. The Creek farmers requested land allotments, reflecting that the cotton farmers were not interested in their hilly mountain farms. They were wrong in their judgment, because the Creek land allotments were overwhelmed and consistently invaded by gold prospectors. In Randolph County, where the "Hillabee Creek's resided, and preferred to stay-put (not leave their homeland), over an estimated five-eight thousand white settlement gold-miners, and squatter immigrant's, invaded Creek land and ran the Creek's off; "their reason for their invasion of the Creek Nation's allotted lands were that they were ill-tempered towards them, and difficult to live with".

Aforementioned, the treaties with the Chocktaw's and Chickasaw's commenced on July 12, 1861, between the Confederate States of America and Chocktaw's and Chickasaw's, at the beginning of the American Civil War. The name of "Albert Pike" is to be remembered as the Southern Confederate deputy appointed negotiator of several Native American Treaties. Besides, he negotiated the Chocktaw's and Chickasaw's treaty, and was deputy negotiator of Cherokee leader "John Ross's" (A White immigrant of European heritage predominantly, and

Slave owner), which was also concluded in 1861, by the Confederacy. The Chickasaw's and Chocktaw's reflected and presumed, that if they like the whites, possessed African-slaves, that white settler's would be favorable to their racism, and accept them as civilized Native Americans. However, Native American slavery was segmented by divisions of worth; therefore, if Africans in their Nations were warrior's or great thinkers, or tribal providers in their survival process, they lived as Native American's amongst them. Their slave system was also based on inner-breeding, enhancements, and sustainability of their Indian Nation's. Additionally, the Chocktaw's and Chickasaw's remembered and strongly resented the Indian's removal thirty (30) years prior, conjoined with their complaints of poor Federal government services to them over the years. Consequently, the main reasons these two Native American Nation's agreed to sign the treaty was predicated on being protected from rival Indian Nations's, by the Confederacy. However, the Choctaw's and Chickasaw's were abandoned by the Confederacy from an Act decreed by the U.S. government, which *nullified* the *64 term treaty, during* and after the *"Civil War"*.

From 1865-1918, southern Chocktaw's were unlawfully ignored by the U.S. Government of Indian Affairs in provisions for their health, education, survival, and sustainability; thusly, the Indian Nation fell into *blatant obscurity*. In the outcome of the Civil War their economic, social, and political problems were ignored entirely. Between the defeat of the Confederates, and slavery that was abandoned; which thusly mandated African freedmen; consequently, the advent of Confederate racist problems multiplied against the Chocktaw's and Chickasaw Indian Nations. The Confederates loss meant that the Choctaw's were helpless people, with an atrocious and defeated future. The Chocktaw's and Chickasaw's Nation's were destined for Oklahoma territories that would eventually be their lawful homelands.

Conclusion of the Trail of Tears

* There were multiple "Trail of Tears", and separate Indian Nations had their own personal ones; along with several tragic forcible exodus that developed insurmountable destruction and deaths among Native American's Nations.

* The "Cherokees Trail of Tears" was a working legal apparatus, due to the United States Supreme Courts lawful decision to allow them to remain in their ancestral homeland, in the Worcester vs. Georgia decision (1832). However, the Cherokee Nation's "removal" received great sympathy from the American eastern newspaper medias, due to their respect for the Cherokees ethnic, economic, political, and industrious business savvy; they were strongly regarded as an "exemplary Indian Nation". However, Western colonial "manifest destiny" expansionism overruled all ranges of lawful vision, and took the Cherokees ancestral land.

* On May 28, 1830, Andrew Jackson's "Indian Removal Act" was signed into law passing by only one (1) vote. *"Davy Crockett, and a Tennessee Congressman"* appealed the decision enacted by "Andrew Jackson". The scheming Andrew Jackson, had literally proceeded in the forefront to institute statecraft in removing the Cherokees from their ancestral homelands; also, conjoined with awarding contracts for designed expulsion route roads. He distinctly mapped out stockades for Cherokee detainment if necessary, prior to the bill's authentication confirmation.

* A Large number of Cherokees were confined as prisoner's in stockades months before their expulsion from their ancestral homelands, awaiting their Odyssey to *Oklahoma*, referred to as *Indian territory* by the U.S. government. They meet this cruel, nefarious, and lawless inhumanity at the hands of immigrant's that were newly arrival's in the "New World"; who were unwanted, hated, dispised, and viewed as contemptible by their British colonizers. Nonetheless, on their exodus to "Indian territory" the Cherokee Nation was given spoiled foods, very little shelter, inadequate clothing and blankets to withstand the freezing winter's, rain and snow. However, most importantly they were refused medicines for sicknesses. Unfortunately, most Cherokee died from diseases, measles and smallpox.

Even though their suffering was insurmountable on their journey to Indian territory, thousands of Cherokees died in the squalor of these "jails or concentration camps" prior to their final removal on their forcible journey to Oklahoma and westward. Lastly, Christianity had been entrenched for twenty plus years within the Cherokee Nation's, before their exodus to "Indian territory"; coupled with their unlawful removal from their original homeland in the "Trail of Tears". Historically, in Oklahoma, North and South Carolina, Tennessee, et.al., the Cherokee's were dispersed throughout the U.S.A. With their own interpretation of the Christian faith that has been with them for approximately 500 years. There are many Cherokee people, families, and communities who have negotiated and brought back to life their ancient Cherokee religion, which is an honorable transformation to remedy the suffering they and their ancestor's endured at the hands of evilness, and hate mongering, and greedy immigrant's from Europe to the "New World." However, we honorably thank those Euro-Americans and other's who have put their lives on the line to salvage the Great traditions of the Native Americans on both and all continents. We thank the many Americans on the North, South, and Atlantis continents who have also suffered with those who have witnessed the reality of unlawful degradation, suffering, and ignorance at the hands of dishonorable laws, government authority (absolute power disrupts absolutely), and tyrants.

By: William F. Williams (A Histojectic analysis of the "Trail of Tears")

CHAPTER XII

A Review of the Revolutionary History of Wine, Coffee, Beverages and Find's from Ancient Civilization's Impact on Modernity

(A Histojectic Analysis By: William F. Williams)

Wine, Beer, Coffee, Beverage, and ancient finding's is introduced as the *"motif"*, with their *ontogenesis"* process, that identifies cultural origin, nationality, geography, identifiable and unidentifiable artifacts; and miscellaneous materials akin to the ontological colonization of civilization's. They have guided archaeologians, paleontologist, classicist, and excavator's to evolutionary historical discoveries that identifies homo sapiens ontological chronology in the universe. Additionally, the discovery of these drink's conjoined with other finding's have established mankind's path towards modernity. Thusly, fostering a systematic and constructural antecedence in identifying historical civilization's. However, the oldest recorded winery on record was discovered in 4100 B.C. ; which identifies an ancient civilization currently in present day Armenian.

Historiography directives edit the Neolithic Period "Chateau Hajji Firuz", as the primary community permanently settled *(as opposed to nomadic existence)*, that established domestication of *"organisms belonging to the vegetable throne"*, and *"domesticated livestock"*; which secured communal longevity and collective sharing. The

Middle East and Asia attribute the geographical discovery of these ancient findings within the scholarship of Western archeology, anthropology, and the progression of the evolutionary process, which supports and promotes historical novelty. History allege that a Neolithic "pabulum" or consortium of food discoveries progressed which created the following processing techniques: spicing, heating, soaking, and fermenting. Therefore, history alleges, depending on the geographical location, that predominantly permanent Neolithic settlement communities are accountable for initially producing bread, beer, wine, and a variety of meat and grain recipes or entrée's we consume today. The appearance of clay pottery was alleged to have been discovered around 7,000-6,000 B.C., which was manipulated by humans, through its' plasticity innate material (clay dirt) to be formed into specific shapes, for specific purposes, such as for storage-jars or drinking casks etc... The pottery was almost entirely indestructible after the heating process of firing the clay to extreme temperatures; causing its porous construction to osmose amoebics. However, at the site "Chateau Hajji Firuz" a yellow residue was found inside clay pottery, and was confirmed to be associated with winemaking. It's alleged that this pottery was discovered in a Neolithic mud-brick house dated 5400-6000 B.C.

The early Neolithic era follow the end of the "Ice Age" about 10,000 BCE, depending on the geographical location, which includes the "Bronze and Iron Ages". Consequently, this period in time opened our ancestral social, genetic, and cultural transformation over past ancient years of human survival. However, the continuity of ceaseless human development, and historical progress has paralleled with the manufacturing discovery of ancient wine, and beer fermentation. Nonetheless, as we analyze and appraise the ancient historical processing of fermented wine, beer and beverages, it's imperative that the exploration of the "responsible civilization's" are widely recognized (in their time and place).

Ancient excavated beverages have been identified through the science of "chemistry", through the analysis of composition and properties of substances and various elementary forms of matter. The aforementioned beverage residue was found through excavator's, anthropologist's, archaeologist's, and scientific researcher's in "ancient drinking vats, and storage casks. Many ancient historical discoveries were recovered from "Midas Tumulus", or tomb of King Midas, in Gordium, Turkey (in the village of "Yassihoyuk); approximately in or near the 8th century, and located near the capital of the "Phrygians in Central Turkey". Additionally, sites in Ancient China located near the 'Yellow River", dating as early as 7,000 B.C.E. Additionally, it's most important to acknowledge *"these findings"* are the direct results of innovative chemical data formalized and defined through the integration and synthesis with newly discovered scientific disciplines. Thusly, vigorously clarifying essential historical dates and finding's, by utilizing "Kipling's" six favorite friend's (by metaphorically reflecting this subject matter from a journalistic approach, as to): *"who, what, why, how, where, and when'.* Example, the discovery that constitutes the "Eurasian Grape" substance or "Vitis Vinifera", that's scientifically acknowledged through the application of microchemical techniques as the source of 99% of domesticated "wines" can reconstruct, and validify what existed originally. Therefore, furthering the scholarship of "Vitis Vinifera's" geographical heritage by identifying a "Near Eastern Fertile Crescent" wine culture, that evolved in approximately 6,000 BCE. However, it's migratory adaptation and assimilation advanced around the globe to civilization's, subsequently (alleged) in *thousand year* intervals, which fulfilled it evolutionary "manifest destiny". Historical research data chronicle that "Egyptian King Scorpion I (circa 3150 BCE), had exported 700 jars of (yellow residue discovered inside these jars) from this ancient wine source, estimated to constitute 4500 liters of "Vitis Vinifera" from the "Jordan Valley or Fertile Crescent"; however these historical facts are further referenced through modern day *"Activated Neutron Analysis"*. During this era, the exporting method would be by domesticated livestock, in transporting such large quantities of wine, either over land back to Egypt or Abydos, or by livestock to ships for transport, or by either means whether by donkey's, camel's, or oxen's, the domestication of animal's is speculated to have been cultivated during or before this era.

The historical narrative of *"wine"* navigates through *exegesis* or *interpretation* into biblical *anecdote or an amusing story,* displayed in the *"Old Testament"* in the *"Holy Bible",* in the Book of Genesis 9*th* chapter. Thusly, ascribed to *"Noah's Hypothesis" or "anecdote" (Genesis 9), "that the wild Eurasian grape-vine emerged into cultivation and "in the course of time"* was domesticated in the region of the "Caucasus Mountains". The anecdote acquired its' epithet or name from the patriarch "Noah"; who is alleged to have planted a vineyard on "Mount Ararat" after the biblical "Great Flood" recorded in the Holy Bible (Genesis 9). Importantly, "Genesis Rabbah Judaism" systematic interpretation of the book of "Genesis" evolved from the "Judaic Sages" approximately 400-460 ce., that produced a comprehensible and earliest or original written description of the "Book of Genesis". Also, in "Genesis Rabbah" the entire narrative is structured and constructed to illustrate the sacred "history of Israel"; however, explicitly and unequivocally referring to the "Jewish People", and their enslaved reality, struggles and recovery (redemption).

Historical uncertainty or skepticism regarding the aforementioned "Egyptian King Scorpion I's (circa 3150 BCE)" exportation of "Vitis Vinifera" is historically validated through the science of "microchemical techniques" and the "DNA" process. Consequently, homo sapien's and most of what they surround themselves with, namely: clothing, habitation, and food items, are essentially *"organic in chemical composition"*. Therefore, *organics are easily obliterated and scattered over time;* only the application of microchemical techniques can identify and reconstruct what originally existed. The process and access that's been developed for ancient "wines" can also be applied to other organic materials; whether DNA, woods, dyes, *resin, drugs, honey, or whatever. However, the catch twenty-two is predicated on their preservation(especially in hot and dry desert whether) or underwater where oxygen is not exposed. The excavated jars residues demonstrated that "wine" had indeed been fermented with a precursor of the wine yeast "saccharomyces cerevisiae" (sugar fungus). Thereafter, the adaptation of wines notably in the Eastern and Middle-Eastern cultures began to reflect and perceive the development and establishment of a winemaking industry around 3000 BCE; with its foundation in the "Nile Delta". Their application was to transplant the domesticated vines from "Southern Levant", the current region of the Middle East, that extends along the Eastern Mediterranean; which includes the coastal and inland regions of modern day Syria, Lebanon, Jordan, Israel, and the West Bank of Gaza. Accordingly, extended research conducted by paleontologist and scientist discovered that the *wine* discovered in Egyptian King "Scorpion I's excavated tomb in Abydos was authentically included in his burial as an Elixir of life; and derived from the "Vitis Vinifera" exported from the "Fertile Crescent" region (in circa 3150 BCE).

Further findings in the tomb of King Scorpion I's were, "terebinth, pine tree resin, grape and fig residue. The fermented wine beverage was said to have been laced with herbs, which included mints, coriander and sage. Furthermore, its historically chronicled that alcohol in the fermented wines was ideal in dissolving "medicinal active compounds"; therefore, instituting the foundation for "Egyptian Pharmacopeia" discovered in the Ancient World. Additionally, in the neolithic period (circa 7000-6000 B.C.) discovery of ancient "Chinese fermented Beverage's", which pinpoints the "rice wine culture" established with equally far reaching results in the development and innovation of "Traditional Chinese Medicines".

The historical cultural pathway that utilizes the subject-matter of ancient discoveries, which includes wines, beer, coffee, beverages, and numerous excavated artifacts, has enhanced our scholarship in the contributions and shaping of World Civilizations from the "ab initio" to modernity. With the advent of beverage fermentation, science has directed safer alternatives in clean water-supplies in human settlements from antiquity to modernity.

The discovery of wine, beer and beverages, has many social ritualistic symbols within societies, such as the celebration of births, deaths, cuisines, social bonds, business transactions, holidays, and life saving medicines as well as deadly poisons. Notably, paleontologist, archaeologian's, excavators, anthropologist, and scientist's have divided historical time-tables from validated and confirmed ancient discoveries; however, analogously historians and historiographers divide ancient discoveries by authentic source materials that validates "matter, substance, civilizations, issues and events from these scientific discoveries to re-establish an accurate time-table of the events.

Historiographer's acclaim and support the hypothesis and conclusion that alcohol developed and sustained all civilization's causing and stimulating a longer life-span and spirited procreation through engenderment progression, that structured and populated civilization's. Therefore, as population's became more advanced and accountable, the fermenting of beverages were intelligently executed by *"community selected skilled and proficient artisans"*. Furthermore, beverages such as beer, coffee, tea, and wines has accelerated, promoted, enthralled, and accumulated economical wealth throughout governmental and cultural interchanges on a global monetary system of accountable sustainability.

The discovery of ancient "beer", "wine", "coffee", "beverages" and an assortment of artifacts, opened the door for bimolecular paleontology, which is the scientific analysis, synthesis, and authenticated measure of identifying and validating ancient *organic* remains. Civilized modernity offers an abundance of social occasions that are ritualized through the partaking of various beverages evolved from ancient civilization's that discovered specific vegetation; furthermore, the geographical location of these findings was initially procured in the East, and Middle-East. Notably, these ancient vegetable kingdoms or plants were cloned repetiously from ancient beginnings in approximately A.D. 10,000.

Coffee

Coffee's composition and content: a *"tree, its seeds, and the liquid refreshment"* made from them. The species of coffee historically documented that derives from *Ethiopia (A.D.1000), and labeled the "arabica"*, which is allegedly the *"highest quality bean", which cater overwhelmingly the majority of the World's requested* imported coffee; notably, it accounts for approximately 85% of all imported coffee in the United States. In natural composition and assembly the coffee tree is a small evergreen of the genus "Coffea"; with ovate smooth leaves and clusters of aromatic white flowers, that ripen into deep red fruits approximately 1/2 to 3/4 inches long at harvest time.

The ancient history of coffee's discovery will always reflect a problematic uncertain timetable, due to the *nature of causality and "historiography's" Authenticated pledge* for factual "data" accountability; because approximate dates of *events* vary depending upon the *"critical validity of the sources"* of eventful materials published. Many historiographer's place the first discovery of coffee to be as early as the sixth century. While other's chronicle that coffee discovery evolved in the eighth and ninth centuries; when civilizations first discovered the effects of coffee. Nonetheless, the history of coffee recorded by numerous historiographer's and historian's narrate and chronicle coffee discovery historically beginning in Ethiopia and parts of Africa; thereafter, disseminating (spreading by land or sea) to Arabia, China (Far East), Ottoman Empire, Europe, and finally arriving in the Americas around 1668.

According to legend circa 800 A.D., an Ethiopian goat herder named Kaldi, observed his goats frolicking over-actively after eating berries from the "dark leaves" of this coffee plant. It's documented that "Kildi" told his village community of this momentous historical experience; thusly, validating coffee as an authentic newly found drink in this Ethiopian village. Therefore, the first human account of coffee was allegedly discovered in Ethiopia.

Coffee, in the Ancient Arab World became such a staple drink in the lives of families, both rich and poor, that Islamic Law" authorized grounds for separation between spouses if husbands cannot produce coffee for their wives. Traveller's to Cairo, Egypt and to other Egyptian Cities from England would state that "Arab's coffee houses are more common on these City streets than our Ale-houses in England". These *coffee houses* in Cairo and elsewhere revolutionized a *"news gossip media"* within the various communities in Egypt, and around the globe. Thusly, institutionalizing the way society socialized, functioned, and interacted within communities, for the "indulgence" of coffee, conversation, and the latest news. Furthermore, the first *"coffee shop"* opened in *Constantinople's, Turkey* in 1475, and was followed by the second in 1554, allegedly.

Coffee entered "Europe" in approx. C. 1600's, through the Port of Venice, Italy. However, the first "coffee house" opened in "Italy" in 1654. It's alleged that coffee introduced the "Age of Exploration" in Europe; However, it's alleged to have been diffused with the "New Rationalism" throughout Europe deemed the "Enlightenment Period". The advent of Coffee symbolized modernity and progress in Europe. Coffee stabilized a venue for scientific assemblage in Europe; and is alleged to have fostered the "Scientific Revolution". Coffee shops in Europe were contestable dialectical gathering sites, during the initial stages of the "Scientific Revolution". The coffee shops were visited in Europe by the likes of "Edmund Halley", "Sir Christopher Wren", and Robert Hooke's, all vital accomplices, designer's, and architect's of the *"Scientific Revolution"*. Hook's is honored and esteemed for inventing the *"Theory of Gravity"*, in a "coffee shop, that launched "Sir Isaac Newton's", *"Mathematical Principles of Natural Philosophy"*. Hooke's was labeled the coffee house "inventor" by the coffee house regular's, due to his fluid academic background as a mathematician, physicist, inventor, and scientist. The coffee house localities further extended into financial gathering circles for informative Insurance news, business news (investments), and a facility to produce news pamplet's, newspaper editing, political dialog, and mailing addresses (post office boxes). It's alleged that the "London Gazette", and "Daily Courant" Newspapers establishments evolved from London's coffee houses. Coffee Houses in Europe instituted an "elite social class", status, and a reserved discipline in character amongst its' patrons in the likes of scientist's, intellectual's, educator's, business merchants, and philanthropist. However, it's documented that between 1680 and 1730 the "London" population consumed more coffee than anywhere else in the World".

The first London coffee house was established in 1648, and the second coffee house established in Oxford, England in 1650; however both coffee houses were opened for business by a Lebanese family. Thereafter, coffee houses in Europe, especially in Italy increased to approximately two-hundred.

In the American Colonies on *May 10th 1773*, the British Parliament passed the *"tea tax"*, which initiated the disapproval and eruption by her colonies seven months later into the *"Boston Tea Party"*, commencing December 16, 1773. This belligerent *legal dispute* by the colonies against taxation without representation, and their disapproval of the tea tax imposed on them, resulted in the social desire for "coffee" consumption, as opposed to tea consumption by the British colonies in America, after the "Boston Tea Party" confrontation. Thereafter, *"Coffee"* consumption in the *"New World"* became the *patriotic expression* of *freedom and independence*, conjoined with the determination to become *"subject's"* of their environment as opposed to *object's*, under British rule in 1773. The colonies "in loco parentis" subjectivity in precept and ordinance, enforced by the British, was the colonies determinant objective in fueling their consolidated might to overcome their oppressor's, which was English governance, and the relinquishing control of their future subservient status to British rule.

During the "Revolutionary War", it's alleged the "Founding Fathers" of the United States of America collaborated their ideology and legal tactics in expository, at methodic gatherings in *coffee houses* during this era in time.

In 1790, history records two-first's, the "wholesale coffee roasting company" in the U.S.A. in 1790; and the first U.S.A. "newspaper advertising" of coffee, as a quality consumer merchandise, rubber stamped as a social necessity. Additionally, by 1850 a "manual coffee grinder" was invented, and found its' way into the American "elite's" kitchen's in America. Furthermore, the "American Civil War" elevated the popularity of *coffee* from the *battle field's* to the American *households* as a staple product. Soldier's went to war with "coffee bean" as a primary source of military rations. In the last three centuries 90% of people living in the Western World switched from tea being the primary drink to coffee being the dominant beverage in households, and also in restaurants, and diners in the Western World. Notwithstanding, coffee also owe its fame and popularity in part to its *"stimulant effect and substance that invigorates its caffeine components".*

Bibliography

"Ancient Egyptian Herbal Wines," The proceedings of the National Academy of Science (May 05, 2009), Vol. 106, no. 18, pp. 7361-7366.

Davis, Kenneth. *A GUIDE TO BUYING, BREWING, and ENJOYING EXPRESSO,* Ultimate Coffee, and Home Coffee. Kdivids@coffeereview.com.

Standage, Tom. *A History of the World* in 6 Glasses (New York: Walker & Company, 2006).

CHAPTER XIII

A Critique Analysis and Interpretation of Evilness in Our Universe

(Analysis and Interpretation By: William F. Williams)

An Interpretation of the Theory and Perception of Evilness !

Evilness represents many philosophical, psychological, and metaphysical derelictical definitions, conjoined with numerous subtexts of consistencies and non-consistencies that defines evil behavior in human beings against other human beings. The interpretation of "evil" behavior is defined through connotations (implying), associations (groups, governance), *genealogy (heredity), theorems, nuances (distinctions), and varying types of symbolizations (types of immoral conduct).

The philosophical question regarding "evil" is defined between the perspectives of common evil, illegitimate evil, or/and by embracing both through kinship. Thusly, embracing the definition of "evil" through "theology and/or evolution"; consequently, one type of "evilness" is evolving from the illegitimate nature, spirit, and soul, of the biblical "Satan"; and the other "evilness"(common) derives from the creative evolution and naturalistic nature of the world (creation). Nonetheless, both evil-actions or interactions is the spirit forces that is directed towards disrupting the entities of (existence, body, individual's, facts, and essence) of universal stability, clarity, and human intelligence. Therefore, disruptive "evilness" embraces wars, deception, chaos, poverty, wickedness, hate, jealousy, depravation, greed, pain (mental and physical), and negative dispositions (within beings). Evilness, as a functional antagonistic behavior, has combated *"positive behavior"*, and *"principled moral universalism"; "and positive earthly spiritual forces"* since time. However, mankind is unable to discover a valid network to extract the defining ramifications that commands "disruptive behavior" within the inborn character of principled "homo sapiens". Therefore, the question asked, "is this disruptive evil discipline" in mankind ingrained in the evolutionary genetics (Darwinism); or from theology (religion's) concerning a god-centered creation; or by intellectual design through empirical evidence of natures discoveries (CSI synthesis)?

The interpretation of the theory and perception of "evilness" is interpreted by residues of Religion, Darwinism, or Intellectual design. However, a forthright analysis of "evilness" will awaken the intellectual consciousness and subconsciousness to decipher numerous elements, circumstances, dispositions, and sociological entities that promotes and supports "evilness" universally, and between "clashes of civilizations". This forthright analysis of "evil" is defined as "a cognitive mental emotional state of fixation (obsession) that's stimulated, enacted, and confirmed by its consequential effect to pacify and release its' incarcerated antidote upon other's; which represents his /her superficial counteracting agent (their cure)". The actor(s) to this "evil" participation fines temporary or permanent justification from the "consequential effects of transferring and transposing his/her psychological afflictions upon another. The rational of "illegitimate evil actions" imposed on society is either through "retributive retaliations, greed, jealousy, poverty, chaos (utter confusion), wickedness, hatred, deceptions (to trick), genetics, abusive behavioral exposure, disgrace, contempt, defamation, lying, murder, mental disorders, fear, and wars". However, the defining affinity for "common evils" is characterized by a "bad state of affairs", such as: illness (physical and mental), natural disasters (disruptive weather), the general "state of things"(the combination of environmental circumstances at a given time), situations (physical positions in relations to your environment; Example, "the present global "International" situations)". These common evils are not the result of "moral agents", but are dependent on the results or responsibility of "moral agents" capabilities of acting with conviction, faith, and tenacity to correct and solve these "common evils" (such as Heads of State, Father's structuring their families, hurricanes, tornadoes, sicknesses etc...). However, "illegitimate evils" are the result of moral agents *wrongful decisions* to initiate "illegitimate evil" upon others. Thusly, these *moral agents* are twofold in disseminating "common evils" and "illegitimate evils"; nonetheless, one evil evolves from *natural (common)* cause and effect, and the other evil from *bastardly (illegitimate)* cause and effect. However, positive "moral agents" are designed to framework *"Explicit Essentials"* through a *"fixed necessity"* for Universal moral laws to (1) set positive characteristic examples towards others, (2) exhibit personal and collective significant morality towards others, and (3) structure a communal, national, and global consciousness that demands moral fortitude, in exchange for one and the same. Therefore, my definition of a "moral agent" is a living *cognitive and perceivable* person that must accommodate, adapt, and adjust to their *responsibility* to bear the weight of their convictions (principles), or cogency, within the scheme of moral laws.

The illegitimate "evil" commands disruptive human behavior on our planet (named) earth, and its life forces nourish and subsist on individual's, and collective universal "ignorance" of "self ", with an appetite that enters and resides in the social torture and oppression of universal life's positive spiritual elements, which disseminates destructive atrocities that blinds and conditions a likeness in attitude through subjective illusory that equates to "evilness".

The basic fundamental hierarchies that covenant humanity is shelter, food, clothing, cleanliness, sanitation, family, and sustainability to survive earthly bound. Therefore, If the aforementioned obligations are not met as a natural covenant for human consumption, utility, and protection, the natural order of human activity, growth, and progressive enterprise equates to "poverty". Thusly, life forces will consume humanity with an extreme exposure to ignorance, negativity, hopelessness, and chaotic Depravations and unethical degeneracy in combating evilness. Therefore, since "evilnesses" appetite, sustainability, and foundation resides in social torture, oppression, and lifelessness inherited in its manifestations to manufacture poverty, then poverty must be first on humanities agenda to eliminate "Global Poverty", within the concepts of fostering fundamental moral decency and respectable behavior within all societal capacities. By eliminating "poverty" humanity counters "evilness" within the global communities to strengthen and develop sound minds, elevate the human spirit, and nourish a Universal mandate towards mental positivism, and moral credibility, to combat the aggressive nature of "evilness".

Theodicy

Is the Price Paid in "Evilness" for Human Freedom over Compensated? (1). Or should "Human Freedoms" be limited to contain "Evilness" in our Society?

Western Religions synchronize, and coexist "love, goodness, decency, and kindness with the biblical doctrines deriving from "God"; contrastingly, "evilness" that derives from the hierarchy of "satanic and demonic" conscious and subconscious activities exercise there vengence deliberately against societies. Therefore, satanic and demonic evilness denotes "illegitimate morals"; versus "common evils" which symbolizes nature's disposition deriving from human illnesses, sicknesses, and various human sufferings; secondly, "common evils" also symbolizes climatic or atmospheric catastrophes, such as hurricanes, tornadoes, earthquakes, and poverty that breeds *"common evilness et. Al..." Therefore, can the Western Worlds "God" be held accountable for "common (natural) evilness", or is he the blame for "all" evilness, both illegitimate (bastardly) and common (natural) evils against global societies?*

Is Suffering a Test and Necessary Observation to Obtain Spiritual Positivism, Happiness, and Humanity in Western Religions?

Religious faith in Western society qualifies its divinity that manifest and divulge the "absolute being", which is characterized by obtaining a "divine nature" for its believer's to "walk by faith" and not by sight". Interestingly, the key component in believing in the Biblical designs of "God's" doctrine (canon), is principled through Theologians asking or persuading Christian follower's to accept religion through the convictions of mythology; which is postulated and argued by many opposed to the faith.

Additionally, the historical biblical "Christian Bible Story" reveals that every human being entering this Universe is entering as "sinners" (evildoer's). However, the "Bible's" example of sinner's is symbolized through the story of "Adam and Eve". Contrastingly, Christian's living faith in "God" is structured through the principles of *"God's lawful Universal designs"; which are compatible with "the love and goodness of spirit from the canons of religious vision, to combat without deviation",* through the *Christian framework mechanisms,* that derails evilness, and criminal behavior from entering the spiritual souls of mankind. The "faith" element in Christian consciousness is a powerful *subjective* force that challenges *objective* credence, "proof that one's "faith" is a living and daring certainty in "God's" grace. Therefore, does Christianity utilize delusions and illusions of evilness, sin, and criminal activity to seduce fear in its believer's to the doctrines, guidelines, and principles of "repentance" that *restores* a subjective spiritual faith mechanism in its believer's who've sinned? Thusly, the restoration of the sinful activity is vacated from the Christians earthly judgemental *evilness* or actions; which qualifies one of Christianity's commandments (tenets) that maintains and upholds their *entry into heaven*, through the *acquisition, essence, and maintenance of an everlasting life*; after their demise, through this *repentive Christian tenet*. The nest question concerning "evilness" is as follows: Is the Christians "repentance" principle a "Band-Aid" that heals evil beings? or a Religious placebo having no spiritual effect on the "evil actions of individuals"? However, this doctrine of "repentance" is legislated through Christian Religious tenets as a spiritual conscious and subconscious remedy; to construct a personal reminder to this" evil perpetrator", that as a Christian they will be pardoned and reinstated as viable

Christian's once more, after their evil activity. However, a conflicting *imagined concept regarding the e*limination of the Christian doctrine of "repentance" could and would possibly be an inducement or motivation, to eradicate the *"transcendental spiritual psychological crutch"*, that enables evil Christian "transgressor's" to rely upon, before and after their *evil activity against innocent bystanders and beings concludes! Notwithstanding, be mindful* that a idiosyncratic *accentuation in most* Religious societies is the construction and framework of *moral established practices; therefore, the Christian "repentance" tenet is indeed a valued creed*, that *provides, delivers, and arrange* its' follower's a *renewed and revived* testament, "that their evil actions conducted towards others will be forgiven through their *Christian repentance canon of faith"*. Thusly, after their repentance they have qualified for the *"pure and glorious" Everlasting Life* after death and *Ascent into Heaven.*

The example of the story of "Job's" struggle against evilness (Satan) in the Judeo-Christian canon, exemplifies and substantiates the rigorous spirit, power, and constructural guidelines indoctrinated in the Christian faith and existence of "God". Consequently, the "tests of all tests" against evilness toward mankind is illustrated in the Biblical Chapter of "The Book of Job". However, this "test of all tests" is conducted between "God" (Goodness) and the "Devil"(Evilness); in "God" telling the "Devil" that "pure" Christian faith in him by his righteous follower's was unwavering, enduring, and incorruptible. The "Devil" (evil) challenged "God's" (goodness), through "God's" follower's and believer's "Job"; who exemplified "the faithful spirit in Christian's, of "God's power and influence over *evilness*; by refuting and repudiating "Satan's" moral degeneracy and decadence imposed on him. However, "Jobs" faith-in-"God's

Christian ethos eliminated "Satan's" sinful and evil transgressions and iniquities against him. Furthermore, "Job's" faith ridden fortitude, courage, and endurance, as witnessed by *"Satan's evilness"* and deceitful hierarchy, forecasted, envisioned, and speculated that "Job's faithful obedience to "God" was a *temporary, fragile, and weak* "divine commitment, that would not endure. However, the Christian Biblical Story in "The Book of Job", emphatically demonstrates "Job's" *substantianable faith in his divine commitment* to the *obedience and righteousness* of *"decency, morality, and goodness over evilness"*; as a principled guideline for all follower's belonging to the *Christian faith*. Lastly, "Job" ascertained the authenticity of his true Christian life's journey by refuting "all" evilness, through his faith in his divine foundational obedience to "God", which dutifully obliterated and nullified the "Satanic" *evilness imposed on him by "Satan".*

Determining "Evil" *Intent* within Earthly Confines

Prior to plunging into the subject matter of "determining and identifying evil (negative) intent", it's imperative to reflect upon "ethics of character (honor and integrity), and ethics of accountability and commitment". Ancient Global civilizations structured ethics of morality, as their calculations for what is praiseworthy and, as their quintessential concern for the construct of responsible moral ethics of obligations and duties. Nonetheless, ethics of duties and obligations focused essentially on natural and routine procedures that accord basic principles to society (persons) challenged with extensive activities of behavior, such as compassion, lawfulness, and care. Therefore, the ideal model characters were those in society who displayed compassion, love, fidelity, lawfulness, care, and kindness; Naturally, the aforementioned morally ethical characters established the social guidelines, that qualified the "ideal moral characters" in Ancient and Earlier societies throughout the globe.

Determining evil intent within Earthly confines requires a cognitive and swift comprehensive "intuition" of one's motives, actions, dispositions, habits, and external physical intent, that must be consciously acknowledged through moral patterns of intuitive, spontaneous, and natural virtues that instinctively opposes one's moral harmony.

Evilness opposes moral harmony and spiritual procurement through its opposing vibes, that contradicts ethical guidelines of cosmic and natural law. Essentially, natural law constitutes the characteristics of people that's reflected in body language and structural physical anatomy; which is the fundamental morphology of reality in observational intuition with human nature, and nature itself. However, the "science of deception" cannot always be measured by the characteristics of mankind or circumstances, through the human possession of procured guidelines of moral virtues and spiritual heart-felt vibes or atmospheric cadence, tempo, or articulation. A colloquial interpretation of determining "the right response, action, or procedure to adopt or interpret when confronted with "evil" situations or circumstances would be to intuitively search within the natural spiritual soul that immediately transmits and translates a heartfelt communication of conscious or subconscious opposition to the situation or circumstance at hand; that immediately contradicts "the natural order of our moral and cognitive clarity". Most importantly, by conceiving the cognitive and spiritual intuition of "intent encroachment" imposed from other beings to self; it's imperative, critical, and compulsory to distinguish between positive and negative natural life forces; even if one has to relinquish an immediate response, to the back-pedalling (execution) afforded by "time accountability". Notably, only intelligent and mature minds (common-sense) breeds mindful experience or precedent to capitalize on daily experiences confronting us over time, rendering self reflective direction to measure one's continuous "cultivating and perceptive" experiences in life's multiplicity of encounters with self (excluding those with a lesser contradiction in life's experiences). Thusly, cultivating and expanding a newly innovative thinkingness cited as the *"deciphering mode utility"*, which emanates from our genetic or inherited birthright, to interpret and decipher categorical experiences within consciousness, recognition, and through interpretive analysis of situational and circumstantial identities of life's encounters. The *"deciphering mode utility"* is merely an *"intrinsic support element"* conjoined with ones *"cerebral capacity to decipher"* evil intent, through ones cognitive utilization of the *ethics of virtue*, which is *directed* from the *ethics of obligation* and ultimately *reflection*. Notably, the "deciphering mode utility" *postulates* and *assumes* that our deciphering mentality detects *"evil intent"* versus *"goodness, honesty, and integrity* through one's *cognitive* interpretation, which *fosters* judicious, logical, accurate and conclusive evaluation between deciphering *"evil intent vs. integrity"*. However, *contradictions* to the "deciphering mode utility", which may fog one's cognitive cerebral postulations that manifest its utility between both agents in situations and circumstances can involve cultural, personality, language and religious differences that fogs cognitive utilization of one's "cerebral capacity to decipher" judgemental accuracy, in putting the correct pieces to the puzzle or, to one's "intent forecast" is not always accurate ! Noteworthy, whatever *cognitive sightlessness* is involved with distinguishing one's intent mechanisms that may not prevail within the interpretation of transcending experiences or circumstances to decipher between "good" intent and "evil", however, requires the necessary understanding that the ongoing cultivation of ethics of virtue is challenging.

Is Morality Decreed From Sacred Religious Directive?
Or
(Is Morality Based On Inner Deistic
Metaphysical Designs)?

Socrates question to Euthyphro in Plato's Dialogue to Euthyphro is stated as follows: "Is something right because "God" commands it, or does he command it because it is right? The Socratic *approach* to this ancient dialogue between Socrates and Euthyphro presents both moral dilemma, and ethical dilemma. Therefore, within their abstruse dialogue one identifies this polysemous (ambiguous) encounter as reflecting esoteric ramifications, due to both Socrates and Euthyphro's exclusive and distinctive subjective reflectivity regarding "God's" divine command; which qualifies both individuals as being incoherent to their encountered dialogue, due to their subjective (internal, or individual reality) non factual answer, by questioning "God's" "command that right is right because Divinity commands it, or is it commanded because it is right"? Socrate's scheming approach to this questionable debate aforementioned was cognitively processed through his elenchus (refutational) debate apparatus; therefore, he perceived that the question put forth in this dialogue could not be answered forthright because it required solid facts (objective certainty).

However, giving rise to his dialectical and controversial subject matter at hand in his encounter with Euthyphro, confirms his ideology and concept that "truth" must be pursued by modifying (reshaping) one's intellectual status through engagement with opposing ideology. Notably, this encounter is the "truth" being pursued as opposed to being discovered! Thusly, defining and symbolizing the "Socratic thought process" through the unanswerable question posed to "God's" command... The initial Socratic perception reflects in his abiding belief in a supernatural commander of Universal construction which was created through divinity; otherwise his confrontation with Euthyphro would be nonessential and worthless dialogue. Both Socrates and Euthyphro subconsciously or consciously postulate that their status as thinker's was characterized through "God's" command; which also characterizes "Socratic thought" through "God's" command; or/and that "God" commands the righteous framework within his Universal designs. Therefore, "God's" commands in Socratic thought, establishes and consecrates "right from evil"; However, an unproven Religious concept and command from Deistic tenets is cryptic (hidden, secret and obscure in meaning to mortals). Importantly, Christian believer's (as in most Judeo-Christian Religions) "must walk by faith, and not by sight", which substantiates their perceptive cognition, as opposed to earthly bound objective facts regarding a "God in Heaven", and his commands and doctrines.

The Western concept of Socrates debate with Euthyphro, is indeed Socratic in nature, in that it is conceived as an infinite or ongoing encounter "process", because the aforementioned questions in title, can only be answered by "God" in Heaven; and not by Socrates on Earth; Thusly, only within his earthly realm of imagination and cognitive scope, or compass he can speculate (a totally subjective conjecture). Nonetheless, Socrates application of dialogue exchanges in *debate encounters* labeled him a "sophist", or a philosophical thinker who was notorious for his cleaver pedagogue and specious debate encounters. Furthermore, he is alleged to have literally dissected, dismantled, and destroyed "all questions brought forth in encountering debates with others, and leaving know argumental alternatives for his opponents to resolve compatible, or in harmony with him; however, he depleted, twisted, and exhausted debating opponents ideas and inquiry in his numerous debates; therefore, labeling him a "sophist". A "sophist" is defined as one who is unconcerned with physical or metaphysical questions. Notably, Socrates primary interests was ethics, "living a good life". Importantly, Socrates established a definitive declaration on virtue or (arete), exclaiming "that virtue is knowledge". If one knows good, one will always do good; notwithstanding, if anyone commits *"evil"* are does anything wrong, assumingly they don't know the difference between *good and evil*. Quite possibly, this supports his debasing of opponents encounters with him, by challenging their "moral viewpoints". Consequently, Socrates alleges, that if human beings conceive the wrong ideology about "morality, love, and virtue, or any other ethical ideal, they can't possibly be trustworthy in society, and are subject to do *"evil"* deeds against others.

Lastly, aforementioned is Socrates essential *"cognitive reflective concentration,"* which is arte, translate as virtue (omitting the accent over the "e"), which signifies "living the good life, love, morality, and virtue "; which is directly connected, associated, and allied with "goodness" as opposed to "living an "evil life". Additionally, "God's" doctrines in the "Biblical Stories in the Bible" old and new testaments, commands that "living a positive and loving life" represents the ultimate human goodness, existence, and sacrifice, that "God" in "Heaven Gave His Only Begotten Son" on earth; which associates, identifies and allies with *Socratic paradox*, as opposed to "Plato's" creative perception. Furthermore, in Socrates assertion that "virtue is knowledge" reflects that knowledge breeds informational order, assets, quality of life, valued ethics, and *"goodness over evil"; qualifies and strongly depicts the caliber of supernatural powers that equates with "God's" principled commands to his Christian follower's.* Consequently, in reflecting subjective metaphoric vision, Socrates was designed in "God's" plans as his disciple, cohort, and zealot, through his foundational place in his history of ideas. The *Socratic Paradox's* was designed in "God's" plans, as opposed to "God's" tenets being designed in Socrates plans. Otherwise, Socrates would have answered the questions in "title", without questioning "God's" supreme guidance; which would nullify his question of "God's" command of "Right's" positional order: "Is something right because "God" commands it, or does he command it because it's right? By asking the question acknowledges Socrates intrinsic inferiority to the tenets of Religious doctrine and to" God".

CHAPTER XIV

Examining "Frantz Fanon's" The Wretched of the Earth

(Reflective Analysis, Examination, and Interpretation By: William F. Williams)

This prophetic psychiatrist, psychoanalyst, and political, social, and cultural philosopher; Franz Fanon, awakened the consciousness of those who defied his perceptual "Einstein", which was the right to illustrate the systematic mental, social, spiritual, cultural, and psychological damage imposed on mankind through greed and oppression. Antithetically, for the oppressed, colonized, and enslaved mentalities of the World, his message enabled a change in spiritual, cultural, social, economic, and political conscious and subconscious insight of past, present, and future transgressions, ruptures, and breaches of human dignity they were denied; which resulted from systematic socially generated neuroses; which was established by their oppressor's to restructure their ethnic nature; and systematically countered their human development to function naturally, productively, and sustainably as human beings. "*Fanon's, brilliant writings and mental reflections concerning colonial domination and oppression of human beings emerged and derived from his academic educational psychiatric eminence, development, and enlightenment*"; *to explain his concept of oppression imposed upon human beings;* however, functionally and foundationally, in the interest of the international and *national liberation of colonized* and *conquered peoples, of which he experienced personally as well.*

Fanons formal training began in his native homeland of Martinique (colonized by the French), and subsequently in France. During World War II he served in the French Army; and thereafter, obtained his medical degree in psychiatry at the University of Lyon. After graduating from the University, he was appointed between 1953-1956 as head of the psychiatry administration of Blida-Joinville hospital in Algeria, which was then a colony of France during that era. Additionally, while in Algeria *Fanon* unified with the Algerian Liberation Crusade in 1954-1961 (approximately), and shortly thereafter became editor of its newspaper *El Moudjahid*, in *Tunis.*

France's colonization of Algeria was from 1830-1962. Furthermore, the initial occupation of Algeria was designed to enhance the declining prestige of the French Monarchy. France owed Algeria the repayment of an outstanding debt in 1827 (approximately), which instigated a question and answer debate between Dey Hussein and the French Consul regarding payment of the debt; that led to Hussein hitting the French Consul "three times with his fly whisk in the face", resulting in France setting up a three year blockade against Algeria regarding this insult to France. Thereafter, French occupation and full invasion of Algeria commenced in 1830, which overthrew Algerian rulership, and was replaced by French rule; however, the remainder of Algerian land that wasn't occupied by French rule was annexed in 1834. Noteworthy, during "Franz Fanon's" medical training at the University of Lyon, he attended philosophy lectures by "Merleau-Ponty", and read "Sartre's" works extensively. He wrote plays and rendered eminent lectures to student societies on "surrealism" and "poetry"; while editing a magazine titled *"Tam-Tam"*. Notwithstanding, throughout his many aforementioned outside interests, he managed to graduate from the University of Lyon in the field of psychiatry in 1951.

Fanon's cognitive rational involving behavioral oppressed methodology and stratagem used by the oppressor's, to dehumanize the oppressed, is reflected, calculated, *identified* and *defined* through Fanon's correlation of *personal experiences* as a Black Man residing in Martinique, France, and Algeria; which is *substantiated* through his medical and psychiatric training. However, Fanon's authoritative academic clinical experiences, and understanding of social, ethnic, ethic, and *neurotic oppressive behavior imposed upon the colonized oppressed;* justifies his urging of colonized peoples to purge themselves of their oppressed state of degradation, through a collective catharsis to achieve their objectives of overthrowing their oppressor's torment, through any means necessary.

Fanon laments the intrinsic systematic application of racism that's both blatant and latent in its meticulous colonial application, that's designed to suck the life out of dependent colonalized souls (oppressed people). A poor harvest due to weather conditions, or an untimely colonial situation such as Black on Black crimes, which results ultimately in blatant disciplinary actions conducted by the oppressor's, to "remind the natives (as regards the oppressed in name and title by their oppressor's) of their expected conduct"; especially when it applies to the economy, or their medical inability to work, which is essentially crucial to the oppressor's economic success. Quite frankly, Fanon expressed many cultural stereotypes that's implanted over the course of time within the consciousness of the oppressed; which characterizes his definition and meaning of "Negrophobe", or Black hatred, suspension, and fear of one another, complexion superiority and inferiority between Blacks, that he personally encountered in his native country of Martinique. Additionally, he argues that both the inferiority and superiority complexes between master and slave respectively, has imprisoned both of them within the core of their superficial belief's. One characteristic is to behave properly as expected, which maintains the inferior oppressed status, which appeases, pacifies, and baby-sits, the oppressor's high brow emotional state of qualifying his unprincipled directives handed down from generation to generation to control, maintenance, and substantiate racism. However, the latent emotional state aforementioned is the oppressor's surreal gratification of the rewards after the successful harvest that yields profits. Thusly, evolving in his "dream world" a fortress that breeds racial contempt for any and all oppressed souls. Thereafter, he emerges victorious after the successful harvest conducted through a make belief paradigm, that "babysits his bewildered consciousness," that conflicts and rivals his habitually inherited heredity of contempt against "blackness, poverty, and black family cultural and community unification amongst his oppressed subjects"; which equates with racial degradation.

Frantz Fanon referenced in one of his clinical medical practices, in *France, which* sponsored a trial and error theory, to comprehend an understanding of her colonized subjects, notably the Algerians. Consequently, through conducting a "cross-cultural" psychiatric clinical experience involving newly arrived immigrant's to France. He denotes that their experiences reflected a variety of analytical discourses systematically structured ranging from "climatic theories of epidemiology, to theories pertaining to psycho-social evolution, that disclosed the Caucasian race as the "reincarnation of a higher civilization".[2] During this "cross-cultural" clinical experience, Fanon's essential argument at the conclusion of this clinical session was that this *"School of Psychiatric Medicine"*, completely ignored the reality of colonialism, and its dogmatic psychological effect it has on the personality, and character of colonized subjects. Furthermore, he immediately referred to the colonized "inferiority complexes" of the Martinican's, and the similar colonized "North African" syndrome; which he identified as a "neurotic structure created by the colonizer's within their reconstructive principles, by promoting colonial servility through the calculated "art form" of mind control. However, initiated and designed through centuries of systematic mental applications, and conceivably through various *energies pertaining to* mental and physical persuasions. Thusly, the total objective demands of the colonizer's is *"profits"*, *sustained* through competitive, and challenging colonized workforces in human form; who has endured a "neurotic and impersonal concept" that must appease or "baby-sit" the colonizer's financial and social consciousness. However, success is clocked within a temporary or seasonal harvesting exhibition that determines the success or failure of both victims, which entails duty relegated to the colonized (inferior), and delegated by the colonizer's (superior), with both enslaved mentalities mastering the concepts of freedom, through one being physical and mentally distorted (slave's), and the other's economic, social, and neurotic mental patient's (slavemaster's); through their cultural manifestation of a neurotic historical creation: insane *colonialism, which qualifies the word "freedom"; which evolves through the oppressor's definitive historical exercised inate neurotic inherited and habitually designed consciousnessness, and latent subconsciousness; through the advent of systematized genocide upon human beings.*

Fanon utilized his and other's (patient's) experiences, conjoined with his medical scholarship to eloquently promote and authenticate his conceptual theory that "racism procreates and breeds" latent and blatant psychologically damage of *sense impressions*, that equally limits the colonized and enslaved people by damaging their unrestricted and cognitive prowess ability to comprehend the "Universe", or "World", which has alienated one's consciousness, spirit, and independence to the World's 'insurmountable, achievable, and attainable offerings of human dignity. Furthermore, regarding Fanon's political, social, and economic outcry against colonialism, he reexamines and analyses the causes and effects of the *negative impacted culturally adverse languages that negatively* affects colonized people.

Fanon alleges that to speak a language... implies above all to *assume a culture,* and to support the *weight of that civilization.* African Martiniquan's, Arab Algerian's, or any colonialized people who speak French, Spanish, Dutch, or other colonized foreign languages, implies that they are lawfully and culturally accepting this language, or *is coerced into accepting the collective consciousness* of the languages foreign cultural nature. Therefore, Fanon's analytic example utilizes the French languages cultural definition of "Blackness" as a correlating word within French culture as meaning "Evil". Contrastingly, in most African languages and cultures, "Blackness" represents a Universal affinity with African cultural civilizations, and its meanings and definitions represents "Attractiveness, Beauty, Strength, and Benevolents...etc". However, after 15th century colonization and globalization of Africa's forced migration, and colonization; the contradictions imposed was "linguistic imperialism"; upon African peoples. Consequently, the transformation of cultural exchange manipulations (slavery and colonization) resulted in the duality of languages, definitions, and cultures. Example, French colonizer's in Martinique imposed its "demonstration of power" through the French language, which was the dominant language; which manifested the "pigeon language" spoken (creating language duality, African dialects mixed with the dominant language of French). Therefore, when duality of languages transpires, it embraces duality of cultures, people, and their superficial virtue ethics of not "being of the World". Notably, the impact of globalization and language continuity, spirit, and energy, would be counter-productive without the appeal to the relocation of populations, or dominate powers colonizing imposition(s) upon civilizations... Unfortunately, one cannot define sensibly globalization without connecting or attaching it to "colonization" or articulate how the latter would proceed. Notably, ontologically (the nature of existence), which presents the "new dynamics of colonial cultural competition, which would ensue selective habitual components that evolves an artificial "nature" maintenance. To enhance economic industrial productivity, which propose differential evolution, regards in essence of the creation and vitality of "how to make and reproduce a slave and slavemaster, through an artificially structured presence of existence; while being identified as, being's amongst being's (human beings); while establishing their artificially inclined cultural World reality of self. Furthermore, Fanon synthesize, and psychoanalyze the two words "Black and Evil", and fosters the acclimation that the "Blackman colonized, restructured, mentally and physically confused consciously, as to his approach to his newly acquired duality of persona, while slowly amalgamating into a Frenchman, or colonized subject. However, continually manifesting African or Arabic residual characteristics. Consequently, to his bewildering transformation of becoming captive by both World's; or most drastically, conceives of himself a universal subject equally participating in a society, that he fails to conceive or internalize its blatant and latently advocation of a whole person from his personal appearance, (which is his Blackness, that momentarily escapes his cognitive, intellectual, and rational consciousness, until he's deliberately reminded, due to prioritized circumstantial social predicaments) due to his deceived mental state, which is artificially, and perceptively emersed through valid amalgamation and disrespected identity, which displays his powerless hereditary existence, which foster his symbolic detrimental, perpetual and coercerced desire to qualify himself, through socially structured common sense ideology to continually impress his transparent oppressor, while serving his starving vanity, that nurtures his illegitimate "World View" of his reality, and experience of the painless injection of the oppressive novacaine in his soul.

However, cultural values are internalized from acquisition (age) into consciousness, which creates a basic disjuncture between/from the colonized Blackmans image of self, consciousness, and physical body. "[3] Fanon surmises, regarding the aforementioned conditional transformation, that the colonized and/or enslaved Blackman (African) is foreign to his traditional cultural (African) mind, body, spirit, and soul; as long as he sleeps on this tragic colonized transformation.

It's historically alleged by historiographer's that a Kenyan writer, Ngugi wa Thiong'o, began a very successful career as a writer, by utilizing the "English language"; prior to writing in his ethnic culture of "Kikuyu". However, in his 1986 publishing *"Decolonizing the Mind"*, it was alleged to be his farewell to writing in the English language. Notably, Ngugi is alleged to have characterized language "as a way people have described the World, through understanding themselves". Again, its alleged that he reflects that "the English language utilized in Africa through publications, *"is a cultural-bomb, that perpetuates a process of erasing memories of pre-colonial cultures and history, and is a means of installing the dominance of newly structured insidious forms of colonialism". [4]* Comparably, this theory correlates with "Frantz Fanon's perceptive reflection that "language and culture" are inseparable; therefore, the absence of the former is the absence of the latter". Our second example that correlates with Fanon's concept of "linguistic imperialism", that is a vital apparatus in dominating and implementing colonialism; which is through enforced control of civilizations. Noteworthy, the African slaves and Native American's dehumanizing experiences in the Americas exemplifies how languages, civilizations and globalization unify colonialization. The African's and American Indian's were both afflicted with identity theft, memory lost, rituals and religious abolishments, which caused cultures to be uprooted, and weeded out. Historically, strict law enforcement engaged their cultural languages to be eradicated. The abandonment of Native American's "native tongues" by the American legislation, before and after American independence to England, explains the correlating importance of language and cultural identity. However, African's brought to the shores of the Americas, were stripped of their human rights of their ethnic languages, rituals and cultural identity, which fostered a capricious cultural amalgamation destined for ethnic reclassification and an unworthy identity branded as "slave" and "nigger". Notwithstanding, the English language in the Americas has been the extended tongue supporting "colonial conquest and discovery, racial cruelty, and mentally neurotic behavior exhibited by both the colonizer's, colonized, and enslaved; due to cultural impositions executed by the colonizer's and slave master's, which manifest neurotic behavior of conquered cultures against their cultural identity and validity. However, with the expulsion of cultural languages, colonization would continually encumber the advent of "linguistic imperialism". Therefore, aspects or visible features of the dominant cultures are inevitably transferred along with the languages in colonizing cultures; which demonstrates sheer "Power". Example, if Yoruba's enslaved Yoruba's, colonialism would be recognized as imperialistic, but without linguistic identity. However, linguistic Imperialism identifies with memory loss of language and cultural self.

Importantly, "Fanon" emphasizes *language* as one of many entities that establishes successful "Military Campaigns", which champions and cultivates colonizations, and imperialistic dominance; which explains the Western Empires *"World View"* of her past, present, and future colonized Universe. However, in Fanon's *Wretched of the Earth analysis, the book is designed to implement the "tools" necessary to dislodge the yoke or bondage, servility, and oppression* of colonization, by instructing the colonized and oppressed people of the *World*, that *"they are the only one's capable of cleansing a new dignity, humanity, and destiny"*. Additionally, he beckoned all oppressed people of this Universe to relish a new consciousness of Universality, through the spiritual journey of overcoming the dualistic, or carbon copy of their oppressors, from which they have experienced social, cultural, psychological, economical, physical, and spiritual dichotomy; which has revised and altered the natural order of their cultural nature.

Wretched of the Earth, is considered by many to be one of the most canonical "tools" implemented to over-throw colonizer's, and oppressive regimes, towards the liberation for all oppressed being's. It is written within a "Marxist" framework, by utilizing vibrant, blunt, and candid writing expressions, and personal behavioral genre, that expressly and eloquently characterize the authors African (Black) experience under colonialism. Fanon relates in this published masterpiece his life's experiences in his beloved Martinique, Algeria, and France; however, he forcefully illustrates his medical psychiatric analysis of the torment and systematic destruction, revision, and cultural elimination necessary to control, dominate, and create an artificial human proxy to beckon to "any" cause that's delegated by his oppressor. Noteworthy, we must all be grateful to France's exclusive academic and prestigious "University of Lyon", which enabled Fanon's academic brilliance and humanity to understand the true meaning of humanity versus dehumanization.

References:

John Springfield, *Decolonization since 1945: The Collapse of European Overseas Empires. (New York; Palgrave, 2001).*

Robert Berthelier, *L' Homme Maghrebin dans la Litterature Psychiatrique (Paris: L 'Harmattan, 1994).*

Ngugi wa Thiongo, *Decolonising the Mind: The Politics of Languages in African Literature (NH: Heinemann, 1981).*

Gerald Vizenor, *Manifest Manners: Postindian Warriors of Survivance (Hanover, NH: Wesleyan/ New England UP, 1994)*

CHAPTER XV

A Brief Synopsis of "The Crisis in 21st Century Southern and Northern Sudan"

(Analysis & Personal Interpretation:
By William F. Williams)

Crisis in Sudan

Sudan is the third largest oil producer in Sub-Saharan Africa, following Nigeria and Angola. In 2010 it produced, an estimate 490-500,000 barrels of oil daily. However, most of the oil reserves is geographically located in "Southern Sudan", however, the pipelines extends into Northern Sudan.

In 2005 Northern and Southern Sudan signed a peace accord, which was directed at ending their twenty-plus years Civil War; which cost both Countries a fatality count of over (approx.) two-million lives lost, over the twenty-plus years war between Southern and Northern Sudan ensued.

Sudan gained its independence from joint British-Egyptian rule in 1956; yet, it was United in governance with "Egypt" for political reasons over several years. The Country shares its borders with Egypt, Eritrea, Ethiopia, Kenya, Uganda, D. R. Congo, C.A. Republic, Chad, Libya, and the Red Sea.

The Crisis in Sudan Critique

Southern Sudan's *first civil war* started in *1962*, chronicled by the *"Anya Nya"* guerrilla movement after mutinying by Southern Army Officer's of the *"Dinka"* ethnic civilization. However, the ethnic crisis (clash) is between The Northern Sudan, who are predominantly Arabs, and the Southern Region classified as predominantly African. The conflict commenced over the regional domination of natural resources, which are "oil reserves", and the distribution of revenues from the oil, between the Northern and Southern regions ethnic groups of Sudan. Notably, the four distinct reasons that perpetuates this crisis is based on geography, economics, ethnicity, and politics. Additionally, there are three resourceful areas or geographical locations that both the North and South rival; which are the Abyei, Blue Nile States, and the South Kordofan/Nuba Mountains. The Abyei, and Kordofan/Nuba mountains has an enormous abundance of rich oil deposits. However, the Blue Nile State pose a politically divided populous, whereas one equally divided people supports Southern Sudan's (SPML), and the other populous divide supports Northern Sudan's "Arab" front. Yet, the "Nuba Mountains" is occupied by both Southern Sudan's African Tribes, and Northern Sudanese Arab's in the Southern Kordofan State.

Ironically, Abyei which is located in the North politically and culturally allied with Southern Sudan, due to its enormous Southern Sudan populated ethnic tribe, the Ngok African Dinka. Notably, during the Northern and Southern Sudan crisis they fought with the "SPLA", against the Northern Sudan Arab's. Therefore, this Sudan conflict is directly linked exclusively between "who emerges victorious" economically; through dominating the natural oil resources; which will grant the subjugator political "Power" and leverage to control both the Northern and Southern geographical areas; Furthermore, "whomever between the two areas (North or South), that emerge victorious in their unpredictable crisis will become the masters of *Sudan's international negotiable trade of oil* resources; and which would ultimately grant the *victor's economical control* of Sudan's oil export revenues. Therefore, the Sudan crisis can be sum-totaled as an economical, political, geographical and "Power" confrontation between these two countries or civilizations, delineated in a nutshell between African's and Arab's.

The oil reserves wealth sharing negotiations between the two Northern and Southern Sudanese countries is crucial, as to them constituting a structural negotiable, compatible, and agreeable economic package enacted, and dispersed from oil revenues between both countries, within an equitable framework. The constrained and constricting issues of the two countries is finding an equitable economic "oil reserve" distribution resolution; which is stifled by North and South Sudan's infrastructural asset accountability, which includes external debts owed, and internal financial asset mismanagement. Furthermore, the utilization of water from the "Blue Nile", must be equitable negotiated to accommodate their oil reserve industrial production. Notably, The whole of Sudan's oil reserves accountability is estimated to exceed 80% of its accumulated income; however, the majority of Sudan's oil reserves are geographically located in the Southern regions of Sudan. Another qualifying "uncompliant issue" for these two adjoined countries attributes to their incapacity to find a solution to settle the demarcation borderlines unity states; between the Southern Sudan region, and Northern Sudan's southern geography; which includes Kordofan States agreed mandate, which includes Darfur, Nubian's far north area, and Beja to the east. Therefore, the crux of land or border control by the two countries regarding the distribution of oil is another crucial factor that must be resolved, to establish a viable and profitable oil industry that will benefit both countries future development.

A territorial resolution was drafted called "The Compromised Peace Agreement" conducted and negotiated in 2005. Thusly, regarded as a referendum or popular consultation. This negotiation was designed for the three aforementioned "oil rich" designated areas negotiator's to choose which sides they want to represent between Northern and Southern Sudan; Consequently, this referendum has instigated belligerence, as opposed to peace, and an equitable "compromise" between North and South Sudan. One dire reason of an *"unnegotiable compromise" between the two countries* derives from "Northern Sudan's (Arab's) President Al-Basir", who dishonored the Compromise Agreement; and seems determined to repossess the unresolved prime oil reserve territories; seemingly, to preserve his "political, economical, social, and Arab pride" for Northern Sudan.

Notwithstanding, the bitter attacks upon Southern Sudan's Darfur region is "speculated to be governmentally sanctioned, and commissioned by Al-Basir's governance. It's alleged that he utilized a militia stationed in Southern rural Sudan, which is populated by African (Dinka's, Acholi's, Masi's, Nuer's, sub group's etc...) citizens, in their constitutionally sovereign Nation of Southern Sudan, to wage a military crisis against them. Al-Basir's militia was composed primarily of Arab pastoral tribes, namely the "Messiria or Misseriya", globally known as the "Janjawiid".

It's further alleged that this militia army of pastoral Arab's terrorized the "Darfur regions, communities and citizens" in Southern Sudan. In reprisal, the SPLA from Southern Sudan (Sudan's People's Liberation Army), from Darfur organized to fight all aggressors against them, which included the "Janjawiid", who are the alleged Northern Sudan's government sanctioned militia, which is accused of murder, rape, and other imposing crimes upon Darfur Citizens. Notably, the SPLA, is alleged to have been organized and structured by *the Dinka African Leader, "Salva Kiir Mayardit",* in 1991, to defend Southern Sudan's citizens. In November 1991, the "Bor Massacre's" ensued against the South Sudan citizens, which estimates that approximately 100,000 people bolted the region, following the unlawful genocide upon them by the Arab's. Unfortunately, famine followed after the massacre in the predominantly "Dinka" community in Southern Sudan. The alleged Al-Basir sanctioned Northern Sudan government attacks in Southern Sudan, clearly reflects "his schizophrenic intent, which" reflects, "that at the same time "Al-Basir" was calling for peace and brotherly reconciliation between the two countries towards a peaceful, and progressive solution", he was sanctioning his "Janjawiid" pastoral militia to terrorize Southern Sudan.

Britain was prepared to ignore its historical responsibility for creating this dreadful Sudan situation? Also, is the international community going to continue to be bystander's to this perpetual genocide occurring in Southern Sudan, at the hands of Al-Basir? Or will this Sudan crisis equate with Rwanda's terrible misfortune, while her Belgium colonizers watch millions of "Tutsi's fall victim to genocidal massacres?

The Government of Northern Sudan

The Sudanese (Arab) government is accountable for this massive genocide, political confusion, and economic stagnation that's occurring in the whole of Sudan. The North's unmanageable political administration is ill-prepared to function adequately, as leaders in this matter of oil reserve monetary distribution, and territory resolve for an equitable settlement persists, between these two adjoining countries attempting their lucid objectives, which breeds economical contempt. One primary consideration for an inadequate proposal concerning this matter of business rest in the balance with Northern Sudan; however, greed, selfishness, and a selective ethnic arrogance, is the culprit widening the political, economic, and social divide towards an equitable resolution between North and South Sudan. Additionally, the accountability of Sudan's government construction and operational designs, does not correlate with administrative mechanisms for a peaceful resolution to this matter; relative to its aggressive militia activities in the destruction and genocidal tactics used against Southern Sudan's oil rich territories, and people. Example, Northern Sudan's administration displayed national government insecurity, and a disconnect, to this vital issue, through their detachment and lack of implementation of the CPA (Comprehensive Peace Agreement, of 2005); which was relegated to end the crisis denoted as the 2nd civil war, between the Northern Sudan Government and the SPLM/A. However, Northern governmental sanctions against the Southern Sudanese increased, and obviously, created compounded instability and missed progressive opportunities for the vital oil reserves regional border states, that's most important for industrialization of oil production to both countries. Furthermore, Southern Sudan's disenfranchised Government or Government of National Unity, isn't financially prepared to support its' border states vital oil reserve regions; which is greatly affected between this tug-of-war, or crisis between Northern and Southern Sudan. However, presently (21st century), both countries, and especially Southern Sudan's socio-economic context is fragile with both state and local incapacities, to acclimate border regions governance issues, of establishing even a micro infrastructure regional facility towards oil productivity and economic distribution, between both countries. Therefore, the "big picture", of an accord or compromise of reconcile, reflects a diverse identity within a framework of cooperation, and mutual legislative respect between the North and South Sudan, as written and forecasted by the drafter's of the CPA; which temporarily ended the infamous 2nd civil crisis in 2005. Reflective hindsight acknowledges that the "intent" of the North did not dignify "any" peaceful, or equitable resolution within their leadership, or in their commitment to this Sudan crisis.

African Union

The African Union's dual negotiating role in this Sudan "holocaust" requires a responsibility of enormous magnitude and resources. Both, the North and South is entangled within a framework of corporate enterprise; while the African Union is desperately trying to untangle this "global tragedy". All the while, the Southern Sudanese people are tragically striving to bring forth a viable independent, and stable infrastructure accountable towards a sustainable sovereignty; Notwithstanding, the Northern Sudan leadership comprehends Southern Sudan's strife, with alarming historical strategic (Arab), and cognitive manipulative assertive legislative brilliance, "that Southern Sudan's uphill National progress towards its goals, which equates with "oil reserve sharing", is between the two; thusly, the North is determined to "wean, as opposed to nurture" its contestant (South Sudan) from an equitable economic "oil reserve payroll", through equitable monetary distributions from oil productivity; however, they are actually in dire fear of a future competitive adversary in the South of Sudan. Therefore, the aforementioned interpretation of Northern Sudan's governance, is "keep the South down, as long as possible, and keep them kneeling, and don't allow them to stand –on – their- two – feet !" Consequently, The African Union's determination, observation, and resolve of this matter has witnessed massive murders, rapes, and extreme chaos, in their efforts to untangle Northern aggression; and Southern retaliation, between an "old historically established Arab culture, and an unestablished historical Southern Sudan African ethnic culture"; however, the South's purposeful goal is to establish an oil producing conglomerate, within its newly independent Nation of Southern Sudan.

The African Union initially fielded and estimated 7,000 troops to patrol (cover) the vast continent of Africa, as peacekeeper's. Notably, in 2007 the U. N. Security Council unanimously adopted a resolution authorizing a joint United Nation's and African Union peacekeeping forces of 26,000 troops to Western Sudan, or precisely the Darfur, Sudan region. Yet, in June 2008, only an estimate of 10,000 peacekeeper's had been deployed. However, the factors contributing to the reluctance of the International Community to supply the necessary equipment correlating with the deployed troops utility and requirements, was deliberately stifled and suppressed by Northern Sudan's deterrent tactics as follows: damaged roads, unclean water, and inadequate facilities to house the peacekeeper's etc... Therefore, these calculating tactics by Northern Sudan, created limited troop accommodations, which prevented the troop's from stopping the genocide conducted by the ("Janjawiid"s, and Northern Sudan, which occurred in Darfur, and killing an estimated 2,000 innocent citizen's. Unfortunately, the African Union's "command authorization" decreed to its' peacekeeper's to monitor "all activity", negative or positive only! As opposed to protecting inflicted and abused citizens, in the Darfur regions of Sudan. Additionally, this legislative decree to the African Union Troop's, "to monitor instead of protecting citizen's", reflected a grave irresponsible, negligent, and incapacitated intelligence administered by the African Union's and United Nation's leadership, within the framework of policing African's global abuses, genocides, and lawlessness.

References:

http://al-Jazeera.net(accessed) (06/07/2011)

http://arabic.al-jazeerz.net

http://www.sudantribune.com/

Huntington, Samuel P. "*The Clash of Civilization*" Foreign Affairs. 72, no 3 1993.

Kuich, Bonifacto Taban. Sudan Tribune.

Mueller, John. *The Banality of Ethic War.* Vol. 25, Issue 1 2000.

Reilly, Benjamin. (2001) *Democracy, Ethnic Fragmentation, and Internal Conflict.* Vol.25, Issue 3 International Security and Counter Terrorism Reference Center.

Tarrosy, Istvan, et. Al. (2011). *The African State in a Changing Global Context: Breakdown and Transformation.* (New Jersey: Transaction Publishers)1

CHAPTER XVI

Americas Compact Designs of the Primary Crime Data Systems UCR / NIBRS and NCV'S

(Critique Histojectic Analysis, By: William F. Williams)

The two primary crime data source systems in America are the UCR/NIBRS and NCV'S; whereby national crime data statistics is collected, analyzed, and presented to numerous security agencies, for the purpose of tracking crime trends, and gaining a close forbearing of what way or manner, these crimes impact America; and the Global communities. Each of these data sources serve as unique methodological procedures for implementations and operational utilization. The two primary elements most beneficial and detrimental to this operation is the overall *collection and processing* of objective *"statistical criminal data"*. Notably, the brevity UCR, represents the "Uniform Crime Report", the NIBRS, represents the "National Incident Based Reporting System", and the "NCV'S, represents the "National Crime Victimization Survey" respectively.

The UCR's primary objective is to generate a reliable set or confirmed criminal data statistics for "law enforcement administrations, operations, and management. Notably, its crime data sources over the years has become one of America's, and the Global Communities leading crime, and social indicators. Its' indicators scope the capacity, accuracy, and data (information) on variation, fluctuation, and constancy regarding the "levels or grade of crimes", accessible to criminologist's, sociologist's, legislator's, municipal planner's, the media, and numerous criminal justice affiliates, and the International justice systems, for their utilization of statistical data for research and civil or municipal planning purposes. These two formable primary crime data sources, "also receive annually, The Federal Bureau of Investigations summation report of crime statistics, which are recorded annually, and reported to "all" or "most", State, City, and Local police department administrations. In response to Law Enforcements needs for more flexibility concerning comprehensive, and concrete data sources, the UCR administration developed the (NIBR) or "National Incident-Based Reporting System. The "NIBR's" operational responsibility is to report comprehensive, and detailed information concerning "all" crime incidents to "Law Enforcement" organizational administration's, crime researchers, government planners, and to the general public. However, the "NIBR" provides a more comprehensible, extensive, and specificity in crime and criminal reporting. However, the UCR Summary Reporting System "collects, analyze, and synthesize the majority of its crime data in the form of "types of criminal behaviors", which are categorized. Furthermore, the NIBR's data system and operation, has a greater ability and range to capture and breakdown data into specific categories, and sub-categories, through the utility of newly structured criminal offensive and defensive word definitions; which represents the advent of a newly enhanced statistical reporting system, that will collect criminal data on each single criminal activity or incident, which includes arrests within allegedly twenty-two (22) criminal categories. Importantly, the significant other that constitutes the primary data systems is the "(NCVS) or "National Crime Victimization Survey". This survey is conducted annually by the "Bureau of Justice Statistics" administration; that provides data on surveyed households that report that "they were inflicted with criminal acts or crimes in their respective households". Additionally, the U.S. Department of Justice "National Crime Victimization Survey's" objective is to estimate the number of unreported crimes nationwide. Consistently, the UCR program detail reported crimes, while both the UCR and NCVS are designated to complement each other as vital criminal data counterparts; within the criminal data system. Also, the UCR administration provides a "reliable" set of criminal justice statistics for the Law enforcement administration, operation, management, and local media sources, as well as to present actual rating statistics of crimes in America, and Globally. Most importantly, the NCVS provides "previously unavailable information concerning crime victims, and offender's, as well as crimes committed, but not reported formally to law enforcement. Incidentally, both aforementioned programs cover forcible rapes, or minor and major abusives, robbery, aggravated assaults, burglary, theft's, and motor vehicle theft's etc... Both crime data systems (UCR and NCVS) employ different and varying methods of defining and categorizing types of criminal offenses against the law; yet, the criminal trend gathering direction or method of acquiring data may differ, but the crime is defined in most instances as the same categorical offense. However, these data system organizations examines the Nations crime problems from different perspectives, as well as global trending and offensive and defensive crimes conducted in different and varying geographical surroundings; Thusly, in many discoveries after investigations of criminal acts, the crime results are not always comparable between data gathering systems. Furthermore, the process of defining types of criminal offenses, coupled with procedural approaches to the exact type of crimes, in many circumstances, can account for variable and fluctuating discrepancies in the results of the type of offense. For example, the "NCVS" includes recorded offenses that's officially reported, and unreported crimes to law enforcement; contrastingly, the UCR program includes "only" crimes reported to the police from their extensive data systems.

Noteworthy, the "NCVS" rates property crimes per 1,000 households; and the "UCR" data system rates property crimes per 1,000 household occupants. Also, the "BJS" data system derives data from the "NCVS", in most causes, and from an overall approximate and speculated ratio of recorded crimes through interviewing, to approximate "types" of crimes mathematically measured from a percentage and proportional annual quota; therefore, the "BJS" are subject to margins of error in their data system; primarily, due to an increase or decrease in local, city, and state population variables. Importantly, the creditable "UCR" data system or program, invariable structures its data on the actual count of offenses reported by law enforcement agencies; Yet, both data systems is "the Nation's two exacting and accountable crime data sources in the United States and Globally, which interacts with Interpol.

The United States breakdown of crime statistics derives from the "Bureau of Justice Statistics", thereafter it plans the annual "National Crime Victimization Survey; and thereafter, from the "Federal Bureau of Investigation", which publishes annual data under its summary stationed "Uniform Crime Reporting" program, and thereafter to its more comprehensive foresighted and motivated "National

Incident-Based Reporting System. Aforementioned, the "(NCVS)" is regarded as the significant other, that constitutes the "primary data systems", which is conducted annually by the "BJS", that provides offensive criminal data on surveyed households that have officially reported offensive criminal offenses against their households, and /or household members. Noteworthy, the "United States Department of Justice National Crime Victimization Survey" *estimates* the number of serious unreported crimes nationwide. The "UCR" program detail and chronicle in their data system "reported" crimes. However, the initial objectives of both the "UCR and "NCVS" were structurally designed to complement each other in their systematic crime data coordination, and sense of administrative direction. The "UCR's" commendable and reliable assemblage, collection, and dissemination of "criminal justice statistics" for law enforcement administration, operation, acknowledgement, and provides statistical fluctuations from ratio-calculated criminal acts per annum in its dutifully assembled. However, the definitive word "fluctuation", denotes criminal offenses speculated annually from past officially accountable offenses, of the same or similar categories within the borders of the U.S.A. However, the "UCR" tallies each criminal incident, but does not maintain information on each and every reported incident. The "NIBRS" reports all incidents to the police, which includes "the characteristics of both victim's and offender's", victim's and offender's relationship, crime's committed, injuries at the incident scenes, weapons used, arrest's made (statistics), and location of the incident's. Notable, the "UCR" does not provide information about simple assaults, such as domestic violence, which is the most numerous and common reported crimes or offenses in America. The "NIBRS" provides information on all simple assaults, which includes domestic violence offenses. However, the "UCR" reports "only" the most serious crimes committed in a single incident; therefore, if both a "murder and rape" offense is inflicted on a victim, only one (1) is reported, not both. The "NIBRS" requires law enforcement officer's to report multiple offenses concerning both the victimized and offender's, which afford criminal researcher's to compare, synthesize, and analyze all multiple criminal offenses.

The forming of the UCR/NIBRS data systems was necessary due to the disparity and variability of sourced criminal offenses data responsibilities aforementioned between the UCR and NIBRS as separate entities; which greatly required information compliant to the criminal justice systems, to maintain public and private criminal statistics on a professional aggregate basis; however, the "UCR and NIBRS formed in 1985. The establishment of the newly innovative "criminal-based National Crime Reporting Data System was managed by the "Federal Bureau of Investigation", which included an "Advisory Policy Board" composed of law enforcement executives assisting in directing and implementing this program in 1985. A contract was awarded to the coordinator's of this program to develop "innovative criminal offensive interpretation to criminal genre characteristics correlating to types of criminal acts, which was complemented by data system elements to redesign this newly conjoined data system. The redesigned data system was revised by adding the following: new definitions of indexed offenses, identifying new types of criminal offenses vital to the indexed data system overlooked in the past, refining all newly structured criminal definitions to correlate with the offenses, developing incident-details with data system elements and merging them with all past "UCR" criminal acts, in order to fulfill the extensive new structured requirements of "incident based criminal reporting; versus, the old outlandish summary reporting formats, that's now newly revised through the merging of "UCR/NIBRS".

Currently, 7,400 law enforcement agencies contribute NIBRS data to the National "UCR" data system program. Also, a newly formulated "handbook" was developed by the "Federal Bureau of Investigation" for acquiring a "Records Management System" (RMS), that's compatible with the "NIBRS". It provides instructions on planning for a system acquisition, and prepared the agency for convergence to the newly innovative system, and to the "UCR/NIBRS". However, further extensive implementations of "NIBRS" is occurring at a pace commensurate with the available resources, cognitive objective reflections, and reconstructed and revised law enforcement agencies limitations of *substandard data,* to professionally improved standards. As of 2007 and beyond, the Federal Bureau of Investigation has certified 31 State's "UCR" programs for "NIBRS" participants. Consequently, the two merging "Crime Data Systems" are continually compacting into one compressed volume of essential "criminal data content" to insure National and International security and safety.

References:

Adapted from Federal Bureau of Investigation. FBI Policy and Guidelines: *http://www.fbi.gov/* (assessed October 21st 2010).

Bureau of Justice Statistics. (July 2000) (updated in February 2001) concerning the effects of the Statistical Crime Analysis and Survey Report 2001.

Kaplan, Abraham. (1964). The Conduct of Inquiry: Methodology for Behavioral Science. (San Francisco: Chandler).

McLaughlin, C. (1999). "Using National Incident-Based Reporting System Data for Strategic Crime Analysis, Journal of Quantitative Criminology.

National Institute of Justice (2004). U. S. Department of Justice Programs. The Research, Development, and Evaluation Agency of the U. S. Department of Justice.

Smalleger, Frank. (2009). Criminology: Today an Integrative Introduction. (New Jersey: Pearson Prentice Hall).

CHAPTER XVII

A Brief Examination of America's "Plea Bargaining" History And "Constitutionality" for Felony Defendants's

(An Exposition: By W. F. Williams)

Research investigation, examination, and exploration of "plea bargaining's" history explains the development, promotion, legal, and economic stimulus of its creation, objectives, and concepts; which is relative to the utility of "plea bargaining" versus a Constitutional-inherent (bred in the American bones) "jury" trial for felony offender's. This analysis examines the vital proponents, components (constituent's), mechanisms (system of governance), and the framework of "plea bargaining's" effects as follows: "the criminal law system, judges, prosecutor's, defense attorney's, and felony defendant's". The plea bargaining concept is engaged as a central unifying ideology within the criminal system of governance; which legally rests on the constitutionality and principles of an indeterminate calculated sentencing structure (measured jurisprudence); which enforce the advent of a newly (21st century) established paradigm (model), that's supportive of a macro economic-political movement, within the Constitution (jurisprudence) of the American Judicial Court System. Consequently, the shift in the legal systems "criminal processing ethics, and procedures is through enforcing the "plea bargain" apparatus and entrapment philosophy within legal boundaries; which has ultimately and effectively designed, shaped, and forged a vanishing "trial by jury", which constitutes approximately ten percent (10%) or less of felony convictions through the Constitutionally decreed "jury system". Naturally, the equation or formulary from one-hundred percent (100%), minus ten percent (10%), equates to exactly ninety-percent (90%) of all felony trials acquiesced through the "plea bargaining" gambit. This swift from Constitutionally designed "trial by jury", to the predominant utility of "plea bargaining" was created primarily to expedite loaded trial calendars of judge's and prosecutor's for the following reasons: maximize successful prosecutions and minimize legal cost; which has elevated the number of African Americans and Hispanic felony convictions; it also solidifies guaranteed convictions; protects snitches(or informers); and liberates the prosecutors optional "plea bargain" deals with the felony defendants, which alleviates overpopulated courts, and lessen overcrowded jails, and prisons, which insures prison space for socially vulnerable low-income felony defendant's.

Therefore, it's presumptuous to surmise that the legal system's process to get as many *guilty* plea's as possible, was conjured, invoked, and formulated by the felony judges, prosecutor's, and defense attorney's; Albeit, the municipalities concurred with the principles of a civic economic monetary solvency "through the plea bargaining" legal felony benefit harvest. Although "plea bargaining" has yet to be sanctioned by the United States *"Constitution"* or through The Philosophy of America, the *"Bill of Rights"*. The legal systems managerial hierarchy ruling class elects to promote an illicit medium, as opposed to lawful and ethical selection, between "legal protective stipulations", such as "jury trials and plea bargaining" as options to all felony defendants, within the scope of the aftermath of either trials convictions, which must equate with incarcerated penalty time spent, on par with the crimes committed through one or the other type criminal process of conviction, or deliberation. Otherwise, as witnessed, the "plea bargaining" criminal process erupts and develop's through an aforementioned multiplicity of unauthorized systematic legal postulations akin to "Human body counts vs. judicial economic cost sustainability, which perpetuates the *primary method* of "plea bargaining", as a legal felony criminal case deposition processing application process in America. Off the cuff, if we equalized the promotion of "jury trials" in the American Legal system, and "plea bargaining", to a fifty-percent stalemate conviction ratio, would corporate America privatize the American' criminal penal institutions further? To be maintained and controlled by wealthy citizens who pooled their money or resources together for the sole purpose of becoming monopolizing authorities over the legal system of government, and U.S. State communities *(through their selective control of who lives in our communities, and who belong there, and who don't; which is based on ethnicity selection, in accordance to the ethnic ratio to criminal activity indictments in America, and these same select private citizen's control and profit from criminal indictments and convictions through the vanishing jury trials. However, this private selective citizen monopoly extends from their penal institutions investment enterprises, to government municipal institutions; and ultimately real estate monopoly in America to decide who should live in what communities; and eventually, they dominate the Global bankrupted Communities and mismanaged impoverished Countries of this World)?*

It's conceivable that "plea bargaining" is a tremendous economical savings to all jurisdictional bureaucratic legal authorities, which alleviates caseload stress on judges and prosecutor's; however, its unconstitutionality enables judges and criminal prosecutor's the "full range of the "guilty plea"; which represents a "felony criminal prosecution" apparatus contraption, to ensnare and entrap both harden, and first- time- felony offenders into the concentration "penal institution" camps that house blatant degradation, and mental disparities; which conflicts with sound and ethical rehabilitation. Especially, for first-time offenders, that could become moral and economic assets to their communities, if given that opportunity to return to their communities ethically correct, with a heightened understanding of their roles within their communities and society.

In 1880-1900, in Middlesex County, Mass., legislative hearings concerning "plea bargaining" through exegesis (reviews) concerning it as a useful means of judicial legislation, became *firmly* normalized in Middlesex County, Mass. Felony court system, in the nineteenth and twentieth (19th and 20th) century; (Fisher, 2003: *Plea Bargaining's Triumph: A History of Plea Bargaining In America*). During this early era concerning "Plea Bargaining's" ontology (philosophy), involving felony convictions and sentencing of criminals through the *Constitution* structured mandate of a *"jury trial", promptly* took a back seat to the *expedited "plea bargaining"* system of sentencing; which resulted in confirmed *"guilty pleas"*, as opposed to long extended and "prolonged "jury trial" preparations, which required added judicial legislative executive labor, resources, and expense. Example, during that early era, if a felony defendant committed a capital offense of murder, and pleaded guilty to the crime, the judges and prosecutor's sanctioned the felony defendant's "guilty plea" of the capital crime, to a lesser type felony, which reduced the sentence of the "death penalty", to a time-extended sentence, as opposed to the legal Constitutional mandated "death sentence". Additionally, as early as the 1800's, the *"nollo prosequi"* decision was a normalized process through prosecutorial procedures, relative to a felony defendant's "guilty plea bargaining", which allowed in numerous cases, felony defendant's to be placed on probation; through felony convictions escaping the Judges bench. Therefore, both historically (1880), and presently in the twenty-first (21st) century, an adequate counsel or defense continually rests in the hands of the prosecutor, judge, and defense attorney's, who ultimately prospers from the "plea bargaining" apparatus. Thusly, alleviating trial court expenses, which fosters caseload tactics through coercive plea bargaining, and ultimately prosecutorial control of the felony defendant's optional selections of either a "jury trial" or "plea bargaining" process; which is legally relegated to every American citizen, through their Constitutional mandated judicial rights. The history of "plea bargaining" in the early 1880's vigilante police stages of mass immigration to the American shores, would definitely dictate the coercion of an expedited felony trial system of government. However, it would also carry the weight of administering and elevating a forthright professional legal system of governance, that correlates with the massive influx of dissimilar culturally populated types of people, which fosters the advent of the sophistication of the "social sciences"; such as the professional, intellectual, and educational concomitance of criminology, psychology, sociology, and economics, to legally sophisticate the determinate legal felony offenses, and judicial sentencing structure, which would have stabilized the U. S. Constitutional rights to a "jury trial" or "plea bargain", without one or the other causing monetary or time expending or consuming fallacies. However, earlier era's in the formation of the American legal system, should have judicially structured the judicial system with legal felony defense guidelines, which would have included criminal felony factors, which balances the factors and circumstances of prosecutor's, judges, and defense attorney's; by speculation or forecasting, the merging Constitutional felony offensive mandated rights, which deals with their criminal defense calendars, expenses, and time consuming legal professional clarity, of fairness and integrity, within their professional obligations to the United States of America citizens. Example, "The United States Constitution, and Bill of Rights, *respectively, through the 5th Amendment's prohibition of compelled and self-incrimination by felony offenders upon themselves by being coerced into accepting the "plea bargain"; and the 6th Amendment's guarantee of impartial juries; Consequently, citizen's would think that the "administration of criminal justice" would be manifested by adversarial litigations.*

Notably, if felon's demanded "trials by jury", and wasn't coerced into accepting the "plea bargain", the felony court system would be required to furnish trials complete with attorney's, judges, full jury box participation, court reporters, court rooms, and the required witnesses. If fifty percent of felony defendants requested trial by jury, the complete legal felony system would shut-down. Consequently, the necessary resources required for the requested 50% jury trials measured against 50% plea bargains, would validate the Constitutionality guaranteed by the U.S. Constitution, and The Bill of Rights for all citizens; however, the number of prosecutions would be minimized abruptly, which would foster a smaller prison population, and less prosecutions for low-level crimes, and poor disenfranchised (powerless) defendant's. Additionally, it estimated that the U.S. incarcerates 1 in 95 American citizens; that qualifies it to be the World's leader in both the percentage of American citizens incarcerated and prison population size. "Plea Bargaining" has become pervasively the major process of criminal case disposition in America. It's alleged by prison inmates that "plea bargaining" categorically contravene defendant's against one another, through inducing many defender's to concede or relinquish "worse plea bargains", than they would otherwise not have accepted. Most importantly, through plea bargains, prosecutor's are interested in maximizing successful prosecutions, and minimizing court costs. Therefore, they are encouraged to prosecute a "disproportionate number of poor and disenfranchised defendant's". Incredibly, plea bargaining has become an elaborate felony ridden "institution" in the American legal system; especially against poor and disenfranchised defendant's. Furthermore, prosecutor's who strive for prestige and superhuman acknowledgement in the felony court systems in America, do so by securing a "larger-than-life" number of felony convictions, and accomplish these feats by preying on the easy cases, which criminal offenses are committed by the poorest disenfranchised citizens found on the streets of America. However, if "all" of their cases were equal in degree of significance and costs, these *status seeking* prosecutor's attitudes would change to prosecuting valid, and real cases of social significance.

Given the realities of felony criminal defense, the notorious overburdened caseloads, economic legal practices, and the demands for speedy caseload processing, provides ample reasons why the felony defendant's will rarely spend time, if any with their defense attorney's before an agreement is reached, and procured with the prosecutor's.

Consequently, this *"rare meeting between the felony defendant and his appointed defense attorney"*, is a deliberate strategic and coercive sentencing ploy; that places a tremendous mental and emotional burden on the felony defendant's, to simply consent to a guilty plea, through the Unconstitutional "plea bargaining" process. Thereafter, the felony defendant concurs to the expected guilty plea bargaining process, without being identified as a problem or burden on the judge and prosecutor's court! The legal felony court system acknowledges and summarize that their "plea bargaining" sentencing process is defined as a prosecutorial, judge, and defense attorney's plea bargaining behest and injunction; however, through the Constitutionality of the U.S. legal system, it is merely an unprincipled economic savings, and resourceful provision that doesn't require an expensive legal litigation cost. Therefore, the unprincipled acquiescence by the felony defendant to plead guilty to the felony offense, whether it's a very minor offense or major offense, "it's merely a trade-off between the felony court system and the felony defendant's, to think that they are bargaining for a lenient sentence, even if there's a possibility that they are innocent of the convicted crime, given to their relinquishing or abnegation of their options for a "jury trial", as opposed to the "plea bargain"

Conclusion

A felony defendant of an offense gets know sympathy from society at large, unless there is vital mitigating evidence or circumstances of his guilt. However, the legal and social entanglement is relative to the U. S. Constitutions 5th and 6th Amendments; and the U. S. Bill of Rights Declaration, that guarantee every U. S. citizen the lawful right to a jury trial. Importantly, neither of the two major documents that "sustain the laws of the land", and philosophy of the U. S. A. concede legal sanctions, or ratify authorization for plea bargain, and its coercive procedural process of *"tic-for-tack"*, we give you this (shorter sentence) for that (plea bargain), in the felony courts criminal processing procedure for felony defendant's. Yet, the contradictionary "plea bargain" process versus "trial by jury" melee, was sanctioned by the "U. S. Supreme Court"; however, with know commitments or amendments to the "U. S. Constitution or Bill of Rights" to defray legal costs, exhaustive or expedited case-load burdens relative to the prosecutor's, judges, or defense attorney's. Therefore, aside from the efficient, expedited, or progressive "plea bargain" procedure, the crux and cancer to this issue of coercive plea bargaining gambits, is its relevance under Constitutional Law. Additionally, in question is the forthright legitimacy or illegitimacy of compelled self-incrimination, through the "plea bargaining" insistence to felony defenders to abide by pertaining to their lawful rights as U. S. citizens. Furthermore, in question is the *"legal intent* or *"mens rea"*, of the prosecutor's, judges, and defense attorney's to tactically structure this violation of the U. S. Constitution by threatening felony defender's with their "gambit of mental and emotional" tricks of their trade, which lashes onto the defendant's psychological and emotional forbearance to qualify the infamous "guilty plea". The coin flipped, and one or the other selections are made between, "heads (you win) or tails (you lose)", which is the deciding factor in choosing "plea bargaining"; which is presented as the major conducive and progressive element in the felony court of law systems; as a vital criminal justice apparatus, that alleviates legal caseloads, economic resources, and time-table factors; in advancing the political arena to a more productive and forthright American institution. However, we thrust upon a "legal control theory" by injecting "plea bargaining" as the major controlling factor relative to the felony criminal justice system; by *"playing down"*, and almost omitting, felony trials by jury selection". Jury trials have become an oxymoron, in the vision and mentalities of the "in-house court professionals", namely; judges, prosecutor's, and defense attorney's. Notably, the creation of the "plea bargaining" process and concept, was advanced by the "Supreme Courts" plea bargain sanctions in the *"Bordenkircher v. Hayes"*, documented felony case. However, when there is little doubt about the commission of a felony crime, and valid evidence is brought forward to convict the felony offender; Naturally, the ethics and principles of the "plea bargain" execution legitimizes the process as a viable utility, to an unquestionable guilty verdict. Contrarily, if a wrongful conviction is handed down through a strenuous and coercive "plea bargain" confession of guilt that leads to a wrongful conviction; then, the wrongfully accused felony defendant's legal ethics, which is mandated through the U. S. Constitution, and Bill of Rights legal ethics, becomes a disgrace to the accused felony defendants social and legal freedoms. The acts of coercion and forceful methods of persuasive tactics on a felony defendant, to plead guilty through "plea bargaining", is a violation of the U. S. Constitutional Law, and Bill of Rights, which ethically and legally should forfeit that specific "plea bargaining" enactment conviction; and depending on the status of the criminal offense, it should be presented for retrial through the "jury" process

CHAPTER XVIII

An Analysis of The Relationship Between Science and Religion

(By: W. F. Williams)

Western culture's between the fifteenth to twenty-first centuries, founded, contrived, and enforced a socially structured cultural *theology* and *science, which created an* antagonistic divide; and thusly from the 15th century forward, reflected their "World View of themselves and the Universe". However, within the latter centuries Theology (Christianity) and Science reached a formal compromise in the 1500's and late 1800's, by coexisting through an alliance.

Notably, up until the late nineteenth century most Western scientist were raised in the Christian faith, and very seldom ever raised negative issues about their inherited Christian or Judeo-Christian upbringing. However, Galileo vs. The Catholic Church (Christianity), revealed his astronomical discovery that the earth was not the center of the World; and literally invoked the "new" over "old" antiquated theories planted in the religious canon of the Catholic Church tenets. His discovery was definitely reviewed as a negative discovery by the Church. However, the Catholic Church approved of Galileo's book as a discussion and exchange of arguments between the two, in reference against a "sun-centered" Universe". However, Galileo's "management of written words in the book", was mistaken to be expressly ridiculing the Catholic Church's *"earth centered model"; therefore, it was alleged that he was directly insulting the "Pope",* which lead to the "infamous inquisition". However, before pursuing the historical differences and controlling factors between "Science and Religion", it's necessary to understand that most human beings reflect that "religion" by character and essence is "anti-science", and "science" is anti-religion; yet, they merely hail contradictory visible features and attitudes concerning Universal "facts of existence". Science interprets, analyze, explore, and involve the physical world; while religion interprets a subjective world outside the scientific physical world; which reflects imagery through the transcendental, boundless, mystical, and spiritual Universe, through (walking by faith and not by sight).

The historical challenges between "science and religion" was/is the quest for social, political, and economic dominance over the other "institutions", as the leading authority between "divine creation", that challenges the concepts of "natural and physical science"; which constitute conflicting beliefs, theories, and philosophies referencing "the ontological creation of the Universe". However, scientific discovery in the earlier centuries was a life-force intrusion in early and modern theology by contradicting "religious doctrines"; which supports the Biblical theory that "God Created the Universe"; as opposed to "Natural Science" creating the Universe; through "Evolution, or Intelligent Design". Noteworthy, in earlier centuries "religious doctrines and tenets" controlled governance and social ethos in the Western World. However, in later centuries "Science perpetually provided serious answers to our physical existence, which continues to open debates between "Religious leaders and Scientist's.

Thusly, historical observation, events, and *mores* strongly reflect exacting chronology of theology embedding its philosophy and ideology into the framework that presently dictates the governance of Western civilization. Notwithstanding, debatable opinions between "divine creation", "physical science", and "intelligent design" will always seek popular and prevailing theoretical discourse, due to personal beliefs, assumptions, and commentary on how the Universe negotiates its existence. Not surprising, the contradictions between science and religion has entangled many elements of social ethos in the historical fabric of Western civilizations. Darwinism, untangled many postulations between physical science and divine creations, in open-ended arguments between the philosophy of science and philosophy of religion. Furthermore, Darwin was laboriously devoted to instituting his veracious (truthful) scientific concept of the physical world, and its affinity to the origin of species with life. However, one miscalculated impediment rebuffed Darwin from fully extracting his theories of evolution, by safeguarding his valued social status and reputation. In 1878, Darwin wrote to Anglican Priest Innes, that he "never published any of his theories against religions or the priesthood". However, in that identical year, Darwin published that Christianity was a "damnable doctrine", and that the Bible was manifestly a false history". Thereby, "validating his scientific intellectual and instinctive theories of evolution"; which (temporarily) hampered his veneration for imminent scientific evolutionary works of discovery, in that immediate time frame of his life. Essentially, Darwin's abandonment of the Christian faith allowed him the theoretical drive, aptitude, perseverance, independence and self-determination, to piece together his ideological puzzle of "Natural Selection"; as the machinery for his evolutionary development.

In noting the Copernican revolution, which supplanted the earth from ancient seat at the center of the universe, that's frequently cited as the beginning of modern science. Not only did Copernican theory rectify a mistake dating to antiquity; by replacing the sun for the earth as the core of the solar system, but also contested the cosmological teachings of the Roman Catholic Church; thereby setting up a new scientific cosmology as the unification of opposition to dogma (religious doctrines, tenets, beliefs, and principles). Nevertheless, the capstone of the Copernican feat is the "morality dramas" that were established and ordained in the trial of Galileo. Whereby, the church is portrayed as willing to impose "heavy-handed censorship", and worse, to suppress ideas and discovery that would one day open avenues and boulevards of scientific freedom.

Importantly, beginning with the recovery of ancient learning in the twelfth (12th) century, which persisted and endured through the Copernican cataclysm, and into the "Age of Reason", or/and "Enlightenment Era"; that during this period, the Roman Catholic Church contributed enormous financial and social support to the scholarship of Copernican and astronomy, than did any other financially sound institution during this era. However, the rationale for such financial sponsorship to astronomy corroborates, and establishes that it was central to Roman authority; because the Roman Catholic Church was designated an assigned an urgent accountability, and obligation to launch through decree, the specific date of "Easter", which was preeminent and peerless for their dynasty or hierarchy.

Remarkably, the relationship between religion and science endeavored within the core element of human existence, which includes the avatar of cultural identity, social, political, and economic assimilation, and reciprocal benevolent dialogue to define and theorize "Intelligent Design versus The Evolutionary Theory of Darwinism"; as we progress into the twenty-first and twenty-second (21st and 22nd) centuries. The competition between "creative design, Darwinism (classical and modern), and Intelligent Design, has emerged into a scientific "controversy", that will weigh on intellectual scientific exploration, research, and interpretations as these three profound discoveries await concrete laureate identities, social status, with time divulging the truth of their societal order. However, understanding that "intelligent design" is the new neighbor on the block, that reference the process of studying and synthesizing "nature", through the effects that an intelligence has on the study of that specific nature being studied; which reflects an inference from "biological data", like "DNA's" libraries of information stored in four (4) molecules, that characterize digital codes to exploit its "intelligent designs" input. However, from "intelligent design", we arrive in Darwin's theory of evolution, and "Origin of Species", which theorize that "life" is the result of a purely undirected process"; and intelligent design scientist, refers to Darwin's "origin of species" as merely an imitation and an aptitude of illusion of their theory of "designed intelligence. Consequently, they infer that the appearance of Darwinism is an illusionary design; and furthermore, insist that classical and modern Darwinism both, appear to be "designed intelligence", but that they are not, because "natural selection" produces the appearance of a "design". Nevertheless, "intelligent design" cohorts insists that "life itself" is "designed intelligence".

Divine Creation on the other hand evolves from mankind's natural instinctive assimilation, which defines religion and science, as necessary utilities for socially dictated conformity and scientific progress. Consequently, through a *maze* of intelligent reflections towards cultural survival, and mankind's reason of persuasion derives through his intellect, to cognitively understand that science and religion creates and emphasizes Universal independence, and dependence, through human control, principles and guidelines. Contrastingly, religious doctrine mandates "divine creation" through the dictates of biblical doctrines. However, the Science vs. Religion argument will continue endlessly, with each side qualifying its merits and virtues to challenge the other to emerge victorious. The truth remains that "all" ideologies can co-exist in harmony.

Printed in the United States
By Bookmasters